ONLY IN NEW ENGLAND

Only in

NEW ENGLAND

THE STORY OF A GASLIGHT CRIME

by

THEODORE ROSCOE

CHARLES SCRIBNER'S SONS

New York

PRINTED IN THE UNITED STATES OF AMERICA

TO

LUKE AND BENGTA

AND HAP

AND DICK

AND RUSTY AND RUTH

WHO KNOW THE POINT

AND OF COURSE

TO

ROSAMOND

THIS BOOK IS DEDICATED

AUTHOR'S NOTE

It is not often that a true-crime historian enjoys the opportunity of living in the very house where the victim was killed; of dining at the table where the victim, all unaware, ate a last meal; of walking in the garden where Nemesis walked; of using the inner door that led to the rendezvous with sudden death.

Not only did I reside for several seasons in such a house, I saw its original furnishings, handled its original implements, read its period books, experienced its Victorian atmosphere—all left virtually intact when the door closed in the wake of that dark death many years ago. At which time the inheritors, for reasons manifest in the case history, sealed the house and left it to time and taxes.

Sealed within the house were such skeletons in closets and secrets under rugs as would delight the heart of the most case-hardened mystery fan. Indeed, the house contained a built-in puzzle which might have been devised (and certainly would have fascinated) such past masters of the who-dun-it as Mary Roberts Rinehart or Anna Katharine Green. The closure of the domicile drew a curtain over one of the strangest unsolved murder cases in New England history.

Like the famous Borden Case, this one involved the unusual charge of matricide. And, as in the Lizzie enigma, this one ended with a sinister question-mark posed over the head of the accused.

Lizzie Borden presumably took an axe—a weapon quite as conventional as she was. The enigmatic figure in the present case, a former State Senator, was accused of slaying his mother with a weapon unique in the annals of modern crime. In reference, a device historically associated with David and Goliath. You put a weight in a sack and either hurled it or whirled it. A "slung shot." (Could this wicked item be the source of the expression "getting sacked"? Etymologists please advise.)

But the Senator's mother may have died by a weirder device than that. I found this out while nosing around the spot generally designated as "X". And the old dark house divulged other previously undisclosed angles to the case. Added up with the benefit of hindsight and happenstance demonstration, they compose what seems to be a plausible solution for a murder mystery almost fifty years on the shelf.

However, some of the official records which dealt with the case seem to be no longer extant. One of the oddest angles—namely, why the case was summarily shelved—remains a mystery. Because of these missing jigsaws, the writer could not pretend to offer a definitive case history or even a study containing facts of sociological or criminological significance. I prefer to present my story as fiction based on fact rather than as alleged fact based on fiction.

All names of those involved in the actual case have been changed. Not so much by way of protecting the innocent as by acknowledgment that all of the facts were never brought to light, and, at this late date, never will be.

To prevent embarrassment of the present owners, I have screened the location of the house, and have altered its exterior architecture and some of its appointments—in no way disturbing the basic arrangements which entered the *modus operandi* of the death trap. But "Quahog Point" is in the State of Erewhon.

Similarly it was necessary to alter trial procedure and some of the testimony in order to preserve background anonymity. But the general substance is factually presented. Footnotes indicate verbatim quotes.

The characters of my story represent types rather than the actual persons involved. Ed Brewster is a combination of several characters who might be found in the geographic region. Any further similarity to persons living or dead is unintentional or coincidental.

The news excerpts are similar in content and tone to the newspaper accounts of the actual case. The letters presumably quoted are similar to those found on locale. The *Police Gazette* material came from issues cited. The actual house contained an old store ledger, and the "cheese entries" are factual. On locale was a grand piano swathed in cobwebs. The actual defendant did keep a jailhouse scrapbook like the one described and in the manner described.

The legends in my story are so much story-telling. They are, however, closely similar to the tall tales told in the actual area. There *was* a mysterious recluse. There *was* a henna-haired charmer. There *was* a normally inanimate object that went leaping about in seeming defiance of the laws of gravity. There *was* a "customer" brought to the undertaker's in a wheelbarrow. The "stubborn Cornelia" story emanated from the locality's champion yarn-spinner.

There was a household like Abby Bridewell's, complete with contentious sons, "bound out" orphan, doltish hired man, and nameless infant reported by an item of concealed correspondence. The victim in the actual case went to her mysterious death in the manner described herein. Relatives and neighbors made statements and depositions much like those in my story (I have researched many of the period, and their styling is fairly standard). In the actual case the elder son faced trial proceedings much like those herein related. The actual judge pronounced on the real case exactly as quoted in my text. And the fantastic denouement of my story follows the actual.

For the rest, this book is fiction. I trust it conveys the spirit, if not the letter, of the real-life drama. If my characters are fictionalized, so were those who played the leading roles on the stage of reality. And when it comes to public images, aren't we all?

T.R.

"Quahog Point"

April 1959

ONLY IN NEW ENGLAND

CHAPTER 1

As SOMEONE once said, heredity deals the cards and environment plays the hand. Even today at Quahog Point there is in evidence enough heredity to demonstrate Mendel's formula to a black-eyed pea. The families that settled there in 1691 are still there. Those original settlers were of basic English and Welsh stock, and the modern derivatives hark back to the source.

The originals came by way of a sailing vessel which ran aground in a booming nor'easter. The survivors crawled ashore and huddled in a cave. Eventually they salvaged enough timber from the wreck to build a communal hut. They lived throughout that pioneer winter on waterfowl and provisions from the ship. In the spring another wreck provided them with a windfall of live beef. The "Pointers" settled down.

Sustenance from the two wrecks seems to have given these chance settlers an idea. According to legend, they became industrious ship-wreckers, and for a number of decades existed on the cargoes of vessels lured ashore by means of false lights and deceptive smoke-signals. Proof of this evil practice cannot be found in colonial records. You hear such stories of the settlers at Nag's Head, of the pioneers on Martha's Vineyard, of the early inhabitants of Block Island. The Quahog Pointers may or may not have lured ships in to the rocks where shattered hulls could be looted and drowned seamen robbed.

The names of those original settlers were honest enough. Grimes. Babcock. Purdy. Jones. Robinson. Bridewell. Meck. Ord. They never went away. You can see succeeding generations of them on the headstones of the local cemetery. Crop after crop.

Of course there are a few new names. Thorns and Bryces in 1775. Smeizers, Goodbodys, Hatfields and Ross crop up in the early 1800's. They are accepted as "founding fathers," but the older families still claim historic precedence. Anyone after 1850 is a Johnny-come-lately. The two or three Portuguese families that moved in circa 1900 were (and still are) foreigners. They may call themselves "Pointers," however, in contradistinction to "inlanders" or "summer people." These last, of course, are intruders.

The ancestral families intermarried, and their collateral descendents intermarried. Eugenicists tell us this sort of inbreeding is bound to show. I found no evidence of it in the surface characteristics of the modern "Pointers." That is, they are not markedly endowed with six fingers, webbed toes and signs of congenital idiocy. However, nearly all of the old-timers were—as one modern old-timer put it—"vaguely related." The Point abounds with second cousins. There may have been an infusion of Indian blood during the colonial period. Perhaps that accounts for the clear black eyes possessed by some of the localites.

Under-the-surface characteristics? The "inlanders" like to say that the "Pointers" have always been odd. City folk are liable to find them uncommunicative, unprogressive, and—yes—unreliable. But perhaps those are the opinions of sectionalism (urban dwellers are confirmed sectionalists), and the sectionalized "Pointers" were probably no odder than the inhabitants of any self-engrossed community, be it Greenwich Village or Montclair, New Jersey.

That the Quahog Pointers practiced "togetherness" cannot be gainsaid. The same "togetherness" is found among the inhabitants of the Carolina Outer Banks, the natives of Nantucket, the movie colonists in Hollywood, brothers of the Rotary, the élite of Washington (D.C.) society, and in any exclusive insular commune whose members (to borrow from Tennyson) "think the homely cackle of their burg the murmur of the world." It must be conceded, however, that the "Pointers" were a little more together than most. The adhesion was imposed by physical geography.

Environment. Isolation was the dominant factor. Quahog Point is out at sea. The town squats at the end of a long peninsula with beachfront on three sides and miles of salt marsh and bayberry ranging along the peninsular leg. On the land's-end headland overlooking the town stands a lonely lighthouse. Gulls swoop everywhere, and in season the marsh ponds are feathered with herons, drakes and mallards.

In the old days—in fact, until recently—the Point was off the beaten track, and at times almost inaccessible. High tides flooded the peninsular marshes and often inundated the wagon-road across the dunes. Winter storms abolished road travel entirely. From January until the roadbed was repaired, Quahog Point was virtually an island cut off from the mainland save by an eight-mile picket line of lonesome telegraph poles. Weather permitting, there was a winter steamboat, twice a week. You could get there on foot if you had to, but it was hard, even risky, going.

So Quahog Point evolved as a togetherish little community. At the period of this story, the resident populace numbered some seven hundred souls. So far as I could determine, that figure had remained roughly constant since the Gold Rush Era. Nineteenth Century Boston grew, and Providence grew. Bangor and Bridgeport grew. But at Quahog Point, remote, isolated, the economy precluded a population growth. Nor did geographic conditions invite it.

The early "Pointers" had engaged in fishing and boat building. But the little harbor under the headland was too exposed for commercial shipping. And why haul timber and chandler's gear way out on a peninsula when yards were convenient at Charles Town, or up the sheltered Narragansett, or down New London way?

Swordfish, mackerel, tuna, cherrystones—when New York was young the choicest seafoods at Fulton Market often arrived in barrels bearing the "Quahog" label. But Gloucester eventually gained the bigger game, the bigger name. By mid-Nineteenth Century, Quahog Point was out of the Grand Banks competition.

However, for a brief period, which spanned the 70's to the late 90's, Quahog Point enjoyed a flush coincident with red plush. Some of the "Pointers" had joined the Forty Niners on the rush to California. As I gleaned it from local legend, these adventurers did not strike it rich in the gold fields. They hit the jackpot as carpenters earning one hundred dollars a day, as chandlers selling supplies at sixty times their wholesale cost, as laundry hands cleaning up at ten dollars a shirt.

One of the "Pointers," a barber named Smeizer, came home with a clipper ship won by shears and razor. Another, Peleg Purdy, made a quarter of a million in 'Frisco real estate. Captain Nathan Bridewell, from Quahog Point, returned with a seabag full of gilt-edged mining stocks. This was the Bridewell who built the Surf and Sand Hotel—one hundred rooms and the longest double-deck verandah on the New England coast. It was the Surf and Sand that made of Quahog Point a fashionable beach resort.

In its Gay Nineties heyday the Point was known as a second Newport. The ledger at the Surf and Sand bore the signatures of Diamond Jim Brady, Lillian Russell, Betcha-a-Million Gates. "Sapolio" Morgan put in with his yacht. An architect as renowned as Stanford White spent several seasons there. So did an artist as celebrated as Charles Dana Gibson. So did a writer as popular as Harding Davis, an impresario as successful as Daniel Frohman, an opera star as famous as Schumann-Heink.

In this period the "summer people" built some ornate homes along the shore. A Temperance Society erected a fountain in the town's so-called Center (somehow the water was never hooked up, and from the day of its unveiling to this, the castiron fountain has remained as dry as Aunt Carrie Nation). Big paddle steamers with names like *Shinnycook* and *Puritan* came over from Montauk and down from Boston and around from New York. John Y. Gillion built the big gray wharf with the promenade pier. Absalom Purdy put up the Bayberry House. The Ords built two beach hotels. The Robinsons erected the fantastic Seagull with the glass-domed solarium, and the Ross family opened the Headlander.

Wiseacres would say the "Pointers" over-invested. Hindsight! Who, in those days, foresaw a revolution in the bicycle shop of Henry Ford? Railroads were the backbone of transportation. And here to stay seemed steamboating ("Take a trip up the Hudson, or down the Bay"). And trolley cars.

So when a syndicate projected a trolley line down to the peninsula and out across the dunes—with a trestle across the marshes and a terminal at Quahog Center—the "Pointers" voted an enthusiastic franchise. Who couldn't visualize the benefits? Instead of a few hundred "summer people," weekend crowds of pleasure seekers. Trolley excursions. Chowder-and-marching clubs coming in. Clambake conventions. An all-season flow of vacationists with money to burn at Quahog Point.

All of the older "Pointer" families went for the trolley. A Bridewell and a Babcock were prime movers, it was said. The Thorns, Smeizers, Rosses, Goodbodys—all of them bought in. Then the Century belatedly turned. A "tin lizzie" put the Lizzie Borden sensation in the shade. Almost overnight steamboating crawled up on the beach and died. America took to the highway in its Merry Oldsmobile, its Winton Six, its Stanley Steamer, its Packard, its Stevens-Duryea. Motoring, as everyone knows, was the ruination of the old-time summer resort.

The Peninsular and Quahog Rapid Transit Line expired while the last mile of track was being laid. Before it was abolished by our recent Hurricane Hazel you could still see a section of trestle rusting in a stretch of open marsh. It was the trestle-work that really cost. That, plus a lot of stock juggling and inflation. Some of the "Pointers," deep in, went bankrupt. Nearly all of the investors lost a great deal of money.

That was around 1910. The year the Surf and Sand saw its reservations drop to a dozen rooms, the Headlander closed its doors, the Bayberry suffered a disastrous fire, and the Seagull went into receivership. John Y. Gillion hanged himself in a cupboard at the back of Thorn's Fish Market. Neill Smeizer lost his fleet of mackerel boats and took a job tending bar in the Anchor Saloon. Joel Goodbody ran off with the wife of a visiting yachtsman. Absalom Purdy was jailed for the Bayberry holocaust (arson). And Earnest Bridewell started another term in the State Senate.

The Bridewells had owned a reputedly sizable block of P. and Q. Transit stock. But they came off rather well. They managed to hang on to the Surf and Sand Hotel. They maintained an interest in the vestigial Quahog Trawler Company (three boats), the residual Quahog Kelp Company (three miles of beach with riparian rights), and the Neptune Chandlery (a yachting supply store). Then, too, there was the Bridewell homestead—the big, gray gingerbread house with the boxwooded gardens, the surrounding orchards, the capacious stables.

Other "Pointers" had to sell their boats, their horses, their surreys with the fringe on top. Some of them, desperate, began to sell acres of beach property, and even articles of furniture to acquisitive realtors and antique dealers—"inlanders." But the Bridewells kept up.

The localites averred it wasn't the doing of the Bridewell Boys, although the Senator was smart enough. They laid the acumen and the credit to Abby Bridewell, the old mother. She it was who steered the family fortunes through the P. and Q. financial storm. She it was who managed the money.

She had managed it, it seemed, when Captain Nathan Bridewell first fetched it home from California. It was she who had handled Nathan's investments, had conceived the Surf and Sand. After he became a paralytic in the 80's, she had done even better with her distaff hand. Now, herself in the eighties, she ruled the estate with matriarchal acuity and discipline. Abby Bridewell was the local Hetty Green.

But with the calendar at 1910, Abby Bridewell did not have long to live.

CHAPTER 2

I FIRST heard of the Bridewell case in 1939. On my maiden visit to Quahog Point. I went there with fish in mind. I came back with my thoughts on matricide.

9

Luke Martin introduced me to the place. Come on, fold up your typewriter for a weekend. You need some oxygen in your system. I know a shore point where it's cheap. We can get a boat and a guide and try for swords. Luke is a champion salesman as well as angler, and he had me hooked. He was abetted by April weather and crocuses in Manhattan dooryards.

We took the Post Road and cut over to Newport where we caught the coastal steamer. (It doesn't run any more.) Quahog Point was one of the regular stops. When we disembarked at the wharf I felt as though I had stepped into the past. The stubby fishing boats at wharfside. The nets. The old-timers posed like the one on the ad for cod-liver oil.

The little town with its cottages and Western-style storefronts. The Center with the dry fountain. The steeple of the Shoreside Methodist Church. The old-time street lamps. The raffish beach hotels with the decaying verandahs and boarded-up windows. The broad "sea houses," lavishly shingled and dormered—architecture of the day when lumber was plentiful and carpentry could be afforded. Quahog Point was a period piece.

Ed Brewster, our host-to-be and guide, met us at the pier. A wide man with an amiable face, he stepped out of a 1920 Kissel that suited the atmosphere, and came over to pick up our gear. Luke had fished with him for several seasons, and the previous autumn they had caught a record tuna.

Ed inspected the sky, frowning. "I don't like it," he said. "My crystal set says rain tomorrow, and so does my knee."

His crystal set and his knee forecast truly. The sundown grew smoky as we drove out to his house. By the time we got there, a damp wind was whipping the undergrowth at roadside.

My introduction to the house was memorable. It seemed a big place in the windy twilight. Elms in the side yard were bowing and creaking. A tall hedge of scraggly boxwood was in motion. Shadows were weaving across the drive, and dead leaves flew. The lamp-lit fanlight over the front door looked inviting. As we scuttled in, a few drops chased our heels.

We were welcomed in by Ed's wife, a French Canadian girl with a hospitable bosom and generous heart. There was a cramped vestibule with doors admitting to a front parlor, an inner hall, a side dining room. We went into the dining room.

Doors opened into a kitchen, a pantry, a stairway going up. At the stairtop another door. Two doors opened into our front room, a capacious bedroom. My first impression of the house: a lot of rooms and an extraordinary number of doors.

At dinner (supper in the colloquial), Ed Brewster told us about the place. But the topic developed from a discourse on Quahog Point. In the course of which I learned that Ed Brewster had been reared there but not born there. So he wasn't, strictly speaking, a "Pointer." His father had worked as head chef at one of the Point hotels, and Ed had come there as a boy, and stayed. He had gone to the little red schoolhouse with the "Pointer" fry. Had worked his way up on the fishing boats. Had finally acquired a boat of his own, and, recently, this house.

"Been on the Point most of my life, but I'm still not one of *them*." He chuckled. "That's all right with *me*."

His wife? He laughed. "Annette's from Nova Scotia. Strictly a foreigner."

Not that they didn't get along with the "Pointers." Everybody liked Annette. The "Pointers" liked (and, I gathered, respected) Ed. It was just that at times they ignored him at Town Council, or wouldn't let him in on some local proposition. As he put it, "still treated him clannish."

"I think," Ed's wife offered, "maybe it's because of this house."

"It was long before I got this house," Ed said.

"But some of them do not like to come here."

"Who cares?" Ed looked mildly annoyed. Then he tilted back in his chair, listening. It had begun to rain.

Luke Martin, happily fed, pointed a cigar. "You've done a good job on this house," he said, looking around. To me, "You ought to have seen it before Ed took it over."

"Two years ago," Ed nodded. "It was a mess." He saw my interest, and enlarged, "Windows broken. Part of the roof gone. Rats. I got it for taxes."

Annette Brewster sighed. "It was a ruin. Plaster falling everywhere. Fieldmice in the furniture. It took a lot of work."

I looked around at the fumed oak. The fine old corner cupboard. The polished brass. "You mean this furniture was in it?"

"Everything," Ed Brewster said. "Pictures. Carpets. The works. We even found a lot of plate silver. But the place was a wreck. Nobody'd lived in it for nearly twenty years."

"They just went away and left it? All these things?"

"See, the family died out," Ed said. "And the natives wouldn't touch it with a ten-foot pole."

"Superstitious mutton-heads!" Luke Martin snapped.

"Well, not exactly," Ed said tolerantly. "You see," he explained to me, "there was a murder here."

"Tell him, Ed," Luke Martin said. "He's been writing true crimes for the Munsey Company."

"Secrets of the French police," I deprecated modestly. But I could hardly disguise the eager tone. Our host's statement had brought the fire-horse neighing out of me.

Ed Brewster said, "It was a long time back. Before the World War. They say there's only been two murders here at the Point. Since the old ship-wreckin' days, that is. One of the cases: a musician at the Bayberry was shot. He'd been fiddling around with one of the local girls. It wasn't much of a case."

"Is there a lot of such fiddling here in the summer?"

Ed thought a minute. "Yes, there is," he said. "And in the winter, too. But these days it's pretty much taken for granted. That shooting was back in the Nineties. Only other murder was the one in this house."

Of course, we were in the Bridewell mansion. The old homestead. But I'd never heard of the Bridewells until that moment. Ed Brewster donated the rest of that evening to the case history.

I heard about Captain Nathan Bridewell and how his ship came in. About the cumulative family fortune. About the uncles, cousins, and aunts. But the story centered around Abby Bridewell, the Captain's widow, and about the two bachelor sons, Earnest and Lionel, who lived with the aged mother here in the house.

"They lived here together, the three of them," Ed Brewster said. "Earnest and Lionel were unmarried. I expect the old lady didn't encourage them to marry—she'd have figured the girls was after the family money. Anyway, they didn't, and when I knew them as a kid, Lionel, he was about forty-five, and Earnest Bridewell was pushing sixty. The old lady was in her eighties. Look, would you like to see them?"

"*See* them?"

Ed laughed at my surprise. "When we moved in here, I found this album. There's an attic full of stuff. Old books. Saratoga trunks. Everything. Come on up."

Ed's wife protested about the dust. But I was thoroughly intrigued. The house was growing on me, and I was curious about its story. Ed hurried into the kitchen for an oil lamp, and we followed him up the stairs. A back room, a back hall—more doors everywhere—and a ladder up to the third-floor loft.

"Here we are," Ed said.

We stood in a nest of lamplight and shadow with rain drumming on the roof overhead. We might have been in a second-hand shop on Third Avenue. All kinds of rummage was crammed under the eaves. Wonderful things. Bird cages, three-legged chairs, carpet bags, dress forms, boxes, trunks, books, broken parlor lamps, a headless statue of Napoleon.

While our host rummaged in a leather trunk, I examined some of the books. A first edition of Horatio Alger—*Sink or Swim.* A copy of *Paradise Lost. The Calf Path* by Sam Walter Foss. Whittier's *Snowbound. The Prisoner of Zenda.* A fabulous booklet entitled *From the Ballroom to Hell; Facts About Dancing* (Glad Tidings Publishing Co., 1894). An old Bible wherein someone had scrawled on the flyleaf: "Matthew, Mark, Luke, John; saddle the cats, and I'll get on." The book covers were sooty and the spines were warped.

I observed that you could sometimes tell about people by what they read.

Ed said, "You'll notice nearly all these books were gifts. Except in the Algers and that old Bible, the leaves are uncut."

I reversed the English on my observation to say you might tell about people by what they didn't read.

"Well, the Bridewells didn't read much," Ed remarked. "But as you can see, the old lady wouldn't throw nothing away. . . . Here's the album."

So I met the Bridewells as preserved between covers of brown plush, brass-bound and embossed with hearts and flowers. They were a numerous clan. Stern uncles and lanky maiden aunts. Little boys posed with elbow on parlor table, and solemn little girls seated on tuffets.

"Those were back in the eighties," Ed said. "The one with the derby is Captain Nathan Bridewell. He had a stroke and was paralyzed for years. Died in 1910."

The deceased sea captain resembled a character straight out of Eugene O'Neill. Chubby features framed with side-whiskers. Button eyes and buttoned-up mouth. He was holding a telescope propped on one knee.

"Here's the last of the Bridewells," Ed said, turning a page. "The ones we're talking about."

Earnest, the State Senator. He was posed like a statue, with hands gripping the lapels of his coat, in a stance of oratory. A gaunt man with a lean face, the stalk of his neck accentuated by a high stiff collar with wings wide open to accommodate the jut of a blade-thin Adam's apple. He wore a pompadour of dark hair, heavily-browed eyes, and a black horseshoe mustache. The flanks of his cheeks were sunken. His eyes, fixed on the camera, had little pouchy hammocks under them. One was informed by the pose that he took himself seriously. He might have been one of the humorless statesmen immortalized in the steel engraving, "Lincoln and his Cabinet."

Lionel, the junior brother, had stepped from the Currier and Ives period into the Turn of the Century. His close-up, circa 1905, bore the imprint of a fashionable Newport photographer. He faced the camera with folded arms and the intense self-interest of a theatrical portrait. His features possessed the clean-shaven, strong-jawed vacuity favored by the nickelodeon heroes of that day. He might have been the aging leading man of a smalltown stock company. His handsomeness was marred by the weathering of middle age and something tricky in the eyes. I was reminded of certain portraits of William McKinley.

Abby Bridewell was a perfect Brady. Although her latest portrait was dated 1907, it might have been taken by Alexander Gardener. She was posed in a mahogany rocker. She wore a black lace cap, a black velvet choker, and a dress that looked as if it were fashioned of black bombazine. Her eyes were direct and uncompromising. Her mouth was a tight little line between dumpling jowls that would have suited one of Disney's dwarfs. But the grumpy, curmudgeon expression was, it seemed, deceptively folksy. I was to learn that this old lady embodied the temper, the sharp acumen, the willpowered determination of a German baroness. It came to me that somewhere I had seen her portrait before. Then I remembered. Pictures of old Queen Victoria.

We took the album down to the dining room.

"Here's where they ate," Ed said. "At this same round table. The room is just as it was, except I took down a big old hanging gas fixture and put in electric lights."

I said, "I suppose after dinner they moved into the parlor."

Ed said, "I'll show you."

He guided us through the puzzle of the three-door vestibule. The parlor was a tight little pentagon which seemed somehow apart from the rest of the house. With its horsehair sofa, its black marble fireplace, its Turkey carpet, mahogany chairs, bric-a-brac, whatnot and needlepoint samplers, it resembled a stage set. Today's decorators generally deplore dark interiors, and the maroon and blue motif of this little parlor proved at once somber and oppressive. The mood was heightened by the picture over the mantel—the framed lithograph of a large and veiny human eye staring starkly over the legend: *International Order of Ancient Knights, Lodge No. 46.*

Meeting mine, the Eye challenged my presence in the house

and made me feel uninvited. It followed me as I crossed to look at the steel engraving of *Morning, Noon and Night*—the child in the bow of the rowboat, the handsome couple at the oars, and the ancient gaffer in the stern, standing upright and pointing at the sad, dim shore in misty distance. In keeping with this gloomy portrayal of man's junket from cradle to grave was the massive volume on the marbletop table beside the sofa. Gustave Doré's *Night Scenes from the Bible.* Tabourets, footstools, wax fruit under glass, an obsidian vase, a statuette of Chief Massasoit, a model of the *Marie Celeste* and a stuffed owl added an ostentatious confusion to the parlor's solemnity.

Ed's wife said from the door, "That eye has to go. It oggles me when I come in here to clean . . . Ed insists on leaving it."

I said, "But the parlor is wonderful. Genuine Americana."

"I've put everything back," Ed said, "the way they had it. Notice the gramophone. I found that out in the barn."

It dominated a window corner. A big, bell-mouthed morning glory sprouting from a little oak-veneer box with a crank handle. It sat on a cabinet containing shelves of small black cylinders—the forerunners of the victrola platter. We tried one later. Out came a scratchy rendition of "Daisy Belle." A voice spoke in preamble: *This is an Edison reck-ord.*

Evidently the Bridewells had junked the gramophone. It interrupted their talk.

"I remember glimpsing them in here talking," Ed recalled, "and wondering what they found, all the time, to talk about. I'd be peddling papers. Coming up to the house, I'd see Earnest with his back to the window, flailing his arms like he's practicing a speech. Lionel would be yapping and the old lady carrying on. I didn't get wise till later that they were quarreling."

"Tell how they went to church," Ed's wife said.

"Oh, yes. Every Sunday. Down to the Primitive Sabbatarian that used to be here. Real Fundamentalist. They'd go in the old lady's surrey pulled by the matched bays. She always drove. Sitting up stiff, like a coachman. Otherwise, they never went out together, unless on business."

"Was that what they quarreled about?"

"All the time. You see, the old lady held the reins, and she wouldn't let go."

Luke Martin had begun to pace the carpet. "Tell about the murder, Ed," he urged.

"Wait," I said. "Ed's doing all right. We're just getting acquainted with the Dramatis Personae."

"How's that?" Ed inquired.

"You're giving us the cast of characters." I was thinking that these Bridewells were walking stereotypes of gaslight Yankeedom. Of course, the old mother and the elder son were pillars of the church. As befitted conventional tycoonery and conservatism. Even handsome Lionel had found it expedient to follow the styles in conformist respectability. But the faces registered by the camera suggested that the fundamentals of Cromwellian doctrine neither softened the heart nor purged the soul of egocentric selfishness.

"Well, of course, I don't actually know they rowed *all* the time," Ed conceded. He added, "You know some people enjoy squabbling. It gets to be kind of a habit. They like a good after-dinner bone to pick . . . I guess the Bridewells got along well enough except about money."

"What else is there?" Luke Martin asked.

Ed's wife chuckled, and Ed looked at her affectionately. Then, "But I guess you're right so far as the Bridewells were concerned. They had—at least for these parts—a lot of money. Root of the trouble, I expect. The old lady sat on it, and the boys wanted it."

The oldest plot situation in the hackney repertoire—the Have holding out on the Have-nots. Also the world's oldest *casus belli.* Inciter of wars and revolutions, it had generated the overthrow of nations and the dissolution of empires since the day of the Rosetta Stone. Now I was to see its disruptive workings in Bridewellia (surely the world's smallest domain) here in the microcosm of Quahog Point.

As Ed Brewster outlined this particle of history, Captain Bridewell had left his entire estate to his widow, enjoining her to make such disposition of the properties to the sons as she saw fit. Abby Bridewell did not see fit. Although willing to delegate certain management duties to the sons, the dowager mother refused to sign over a dollar's worth of property, and she ruled the family treasury with an unyielding scepter.

Ed said, "She owned everything. The hotel and the other businesses. If the sons made any money, they had to hand it over. She wouldn't let go of a dime."

And I could not help but visualize the old lady in her rocker as resembling one of those period-piece, castiron penny banks whose only gesture was to make a deposit. Give her a coin, and the automatic response was to pop it into her mouth (or perhaps a slot in her bosom) whence it would be swallowed with a tiny clank. Thereupon she would settle back with a fixed expression of satisfaction. You couldn't get a cent out of her without resort to a hammer or a screw driver.

Coupled with her penury was a relentless determination to direct the lives of her sons. Our narrator opened the album to an early picture of Earnest Bridewell standing, hand in bosom, on white steps in front of a granite pillar. Earnest, it seemed, had attended college—Ed thought, perhaps, Bates. As a young man, then, he had practiced law for a spell.

"I guess there was never much law to practice here at the Point, though," Ed said. "They say Earnest was a pretty good lawyer in his salad days, but there wasn't any salad. I've heard old-timers say the old lady wouldn't let him set up in the city. Wanted him to tend family affairs at home. After the old Captain was paralyzed, she installed him—Earnest—as manager of the Trawler and Kelp Companies."

It was Abby Bridewell and her money that originally put him in the State Senate, and voted him to the board of the P. and Q. But Abby told him how to vote when in the Senate and on the Board—of that, Ed Brewster was certain. "She had him under her thumb, I'll warrant that."

"What about the other one—Lionel?"

"I've heard my father tell," Ed said, "that Lionel Bridewell wanted to go into opera. Back when he was in his twenties. Abby let him study for a time up in Boston."

He displayed an early picture of Lionel posed in profile, chin in palm. The man had the build and features of an American Apollo—and knew it.

"He had a voice," Ed said, "but it seems he didn't have no talent. There was some kind of trouble up in Boston—woman, apparently—and the old lady ordered him home. He got the management desk at the Surf and Sand. Just a clerk's job, really. The old lady kept the say about the hotel."

Ed confided that he had gleaned most of these biographic details from a box of letters up in the attic. "The old lady saved her correspondence by the bushel. Some of it dates back to the Civil War."

"Did you read it all?"

"Most of it. And then I heard talk in the village. . . . But you get the picture."

I did. The mother-ridden politico. The frustrated baritone. Romulus and Remus, middle-aged, bound by maternal cordage to the ancient She Wolf. But the apron strings in this case were purse strings.

"Stingy?" Ed held out a fist. "I recall one time I missed their newspaper. End of the month she came down to the printer's office and demanded two cents off her bill. She used to go down to Thorn's and buy stale fish. She was tight, miserly, mean, saving, scroungey, nickel-pinching and grasping."

Ed's wife protested, "She couldn't have been that bad."

"She wasn't one of these sweet-type mother tyrants," Ed assured. "She was the kind who peed carbolic acid."

"Ed!"

"But she had brains."

Luke said, looking significantly at his watch. "Tell about the murder."

"She got her brains knocked out," Ed said.

"Where?" The abruptness of his statement had brought me upright from a chair.

"Cellar stairs," Ed said. "Here, I'll show you."

We went through the vestibule to the dining room, through a pantry into the kitchen. One of those wide old-fashioned kitchens roomy enough for three or four rocking chairs in addition to a six-foot sink, a king-size range and a red-and-gold coffee mill.

There were doors to a back store room, a back washroom and a side porch. But the one that fascinated me was a small, heavy door at the right side of the kitchen. It was reinforced with iron bands, and the hinges had the look of Revolutionary War metal-smithing. The handle was an iron hoop.

"This is the oldest part of the house," Ed said. He tapped on the door. "Timbering's hand hewn."

He swung the door open and switched on a nearby kitchen light, and we looked down.

Steep and narrow steps descended into a well of darkness. A smell of must came up the steps. An exhalation of raw earth and cobwebs and stale air more than faintly forbidding. Streaked with shadow, the wall of the stairway revealed primitive masonry—lumpy cobblestone imbedded in cracked plaster. On the open side a wooden handrail reached up out of the dark like a bony arm.

Ed said, "She got it coming up the steps."

"When?"

"Spring of 1911."

"I mean, time of day."

"Evening."

"What was the weapon?"

"They found a heavy bag." Ed shaped a pouch with his hands. "With blood on it."

"So she was sandbagged!" I was surprised by the unusual device.

"Bag of lead. Heavy buckshot."

"Who did it?"

"Nobody saw it done. But suspicion fell right off on Earnest Bridewell."

"The State Senator."

"There were other people, too," Ed said slowly. "The case had angles. Four or five parties were suspected. If you—"

"Ed," his wife interrupted, "these gentlemen want to get up early in the morning and go fishing."

Ed closed the cellar door. He said, "Goodnight, boys. See you in the morning."

CHAPTER 3

We did not get up early in the morning and go fishing. I was awakened by a summoning aroma of bacon and eggs. The gloom suggested five A.M. Then I saw the watery windows and heard the downpour. My wrist dial pointed to nine:ten.

We ate breakfast with the lights on. When it rains at the shore, it really rains. From the window I could barely see the boxwood hedge. The dooryard was a lake. The April garden resembled greenery afloat at the bottom of an aquarium.

Ed came in from the barns, looking glum. "Whoosh," he said, taking off oilskins. "You can hear the surf a mile away. I'm sorry, Luke."

Martin glared at the window. "I'm going back to bed." He stamped up the stairs, fuming. Never frustrate the Compleat Angler.

Ed told me I was welcome to his library, and he showed me into a small sitting room behind the dining room. He said it used to be the sewing room. Only room in the house he had tampered with and done over. His tamperings were tasteful. Pine paneling. Bookshelves. Fish and wildlife prints. A rack of guns. A touch of Abercrombie and Fitch in a mansion out of Currier and Ives.

When he excused himself (chores), I settled down with a book on shotguns. But I couldn't become less interested. The room was comfortable, but with the gray rain blowing against the windows, I felt shut in, uneasy. I thought of donning oilskins and walking down to the Center for a look-see. No. Nothing is twice as depressing as a shore resort out of season unless it be a run-down shore resort out of season.

And abruptly I was thinking: "Bag of shot. That's an odd weapon!"

Ed and his wife were busy somewhere out back. I roamed into the dining room, into the queer front vestibule, into the parlor.

In the rainy gloom the parlor had somehow contracted. The black marble fireplace monopolized the wall space. The sofa crowded the chairs. There were too many bits and pieces in the whatnot. The gramophone's absurd morning glory thrust its neck out obtrusively.

Ed Brewster had left the family album on the marbletop drum table beside the sofa. I picked up the album and sat down. As I did so, all the furniture seemed to crowd around me. When I thrust out a leg, Abby Bridewell's rocker kicked me in the shin. The Eye over the mantel, protuberant, staring, watched me. I opened the album to a Brady-type photo of Abby Bridewell flanked by Earnest and Lionel, and three more people crowded into the overstuffed room.

I could almost see them—Abby in her matriarchal chair—Earnest at the fireplace—Lionel replacing me on the sofa. Time: 3:00 P.M. They have just completed one of those Victorian repasts that went from soup to nuts, complete with mutton and dumplings, boiled potatoes, ham simmered in milk, fried eggplant, glazed carrots, boiled coffee, spiced pears and a glutinous floating island. Weighted with custard, calories and contention, they make preparations to digest the surfeit.

The old lady, smelling of mothballs and cologne, begins to rock. Earnest palms a pepsin tablet and loosens his satin vest. Lionel, working a regurgitative toothpick, looks from one to the other combatively. As though by mutual agreement the argument begins.

Earnest thinks they ought to buy a car. It doesn't look right for a man in his position to be going around in a buggy.

Abby: What's wrong with a buggy?

Earnest: You don't see many buggies in the State capital today, Mother. All the important people are driving automobiles.

Abby: Is that what makes them important? Dah!

Earnest: Mother, please!

Abby: Anyway, you're only there while the legislature is in session.

Earnest: But some of those people come here every summer. If only for looks, we ought to have an auto.

Abby: And buy gasoline?

Earnest: We can get an electric.

For once Lionel agrees with his elder brother. Certainly they should have a car. Up by the Light one of the summer people has one for sale. A red sports job with brass headlamps. A genuine bargain.

Abby: You don't know how to drive.

Lionel: I could learn, couldn't I?

Earnest: Why don't you keep out of this? (To his mother): We could get a chauffeur.

Abby: And double the cost? No!

Lionel and Earnest: But, Mother!

Abby: You've each got a good-enough buggy, and there's the surrey for social affairs.

Earnest: Look here! I'm getting sick and tired of having to debate every expenditure with you, Mother. You know our position in this community. That surrey is positively antiquated!

Lionel: Have it your way, Mother, we'd go to town in an ox cart.

Abby: Thanks to me, you don't go on foot. Either of you.

Earnest: Look here! Don't compare me to *him!* I'm getting sick and tired of having to answer for Lionel's arrears.

Lionel: *Whose* arrears?

Earnest: Yours!

Lionel: I suppose it was the hotel that ate up all the profits of the kelp business last year.

Earnest: I suppose it was the kelpers ate up all the hotel profits last season!

Abby: Now don't get your bowels in an uproar. You're neither of you showing a profit this year, and there's no use talking. You'll get no *automobile* out of *me!*

Or perhaps they debated finance on a higher plane. Stocks, bonds, debentures, percentages, mortgages. Or the current price of eggs. Given any difference of opinion, and contention in that close little parlor must have been inevitable.

Here they sat, those three, throughout the long Sunday afternoons (no work on the Sabbath for Sabbatarians)—throughout the longer winter evenings—evening after evening, winter after winter, year after year.

To be sure, Earnest Bridewell repaired to the State Senate for a few weeks annually. Lionel Bridewell remained away from home on occasion. But back they came, obedient pins to the maternal magnet. Or it might be closer to the truth to describe the magnetism as financial. Certainly love was not the attraction. The old homestead was at once a treasury and a trap.

How they must have rubbed each other raw in this isolated house on the edge of this isolated community. People with no intellectual attainments to provide mental escapes. People without recourse to such modern opiates as television, movies, or telephone. People who did not have the abstract whipping-boys we enjoy today—the image in the White House—Atom bombs and Outer Space—the convenient devils of Communism and Soviet Russia. None of these satisfying outlets was open to the Bridewells for an escape into the vicarious or for the venting of spleen.

Nor were they given to the reliefs of arts and handicrafts, nor even the petty household tasks that constitute occupational therapy for the average mortal. Nine months of the year (the hotel being closed) Lionel Bridewell toiled not, neither did he spin. Earnest, self-important, was above manual labors. Large frog in small puddle, he doubtless considered such homely occupations as the shoveling of manure or the mending of nets as beneath his dignity and station. As for octogenarian Abby, it seemed she spent most of each day in her rocker, playing monarch of all she surveyed. The house, I would learn, was served by an "outside couple"—a man-of-all-work, and a Cinderella who did the cooking.

So here sat Abby Bridewell and her sons—three minds with but a single thought. Money. Here the old lady thumbed through her account books, engrossed with balances, interest rates, sums, percentages. I could imagine her with pad and avaricious pencil, adding, multiplying, figuring.

I could imagine the sons also doing some figuring. Importunate Earnest juggling investments in his head. Covetous Lionel quietly calculating. How many dollars added up to a trip to Paris, and if your mother were four-score years and some, what were the estimates on her life expectancy?

And how many pounds of lead are in a bag of shot? When did *that* problem enter into the mental arithmetic?

The calculator must have been a devious and offbeat introvert to come up with such a *modus operandi.* Of course, matricide in itself is a peculiarly abnormal crime. And one particularly rare in America where, for all the high incidence of juvenile and adult delinquency, the Mother Image has been the Whistler version, persistent even in a day when Mother may emerge from a beauty parlor looking like Marilyn Monroe.

But to sandbag Mother! Why this brutal assault and battery when a bag of shot could at least have been fired from a gun? Certainly possession of buckshot implied possession of a shotgun, and it seemed equally obvious that a shotgun was a quicker, surer and more impersonal means for an execution.

Gunfire meant a blast? Keep the buckshot in the bag by way of a silencer? But if murder had to be done, and silence were the desideratum, why not cyanide or arsenic—rat poison being handy to any country home—or asphyxiation while she slept (Mother forgot to turn off the gas; it was an accident)—or even, as she dozed, the gentle application of a smothering sofa pillow? But to catch her toiling up the stairs and hit her over the head! A Lizzie Borden might have given second thought to such an ambush. At least Mr. Borden was asleep when the axe fell, and Mrs. Borden was only Lizzie's stepmother.

I turned up Earnest Bridewell's picture in the album—the one wherein he stood in oratorical stance. While I was studying the portrait, Ed Brewster looked in from the vestibule.

"Sitting here in the dark?" He flicked on the lights. "Look, don't hesitate to use the house facilities. It's a dismal day."

"Time on my hands," I said, and held up the album. "Just browsing."

"I thought you might like to see the barn," Ed said. "There's some interesting old vehicles and sleighs out there. I got to go out and get a casting rod for Mr. Martin, case the weather clears and he'd like to try for stripers tonight. Like a breath of air?"

It sounded refreshing. Ed rigged me up in oilskins, and we went out through the kitchen. As I followed Ed out to the porch a gust of icy rain smote me in the face, and the wind wrenched the doorknob from my hand. The door flew wide, admitting the gale into the kitchen. Dish towels blew and the morning paper went sailing over the range. I had to struggle to close the door. It was that kind of day.

"Yesterday it's April. Today it's March. Typical Point weather," Ed said. "You can't count on spring until July."

But there was a salt tang in the blowing rain—better than the stuffy staleness of the Bridewell parlor. Earnest with his bag of shot had got me down.

I like old barns, and this one was a museum. While Ed hunted for the surf-casting gear, I roamed around in the cavernous gloom, peering at the ghostly contraptions and conveyances of a day that had passed away.

The barn housed a row of empty stables where horse-collars hung from the eaves, massive oxen yokes loomed in dusky corners and the walls were festooned with dangling harness. Beyond the stalls were the period vehicles—an ancient springer wagon, two high-topped buggies, a two-wheel ox cart, the family surrey. Overhead, suspended from high rafters, was a cutter of the type we used to call a Santa-Claus sleigh. And in a far corner was a one-horse shay.

A sadness lingered over these relics of yesteryear. The horse-collars were motheaten, the harness buckles brown with rust. Dust and decay had brought the conveyances to a standstill. There were no matched bays in the barn, no dobbin to draw the shay. The shay itself had collapsed like the one in the poem. And even that once-famous poem had departed from the national memory. Who recited Whittier any more? Or Longfellow? Or Lowell?

I went over to inspect the ancient shay.

Put on your old gray bonnet.

I picked up a leather feedbag and brushed off the cobwebs. A few dried flakes adhered to the rim of the bucket. Oats. And what had happened to the horse-blanket industry? To the carriage shops? To the wheelwrights, the blacksmiths, the salesmen who peddled buggy-whips, the street cleaners with their push-barrels, and the artisans who made the long-handled brushes?

Oh, why should the spirit of mortal be proud . . . ?

Ed came over. "Did you say something?"

"If I did, I was thinking out loud . . . Do you remember horse-drawn fire engines, Ed?"

"Sure. They had one here. My old man was a Volunteer."

"With sparks coming out of the top?"

"Hell, this Quahog pumper sparked so it once set the Town Hall on fire."

"Did the Surf and Sand have a beach wagon?"

"A big yellow one with red wheels."

"Coast Guard must have used horses, too."

"You bet. You should have seen them run the surf boat down the beach."

"I don't see any saddles around the barn. Didn't the Bridewells ever ride?"

"Lionel used to have a horse. Smart roan with a star forehead. A single-footed pacer."

I picked up from the floor a heavy loaf of rusty iron with a scrap of leather buckled to its nose.

"That's a horse-block," Ed said. "The kind they used to throw out of a carriage when they parked the team at the curb."

"I know." Another piece of an entire civilization gone down history's drain. I handed it to Ed. "It would make quite a weapon, wouldn't it?"

"It would," Ed said, hefting the weight.

"But then, why not a plain old-fashioned hammer?"

"Eh?"

"I've just been thinking. I've never heard of anyone killed with a bag of shot."

"Oh, that," Ed said. "Old lady Bridewell."

"I suppose she was killed for her money?"

Ed nodded, "That was what the Prosecution claimed. The boys had been trying to get it for a long time, and the old lady was what I guess you'd call adamant."

"Murder seems the hard way under the circumstances. Close relatives and offspring usually try other means."

"Well, they did." Ed tugged his nose in recollection. "It all came out after the murder. Lionel, he'd been trying to break the old man's will. Writing to lawyers up in Boston for some years. Threatening a law action. And Earnest, he'd been taking another tack."

"What was that?"

"To have the old lady declared unfit to manage the estate. You know, non compost mentis. He'd been working on some sort of gimmick to get his mother committed to an asylum."

"That's a standard move in that sort of game."

"Only it didn't work," Ed said. "Neither did Lionel's scheme. Seems old Abby got wise to both attempts, and promised a legal showdown."

"But at her age why kill her? Wouldn't it have been simpler just to wait for her to die?"

"Abby Bridewell?" Ed shook his head. "That old lady was too stubborn to die."

"But she was well over eighty," I said smiling.

"And on her way to live a hundred," Ed said. "Told everybody she was going to, and she might have done it, to. Like I said, she was stubborn. All her family—the Joneses—was stubborn people."

"Stubborn?"

"Well, I'll tell you," Ed said. He dug a pipe from his pocket, sat down on a wagon-step, and motioned me to another. "You never knew people like them. Let me illustrate. . . ."

CHAPTER 4

ED BREWSTER speaking:

"One day—this was back some years ago—I'm down to Gillion's Wharf. It's a gray November afternoon with a norther making up. Kind of like today. The steamer's there at the far end of the pier, waiting to go at four, and nobody much else except me. I wanted to see the captain, who's gone into town to Smeizer's or somewhere—wanted to give him a special delivery to post for me when he gets to Newport. That's beside the point. The point is, I'm there at the head of the pier, sitting in my car by the deserted taxi stand. I'm a good half hour ahead of sailing time, but I didn't want to miss the captain, who's liable to take off early on a day like that when passengers are unlikely as hen's teeth. Especially with weather building up and a sea running.

"I'm thinking: There won't be no passengers for Newport today—not from this God-forsaken resort. And I take a drink from a fifth I've brought along to keep me company and from catching pneumonia there at the pier. But I'm wrong. Just then I see this man coming around the bend of the road down from town. He's wearing a black sou'wester—so I know it isn't the captain, who wears a yellow one—and he's carrying a suitcase. A little man, hurrying along with his head bowed to the blowing rain.

"I'm wondering who he is, and why he didn't come down in a taxi—it's quite a long way from the Center, as you know, and he's getting soaked, not wearing a raincoat, although he's got on rubber boots. But I guessed none of the cabs were out, bad day like that, or maybe he couldn't wait for one.

"Anyway, he comes down the road, lugging this bag. I think

he's going to hurry on past the car, when he glances over my way, sees me sitting there, and cants across the road to speak to me. He's up to the windshield before I can get a good look at his face, and then I seem to recognize him. That is, he looks familiar, like somebody I've seen a long time ago, only I can't be sure.

"While I'm wondering who it is, he puts down the suitcase and taps on the side window. I run down the glass, and he looks in. He's got a brown face, quite an oldish man, real sea-going like, with squinty blue eyes. He starts to ask me what time the steamer goes or something. Then it comes to me.

"Wallace Ord! Like that. Man I hadn't seen in I don't know how many years. A Pointer. One of the Ord family. He'd left the Point to follow the sea when I was a kid, years ago. Why, I'd thought he was long since dead.

"I said it like that. 'Why, it's Wallace Ord!' and I opened the car door to let him in. He hoisted his bag, and he got in, spry as anything. 'Hello,' he said. He squinted at me. 'I'm afraid you got the advantage,' he said. 'I've not been around here for over seventeen years. Don't seem to know too many of the people.'

"I told him my name, and he laughed and patted me on the shoulder. 'What do you know! Well, a lot of water has sure run under the bridge.' I said it sure had. Must have been in grammar school, or maybe high school, since last I'd seen him. He nodded, and expelled a deep breath. 'Funny, ain't it,' he said. 'But the Point seems the same. The people ain't changed either.'

"He sort of grunted after he said that, and looked hard at me without seeing me. He looked sort of angry. Then his eyes came back into focus, and he fixed a look at the bottle I had balanced between my knees.

" 'Oh, excuse me,' I said. 'Have a drink, if you want one, Wallace.' He had one. A good long one. When he hands the bottle back, he's coughing. Then he burst out laughing. He threw his head back and laughed so hard, it made me laugh, too. He had to pull out a handkerchief and wipe his eyes. Then he sobered up, sudden, and reached for the bottle again. He took another long pull. This time, handing it back, he didn't cough and he didn't laugh. He looked mad. 'Dear old Quahog Point,' he said.

"Me, I didn't get it. I'm wondering if the guy is a little nuts. I'm wondering a lot of things. His wife lives there at the Point, see. Cornelia Ord. I'd guess at the time she was close to sixty. She lived at this farm way out along the shore.

"The thing was, she'd been living alone there for years and years. Raised a few chickens and what not. But all by herself, with a bunch of cats. The town kind of looked after her, and folks would drop in to see how she was. But I'd always thought —assumed, you know—she was a widow. Never stopped to wonder whether it was grass or sod. Just a widow.

"Then here was Wallace Ord—her husband—all the sudden sitting by me in my coupe there at Gillion's Wharf. What with the two of us alone there in the cold rain, it was kind of creepy. I didn't even know he'd come back to the Point. I began to wonder where in hell he'd come from, and how he got here.

" 'I expect you're wondering what I'm doing here,' he says, like he'd been reading my mind. 'I expect you didn't hear I came in on the morning boat.'

" 'No I didn't,' I told him. 'But I didn't get down to the Center this morning. Anyway, Wallace, that's your own business.'

"He agreed it was his business, and he appreciated other folks not minding it. 'There were only a couple of other passengers on the boat this morning, and I didn't speak to them,' he tells me. 'Didn't know any of the crew, and this skipper is new to me. Last time I saw this Newport steamer was seventeen years ago. I expect you're wondering why I came back to see Cornelia.'

"I said, 'Tell you the truth, Wallace, I always thought you'd died. I mean, you'd gone away to sea and had died somewhere. It's been a long time.'

"He reached for the bottle and took a short one and handed it back. 'Look,' he said, 'how well do you know Cornelia?'

"I said I saw her around from time to time, but never had much occasion to go out to the Ord farm. 'She seems to get along all right by herself out there, Wallace.'

" 'She does,' he agreed. 'By herself. That's why I left the first time. Part of the reason, anyway. She's got the farm and some chickens and a herd of cats, and that's enough. She'll never be in want. Now I'll tell you the real reason why I left her back in Nineteen Hundred and Nine. You got a minute?'

"I said I wasn't going anywhere, I was just there waiting. So he told me. He said that him and Cornelia were married just after the Spanish War when he got out of the Coast Guard. He lived at home back then, out at the farm, and he lived there with Cornelia for the next eleven years. They got along all right, except his wife was kind of bossy. It was this way. Wallace would come back from work at night—he had this job at Grimese's Boatyard—and he'd settle in his chair with the newspaper to wait for supper. Or he'd get on his slippers and light his pipe. Or he'd go lie down on the lounge. Well!

"The minute he'd settle, or get on his slippers, or lie down, Cornelia she'd start giving him orders. Wallace, you got to fix the kitchen pump. Wallace, go back down to the Center Store, we're out of tapioca. Wallace, get out there this minute; you got just time before supper to shovel a path to the outhouse.

"As Wallace told it, he didn't mind the *chores*. Everybody has to do chores, and he didn't object to his share. What bothered him was Cornelia always give him an order of some kind just as soon as he got his *shoes* off or got himself relaxed in the Morris chair.

"He didn't say nothing about it, though. He just went on, day in, day out, bearing it. He never tried to add up the number of times, or anything like that. He just took it, the way Job or whoever it was in the Bible took a lot of things. But there's a limit, as Wallace says. He wasn't sore, exactly. It just got to be too much. A camel can carry so many straws, was how Wallace explained it. Then one too many breaks its back. It just takes that final one.

"Wallace knew it was coming sooner or later. Sooner or later, he wouldn't be able to take it like he'd been. Time was coming when he'd have to put his foot down. Have to teach Cornelia a lesson.

"Well, here's what happened. It was late in the November of

Nineteen Nine, and he was working hard at the shop. On this particular Friday he comes home dog tired. It's a cold, rainy night, with a norther making up, same as there at the pier, and he's almost frozen to the bone when he reaches home that Friday evening.

"Into the house by the back door—the kitchen cozy and warm. 'Evening, Cornelia.' 'Evening, Wallace.' She's at the stove with her back to him, busy. He waits. She doesn't turn. He takes off his things and hangs them up. Gets into his slippers. Picks up the paper. Drops into a chair at the kitchen table. A pot on the stove smells good. 'I sure got an appetite, Cornelia. What's for supper?'

" 'Fricasse,' she says, turning around with a bowl in her hand. 'I'm makin' biscuits. But you won't get no supper, Wallace, till you go out to the woodshed and fetch in an armload of wood.'

" 'What's that?' he says.

" 'You heard me,' she says. 'Go out to the woodshed and fetch in an armload of wood.'

"As Wallace explained it, it was an order. Not please fetch some wood, or do you mind bringin' in some wood. Just plain, flat *go get some wood.* Like a Coast Guard petty officer might speak to a seaman third. She always spoke to him like that, and if he delayed a little, she might say hurry up. That night she said it. 'And hurry up.'

" 'I got up out of my chair,' says Wallace. 'I went to the door where I'd left my boots. I put on my boots. I put on my overcoat. I put on my sou'wester. I reached down the lantern, and I lit it, and I went out the door, closing it behind me. I went down the path to the woodshed in the ice cold dark and rain. I went into the shed.

" 'It was cold as Greenland in there,' says Wallace. 'I had to blow on my hands so's I could pick up the axe. I put down the lantern and I blowed on my hands, and I went to the chopping block and picked up the axe. I looked at the axe, and I looked at that there pile of wood, and all the sudden I made up my mind. By Godfrey, I just couldn't take it from Cornelia no more.'

"What did Wallace Ord do? Why, he just wheeled around,

and he drove that axe into a corner post of the shed, just as hard as he could drive it. Wham! Like that. Deep into the corner post so the blade was almost buried up to the head.

"He left the axe driven into the post like that, and he turned and walked out of the woodshed. He walked up the path to the house, but he didn't go in. He'd picked up the lantern, and he kept on going down to the front gate. Reach the gate, he turned right in the road, and he headed for town. He walked straight into town and down through the Center—wasn't a soul abroad in the freezing night and rain—and he kept on going right through town.

"He walked out to the moor, and he kept on going across the moor. He followed the road on across the dunes, and he kept on going across the dunes. He didn't stop when he reached the inlet. He'd kept a rowboat down there, in a duck blind, and he rowed his boat across the inlet and left it on the other side. Over there he hit the peninsula road, and he just kept on walking.

"He kept on walking, and he didn't look back once. He walked all night, with a nor'easter blowing and the scud like to sweep him off his feet. Just before morning, the lantern give out, and he tossed it into the bayberry. He didn't care. He knew every foot of that peninsula road like he knew the back of his hand.

"Funny. Wallace says he wasn't tuckered. Come daylight, he felt fresh as a daisy. An all-night hike like that would have fagged him ordinarily. But he felt great. When he reached the main highway—the country turnpike that cuts inland—he was going strong. A van came along and picked him up. Took him all the way to Newport.

"He had a couple of bucks in his pocket, and he ate a breakfast that tasted like a Thanksgiving dinner. Two servings of everything, and three cups of boiling coffee. He hadn't even caught a cold. He went down to the waterfront to a place he knew, and asked about a ship. They didn't have anything special, but there was a coal collier lying in—an old barkentine that had been dismasted, with bunkers built in her, and an auxiliary engine. She was to go on a tow line down to Norfolk, Virginia, to pick up a cargo of anthracite. If he could run an auxiliary engine, they needed a hand.

"Wallace told them he could run any kind of marine engine. They signed him on. The coal barge wasn't much, but he felt as though he'd stepped aboard the *Mauretania.* Outward bound, the empty barkentine rolled her beam ends under if a launch went by. Wallace Ord went down the Narragansett like Thomas Lipton on a yacht.

"He'd only signed for the Norfolk passage, so at Norfolk he left the collier and got a deckhand job on a freighter bound for Paramaribo. And that was how it went. From South America he shipped to New York on the Munson Line. He sailed on Luckenbach freighters for a year or two out of New York. Then went to the West Coast, Panama Pacific, and after that got an Orient run on one of the Dollar liners.

"Cornelia? He never wrote to her. Five years. Ten years. Fifteen. Never wrote her a single line. He sailed to India. Japan. Australia. Back to 'Frisco. Out again. Not one letter to Cornelia, although he thought of her occasionally. Then, unexpected, he heard of her. Honolulu, of all places. It was during the World War. In a bar there he ran into one of the Purdy kids—just a youngster when Wallace had left the Point—but the kid recognized him there in Hawaii. This John Purdy was an Army sergeant out there at Schofield Barracks. He was sure surprised to see Wallace Ord in Hawaii, and vice versa.

"They talked about the Point, and Wallace asked about his wife, Cornelia. The Purdy boy said last time he'd seen her she was running a bean dinner at the Shoreside Methodist, same as always. He told Wallace the farm was about as usual; Cornelia did all right renting rooms to summer people. So she was okay. Wallace was glad to hear it.

"Wallace didn't bear any ill will. He'd been gone close to seventeen years. He figured that was about long enough, and Cornelia had learned a lesson. So he started home. He came back by way of Singapore, Bombay, Suez. Gibraltar, Liverpool, Halifax—that run. As he put it there on Gillion's Wharf, he got in just that morning.

"Wallace says it as if he's only been around the corner instead of a few times around the world. But seventeen years is a long time away. 'And you went out to see Cornelia?' I asked him.

"He gave me a straight look. 'I did,' he says. 'There wasn't no taxi at the pier this morning—the other passengers had their own car waiting—so I walked. It wasn't raining, then. Just cold mist, the fog comin' in. I lugged this here bag into town. Didn't go through the Center, but took the side road the short way—the drift road across the bayberry past Hatfield's Pond. Then it was solid fog along the shore road and I didn't pass a soul. I got out to the farm about noon.'

"Wallace gazed off in that direction. 'Fog was so thick I could hardly see the house from the gate. But when I went up the path everything looked about the same. I see smoke climbin' out of the chimney, so I figure Cornelia is fixing dinner.

" 'I went around by the kitchen door,' Wallace says. 'Sure enough, through the window I see Cornelia at the kitchen stove. She's got the lamps lit, it's such a dark day, and it's almost like that Friday evening seventeen years ago. Looks to me like she's almost wearing the same apron.'

"Wallace shakes his head, kind of doleful. 'It sort of touched me,' he says. 'Well, I done something almost like I'd planned it. I hadn't planned it, but it just seemed like the thing to do. I put down my suitcase at the doorstep, and I walked down the path to the woodshed. Same old woodshed, except a little more in need of repair, maybe. Same old door standing a little open. I go in. I look around. What do you know? There's this hatchet—one I didn't remember—stickin' up in the chopping block. And there's my axe driven into the corner post, all covered with dust and cobwebs, right where I'd left it.'

"Wallace stopped to take a drink. He coughed and cleared his throat. 'The thing touched me,' he says again. 'The axe, I mean. It comes to me that she's left it there all these years, sentimental like. Cornelia. Well, I got the axe out of the post, and I blew off the dust. I went over to the woodpile, and I chopped an armload of kindling. I carried the wood up to the house. I walked straight in the kitchen door.

" 'Hello, Cornelia,' I says. 'Hello, Wallace,' she says from the stove without turning around. I go to the corner and put the wood in the woodbox. I hang up my hat. I take off my coat. I take off my boots. I go to my chair at the table, and stretch out, and light my pipe. 'All right, Cornelia,' I say, 'there's your gosh dang armload of stove wood.'

"For the first time Cornelia turns around and looks at him. She gives him a smile. Then, as Wallace tells it, she goes to the cupboard by the stove. She takes down a plate of something that looks like little black walnuts. She carries it to the table and sets it down in front of him. He touches one of the hard little nuts with a finger, and looks up at her, inquiring.

"Cornelia gives him a cold nod. 'And there,' she says, 'are your gosh dang biscuits.'

"Wallace Ord stares at her. He can't say a word. As he tells it, 'I didn't say nothing. Nothing at all. I got up out of my chair and went to the corner. I put on my hat. I put on my coat. I put on my boots. I went out the door and closed it behind me. I picked up my bag and walked down to the road. And here I am,' he says, 'and what time does the steamer go? I'm not never comin' back to Quahog Point again.' "

And that was my informant's story. The steamer captain came up in a cab at that juncture, and Ed Brewster got out of his car to give the captain the special delivery. Wallace Ord climbed out of the coupe and started after the captain down the pier. Then, as the little man in boots and sou'wester moved off, he looked back.

He called back over his shoulder something that sounded to Ed like: "God preserve you from a stubborn woman.

CHAPTER 5

As WE entered the kitchen Ed's wife exclaimed, "Men! I've been ringing the dinner bell for twenty minutes."

Ed said, forcing the door shut with his shoulder, "You know the wind in these nor'westers always comes in this direction. No use ringing a bell in the teeth of a gale."

"Well, there isn't much left on the dining table. Mr. Martin and I went right ahead. He's eaten and gone."

Ed's wife explained that Luke had called a cab to take him down to the Center to the telephone exchange. Business call to New York, and he preferred not to use a party-line phone.

"He said he might have to wait some time for an answer; would you boys meet him around four-thirty at the Anchor Saloon?"

We sat down to a feast of New England clam chowder that went far to dispel the weather's gloom.

"Hot biscuits," Ed noted with a grin.

Annette Brewster demanded, "Don't you always get them?" She said to me, "It's a fixation with my husband. If they don't melt the butter, he has a mad bird-dog fit. Men!"

After the table was cleared, Ed steered me into the parlor. There he opened the Bridewell album to the picture of a tall, square-shouldered woman posed on the front steps of a farmhouse. From the high-collared blouse and ankle-length skirt, I guessed the date to be 1900.

"That's Cornelia?"

"That's Cornelia. Abby Bridewell's side of the family. Earnest and Lionel's cousin."

Down South they would have described the relationship as

"kissing." I doubt if the adjective could have been literally applied in this instance. Cornelia Ord was not quite lamp-jawed, but her expression was formidable.

"You know," Ed observed, "I was kind of surprised to find her picture in this album. They didn't get along, her and the old lady. Especially after the auction."

Out came Ed Brewster's briar pipe, and with it another vignette of Bridewell history. It seemed that Cornelia Ord, grass-widowed by her husband's initial departure, had appealed to octogenarian Abby for a loan. Abby Bridewell held a mortgage on the Ord farm, it appeared, and in the bad season of 1909, with her husband gone and summer guests equally *in absentia*, Cornelia was hard-pressed.

Abby Bridewell turned a stone-deaf ear to Cornelia's appeal. Instead of offering a loan, the dowager aunt presented her niece with a demand for interest payments overdue. The demand was backed with a threat of foreclosure if Cornelia failed to meet the obligation.

"She had to meet it with this auction," Ed went on. "I can just remember it. There was a lot of stuff piled in the front yard, and to us kids it was like a circus. They bid off one of those big square grand pianos you don't see any more—it went for a song. An antique dealer from somewhere got it. I remember them carrying it aboard the steamer. It looked like a big, shiny, black coffin."

I could not help quoting: "Lay not up for yourselves treasures upon earth, where moth and rust doth corrupt, and where thieves break through and steal—but lay up for yourselves treasures in heaven . . . for where your treasure is, there will your heart be also."

"Gospel of Matthew," Ed said quickly. "Hmm . . . The way I heard it, Cornelia Ord's heart was in that piano. Anyway, she never forgave Abby Bridewell. Especially when the old lady sent off to the city and bought the piano and had it shipped back to Quahog Point where she put it in the ballroom of the Surf and Sand for Lionel."

That, I agreed, was rubbing it in. I could readily believe Ed's recollection that there was no love lost. Stubborn Cornelia continued to sit in the Bridewell pew with her aunt and bachelor cousins. She came to the Bridewell house for Sunday dinners. As Ed suggested, "Why look a gift hen in the teeth?" But her status was plain to the townsfolk. From independent relative she had been reduced to poor relation—an embarrassment loudly and perennially advertised by the grand piano in the hotel ballroom.

"That was one place she'd never go," Ed Brewster said, chewing his pipe-stem. "Heard my father say wild horses, nor even the team they used to have at the Coast Guard, could have got Cornelia into the Surf and Sand. She was the sole and only Pointer who wouldn't attend the New Year's ball."

The New Year's ball. I gathered this was a custom dating back to the Garfield era. Year after year the Bridewells had opened the Surf and Sand for the occasion. Caterers were brought in from Newport. Hams, turkeys, pheasant, lobsters, baked goods, condiments and gallons of punch were moved in. For two days prior to the banquet the hotel furnace was stoked and the help worked overtime to put up festive decorations. It was an extravagant affair. All of Quahog Point was invited, and all of Quahog Point was expected.

"Everyone had always went." Ed made an inclusive gesture. "The whole town. Afraid not to, more or less."

"Afraid of Abby Bridewell?"

"Well, maybe some were. It wasn't just that she owned a lot of local property. She pulled strings at the Town Council and all that. Who's to be Postmaster. Who's to be dog catcher. Besides, quite a few of the townspeople owed her money. You know."

I could imagine.

So, as Ed expressed it, they "cow-tailed."

Particularly in that winter of 1910–11, after the ruinous collapse of the P. and Q. Transit Line. And most particularly with the come-down of Cornelia Ord as a local reminder of the embarrassment in store for the obligated who incurred a certain creditor's displeasure. The debtor who can't pay his bills must perforce pay his respects.

Ed went on, "Like I say, except Cornelia everybody was there that New Year's. I went with my father, who catered the lobster thermidor. I can still see, mind's eye, the tables and all the food under a big crystal chandelier the size of an inverted Christmas tree. Earnest Bridewell's there in a dress suit. Lionel's at the piano, ready to sing a solo. Old Abby sat by the door in one of those big hotel-lobby chairs, and everyone went by her, cow-tailing."

I too could see it, mind's eye. The chatelaine greeting her subjects.

Subject: Glad to see you, Abby.

Chatelaine: Yes, yes, Cora. Another year, another dollar?

Subject: You're lookin' mighty well, Miz Bridewell.

Chatelaine: So would you be, Sam, if you ate more and drank less.

Subject: Evening, Abby; that new dress on you is becoming.

Chatelaine: Thanks, Henrietta; and I always liked that one on you.

Earnest Bridewell: Silence, please! My brother has consented to sing.

Lionel Bridewell: "I dreamed that I dah-dwell-elt in mar-arble halls. . . ."

Subject: Your Lionel certainly has a voice, Miz Bridewell.

Chatelaine: So has Earnest. You should hear his favorite.

Subject: What song is that?

Chatelaine: How he loves the dear silver that shines in my hair. Happy New Year, everyone!

And that (as my informant phrased it) was the last "shee-bang" Abby Bridewell ever gave.

CHAPTER 6

WINTER swept in. The old-fashioned Whittier-type winter.

Quahog Point was set adrift by a series of blizzards and gales that buried the peninsular road and left the village at land's end as isolated as Nome. Community "togetherness" now mutated into household "togetherness" as neighbor became remote from neighbor, and each homestead dug in.

It was not the worst winter in local memory, but it averaged a number of weeks below zero. There were days when the natives on outlying farms could not get in to the Center. And days when villagers in the Center could not get across the street to Post Office or General Store. Pumps froze and wells solidified. A man had to dress like an esquimau to go from house to barn, and a trip to the village was like a journey to the Arctic.

Oh, those good old invigorating Currier and Ives winters of chalk-white snow and icy blue ice. To be sure, there were discomforts. The January cold petrified your wrists, and if you walked half a mile through the February drifts your ankles ached as though they were sprained. Houses lacked central heating and indoor plumbing. As Ed Brewster expressed it, a four-below night was no time to have the runs. But indoors you could be cozy. What if the feather bed became lumpy, and you cried out when your bare feet touched the floor next morning? Such minor hardships bred character.

Like Abby Bridewell's.

And Earnest Bridewell's.

And Lionel's.

Once more I could visualize them snugged in here in the parlor, elbowing each other raw. Prisoners. There was no escape. The windows were barred with icicles. The house was walled in by polar weather. Out in the vestibule you could see your breath. So you sat here by the fire counting your money, or counting your chances for money—thinking your thoughts.

Abby in her rocker. Each creak an irritant to a man whose nerves were in high tension.

Earnest pacing with hands behind his back. Cracking his knuckles as counter-irritant.

Lionel drumming on a sofa arm and wiggling a restless foot.

And by mere spontaneous combustion the quarrel explodes. About the high cost of living. About the price Lionel paid for the horse. About Earnest's proposal to sell the Trawler Company.

About anything at all, or nothing at all—a quarrel just for the sake of quarreling. But voices rise, pitching off-key. Tables are banged. Fists are shaken. Faces distort like rubber masks—the old lady's squeezed up into a clench—Earnest the color of apoplexy—Lionel squinting venom.

"I tell you, Mother, those bills were paid in full—!"

"Don't lie to *me!* Those accounts were padded!"

"Of course they were padded. Not only that, Lionel shorted the hotel dining room!"

"Me? Shorted the—hah!"

"*Lionel!* If you cheated again—!"

"Now listen to me! Why don't you ask Earnest about the Neptune stock? Ask him what happened to those New Bedford Water Bonds!"

"You know damned well why I sold those bonds!"

"Why you *said* you sold them, yes!"

"You're both lying!"

"That's not true!"

"Quit shouting!"

"Who's shouting?"

"Keep your voices down, you fools. Do you want the help to hear?"

So, as suddenly as it commenced, the tempest subsides, its wind expended.

Abby Bridewell rocks.

Earnest paces, cracking his knuckles.

Lionel wiggles his foot, and drums.

Something had to give.

Ed Brewster touched my arm, and I suppose I jumped. He grinned. "What were you thinking?"

"I was thinking that in the old days it took a heap of living to make a house a home. One of the virtues we have today, at least, is a chance for individual privacy. If you don't like the trend of a fireside chat, you don't have to listen just for the sake of keeping warm. You can go up to your own steamheated room and slam the door. Families aren't confined in a little, airless parlor for weeks on end like mice in a cheese."

"Cheese!" Ed snapped his fingers. "That reminds me." Abruptly he rose from his chair.

"I couldn't possibly—" I began. "All that chowder."

He shook his head. "It's not what you think. Wait here. I want to show you an old ledger."

He returned carrying an armload of warped books and yellowed newspapers—relics from the Bridewell attic. He said, "I got this down last night after you went to bed. Thought you might be interested, then forgot to show you. It's from one of the old trunks. Some of it's funny."

He placed the offerings on the table, then selected a large flat book, and drew up his chair.

"Take this ledger. Dates back to 1879. The Bridewells owned a part interest in Babcock's General Store. This is the old account book. I want you to see something."

He blew a mist of dust from the cover, and, opening the ledger, spread it across his knees, displaying a ruled page. The paper had gone brittle, and a corner of the page crumbled under Ed's thumb. The ink of the handwritten entries had faded to a delicate brown. One no longer sees bookkeeping artistry, and I stayed Ed's hand in order to admire the beautifully enscribed column of figures, the fine Spencerian penmanship devoted to the commerce of 1879.

Each page was like that—a model of perfect accounting penned with meticulous care. Monks would not have lavished more time and scrimshaw on an illuminated Psalm from the Scripture. What grocer today would bother to add curleycues to the capital "B" for bread, or would design a lacy "L" for lima beans, or take half a minute to draw decorative whorls around the "M" for molasses?

"Interesting, isn't it?" Ed Bridewell chuckled. "Look at the prices. Here—January 1892. Coffee, eighteen cents. Eggs, twenty a dozen. Liver, twelve cents a pound. Tobacco, ten. Here—April 16, 1894. Old man Hatfield bought a pair of galluses for forty-five cents. His wife got some button shoes for two-fifty. Cal Robinson got a barrel of potatoes for four bucks."

"And steak at those prices! Look," I noted. "A flitch of bacon. You never see that term today."

"Who could afford it?" Ed grinned. "Here's something else you don't see any more. Nemo corsets. Prudence Jones bought this set, see?—whalebone—for six seventy-five. You don't see people buying quinces, any more, either. But here," he pointed, "this is what I wanted to show you. Notice this cheese?"

The purchase was charged to one Otis Purdy—eighteen pounds of cheese. Ed tapped his finger on the date—July 9, 1896.

"Now, look," Ed said, running his finger down the page. "Here we are again. July 23, 1896. Otis Purdy—twelve pounds of cheese. And here. August seventh. Otis Purdy. Twenty-one pounds of cheese."

"The Purdys were certainly fond of cheese," I said.

"That's not the half of it. See, in September—here—Purdy bought fourteen more pounds. In October twenty-one pounds. In December, forty-five pounds of cheese, Otis Purdy."

"Did they run a boarding house?"

Ed shook his head. "And only four in Otis' family, not counting the baby. But that's nothing. Here's the Bryce family. Same period, Old Man Bryce bought twenty pounds of cheese in July, twenty-nine in August, twenty in September, same in October and November. In December, 1896, he bought sixty-one pounds of cheese! Same month, Saul Smeizer bought eighty-one pounds of cheese."

I had to laugh. "How could a family eat eighty-one pounds?"

"You think that's a lot?" Ed pointed. "Horatio Meck—local undertaker back then—*he* bought one hundred and four pounds of cheese in January, 1897. The following March he bought ninety pounds. For just him and his wife."

"But no man and his wife could consume one hundred and ninety-four pounds of cheese in three months!"

"It's like that all the way through the ledger." Ed grinned. "I estimated the Thorns bought almost a ton of cheese in 1900. Robinsons, that year, are charged for over a ton and a half. I added up the Ross total. Nine hundred eighty-six pounds."

I stared at the ledger. "What kind of cheese was it?" And then it dawned on me, and I looked at Ed Brewster.

"Sure," he nodded, closing the old account book. "You get it, don't you?"

"The kind you drink with hot butter on a winter evening," I said. "Or take on the rocks. It's good with branch water and ice in the summer."

"Most of the Pointers took it straight," Ed said. "It was good stuff up from Bermuda or the Bahamas way. There wasn't so much of it around when I come to the Point in 1905. But I recollect seeing some that come up from Jamaica labeled Jay Wray and Nephew."

"And that's how they could sell it for the price of cheese."

"The best," Ed said. "Tax-free contraband. Right off the boat. I figure from the code, here, that two pounds was a quart. . . . Notice that the Bridewells never bought any?"

"Didn't they drink?" I asked. "Or was it that they didn't approve of smuggling?"

Ed frowned at the ledger reminiscently. "Lionel was a toper on the sly. Drink whenever he could buy or cadge it. I recall seeing him propped up in the lobby of the Surf and Sand, stiff as a cigar-store Indian. Earnest would take a glass now and again, but up at the State capital he orated as a white-ribboner and voted for Prohibition. The old lady, she belonged to the Anti-Saloon League. Funny, too, when you consider it."

Ed considered it with a lopsided smile. "You see, the Bridewells were part owner of the store, so the old lady had an interest in smuggling."

The phone in the kitchen had begun to ring.

"That," Ed guessed, "will be Luke Martin down at the Anchor. Come on. You can see where most of that liquor was brought in."

A gang of rum-runners, tough as a fist full of spikes. A schooner as black as tar. Muffled oars and a yo-heave-ho in the dark of moonless nights. It had been going on for years. And then one night there came a pay-off—a weird pay-off in the light of a bull's-eye lantern. Ed Brewster wove these elements into a folktale as we drove townward in his Kissel through steel-colored downpour.

He prefaced the story with the caveat that he could not vouch for its factuality. The events had reportedly occurred when he was "knee-high to a nipper." As far as he was concerned, he had heard of them through hearsay in a community where hearing and saying did not always add up to truth.

But this happened (it was said) in the summer of 1906. Theodore Roosevelt was President and times were bully. Quahog Point had not yet speculated in a trolley line. In the cities automobiles were stared at by jokers who shouted, "Hire a horse!" Shore resorts were at their peak. All the Point hotels were full that summer, and so were many of the paying guests. In spite of Billy Sunday and Clarence True Wilson and little girls who recited "Lips that touch liquor shall never touch mine," the incidence of alcoholism reflected a booming traffic in the wares of John Barleycorn. At Quahog Point the gilded bars were at high tide.

Then trouble entered Paradise. At the height of the season a price war started. The Seagull featured imported Scotch at a dollar thirty a bottle. The Bayberry advertised it for a dollar twenty. At the Headlander the price went to a dollar. Waterfront cafes and beach restaurants joined the contest. Champagne, 90-proof rye, brandy, bourbon and other choice refreshments were equally reduced on the local market. Finally the Anchor Saloon offered Jamaica rum at ten cents a glass. That did it. Quahog Point was on the verge of civil war.

No one could or can gainsay that wars are, basically, fights for markets and for economic vantage. In our best of all possible worlds, price-cutting invariably leads to throat-cutting. That "Pointers" were at swords' points in their own fly-speck world—this facet of the story was (and is) known history. That the price war threatened to ruin the "cheese" business at Babcock's General Store remains a rumor plausible if not verifiable. But the tale had it that the Bridewell interests were thus jeopardized. And one of the throats threatened by the ugly situation belonged to Lionel Bridewell.

Just how Lionel became involved was a matter of considerable conjecture. He was not the first frustrated baritone to take to drink, however. He had evidently early discovered (along with the people of Birmingham) that the quickest way out of town was a bottle. A year or two before the one in question, he had begun to imbibe with intoxicating frequency. In consequence his mother had reduced his allowance to a pittance and had instructed the staff at the Surf and Sand to serve him nothing harder than well water.

The same official mandate went to all the hotelkeepers and liquor dispensers in town. Whereupon Lionel discovered that he was stranded in a desert as arid as the fountain in Center Square. Still, there remained one dispensary source beyond the limits of "local control." This was the source that lay just outside the maritime three-mile limit. The offshore source of many a cargo of Scotch, rye and rum that reached the local beach.

This sub rosa fountainhead fed a pipeline to the Anchor Saloon —a lonely tavern situated about a mile from the village. Occupying the lee shore of a secluded sandspit, the Anchor was admirably suited for illicit operations. There, when the moon was up, you could find New York, Boston and Fall River businessmen enjoying lively evenings with their secretaries. There, when the moon was down, you could hear the plash of muffled oars, and if you looked toward a wharf at the end of the sandspit you could see dark activity. And moon up or moon down in the early part of the summer of 1906 you could glimpse Lionel Bridewell at the Anchor bar, his elbow in the semaphore position.

One of the hardest things to conceal is a pint of whisky in your system. Old Abby knew her son was drinking, of course. With characteristic promptitude and temper she set out to put a stopper to the proceeding. Woe betide the barman who had dared to violate her local decree.

It did not take the old lady long to get wind of Lionel's oasis. Three times within a week she swept through the swinging doors of the Anchor Saloon, bursting into the taproom with the violence of a revenue raid. Three times she found no visible sign of her errant son on the premises.

For Lionel, exercising an alcoholic craft, had prepared for emergency. He had cultivated the good graces of a girl in the establishment—an entertainer who sang ballads and strummed a mandolin. Facing the taproom's entry, this barroom balladeer sat on a platform with eye-level above the swinging doors. In that strategic position she had a clear view of the road which approached the tavern. Lionel arranged a warning signal. If the girl saw his mother coming, she was to break into a soulful rendition of *Where Is My Wandering Boy Tonight?* Whereupon the wandering boy would make a back-door dash to the concealment of the men's privy behind the tavern.

It worked three times, but a fourth attempt failed. For the simple reason that the escapee found the door of the outhouse bolted on the inside—an eventuality he might have foreseen—and Abby Bridewell caught him (as my story-teller phrased it) with his trousers up. On the spot there ensued an inelegant scene between mother and son (duly reported by the unseen eavesdropper offstage). And a violent climax followed when the old lady stormed back into the tavern to have it out with the publican who had dared to break her commandment in respect to thirsty Lionel.

Proprietor of the Anchor Saloon was elderly Jonah Grimes, described as a frayed individual who shaved with a clamshell and wore a soiled sweater tied around his middle for an apron. At first he protested that he had sold Lionel nothing stronger than tonic. Pinned down, he admitted to Moxie. Abby snatched up the conspiratorial mandolin. "Tell the truth, Jonah Grimes, or I'll crack your bald head!" His nerve unraveled. Cornered, he confessed to selling Lionel hard liquor.

To unregenerate Jonah, Abby delivered a temperance lecture that had the fiery eloquence of a Gatling gun. In conclusion she advised the victim that he was going out of business.

"You're through for good, Jonah. I'll close up this saloon of yours, sure as you're born!"

"But, Abby—! You can't!"

"Can't I? Wait until your license comes up at Town Council next October!"

"You wouldn't dare!"

"*What?*"

"You wouldn't dare padlock the Anchor."

"Wouldn't I?"

"No, you wouldn't," declared Jonah, his voice squeaking in fright. "I don't own the Anchor no more, Abby. It belongs to the Syndicate."

"Syndicate? What Syndicate?"

Jonah glanced around the taproom in alarm. He lowered his squeak to a hoarse, "You know . . . The Ox. I sold out just last spring. This place belongs to Ox."

Abby Bridewell had, indeed, known of Ox. Everyone in Quahog Point had heard of Ox. Heard, but few had seen. So far as most of the natives knew, the man called Ox was only a rumor.

But the image fixed in local mind was that of a hulking bucko who embodied the personality of Edward Teach with the craft of Captain Kidd and the morals of Beelzebub. This much about him was certain: he wore a beard and he was built like John L. Sullivan. And this: his was not a temper to tamper with.

Nobody knew where Ox came from. He had been coming from there for a long time. Some thought he haled from St. Kitts or Nevis; others thought his home port could be Bermuda. His cargoes indicated a West Indies origin, but Quahog Pointers who did business with him did not ask questions.

Dead of night—that was Ox's time of operation. The black schooner appeared out of nowhere like a shadow, and the flicker of a starboard light signaled the arrival. Presently the boats came in to the sandspit wharf beyond the Anchor Saloon. Presently they left. At daybreak the black schooner was gone. The "Pointers" spoke of these doings in furtive undertones. He moved warily and respectfully who dealt with Ox and Ox's syndicate.

"Ox!" exclaimed Abby Bridewell. "Syndicate! The next time he comes here, Jonah, you can put a flea in his ear."

"Ma'am?"

"Tell him," Abby Bridewell ordered, "that he's through!"

"Abby, I never see him."

"Tell his sailors, then! Send a carrier pigeon! Do what you want, but this tavern gets padlocked come October!"

According to local history, it was that ultimatum which started the price war. Whoever Ox was, he had no intention of being dictated to by eighty-year-old Abby Bridewell. No doubt his spies advised him that she was a power in Quahog Point; that her son was a State Senator; that the old lady must be handled with kid gloves. So this rich old granny thought she could scuttle the Syndicate, did she? Owns a big hotel, does she? Competing with us under the counter at that hick general store? We'll cut the business right out from under her. Next shipment that goes ashore, flood the market half-price!

It was a combat Abby Bridewell had not anticipated. One that hurt, too, striking at her pocketbook as it did. She stood up to it grimly until late in August. Then she put out a peace feeler. The liquor war was ruining Quahog Point, and the old lady requested a truce. She was willing, it seemed, to vote another year's license to the Anchor Saloon provided its bar remained out of bounds to her son.

The message, conveyed through appropriate channels by Jonah Grimes, brought the sort of answer one might expect from a buccaneer. Never try to appease a pirate.

Ox agreed to call off the price war. But, borrowing a leaf from Barbary predecessors, he attached a little rider concerning protection money. The Syndicate would make peace for an appropriate fee. Ox would not accept dollars for it, either. On this point he was explicit. His note specified that the pay-off must be made in British exchange—in short, pounds. The first installment would be due on the first night the moon was down. Ox demanded a payment of three hundred and fifty pounds.

And at this juncture the story blurs. Apparently negotiations were conducted by Jonah Grimes, manifestly an unreliable reporter. Still, as go-between he could conceivably have been a witness. Be that as it was, something happened on one moonless night late in the summer of 1906. It happened on the wharf at the end of the sandspit within listening distance of the Anchor Saloon.

A light winkering from the rail of a black schooner three miles out.

A springer-wagon coming down the beach road in pitch dark.

A ship's clock in the tavern striking four bells.

Time: 2:00 A.M.

Its wheels creaking furtively, the wagon moves out along the sandspit and halts in black-out at the wharf.

Shadowy figures sweat and strain in the pitchy dark. Then silence, broken only by the occasional stamp of a hoof, the faint twitch of harness. Silence and the sound of wavelets slapping the wharf's underpinnings.

Then presently the creak of oiled oar-locks. The silhouette of a dory stenciled against midnight. A glimmer of metal and the white of grinning teeth in the outer darkness. A low voice hails, "Are you there?"

From the wharf a woman's voice answers, "Here."

"Have you got it?" calls a basso voice from the dory. "Have you got the three hundred and fifty pounds?"

"Yes, I have," answers the woman. "But before I hand it over, I'd like to see who I'm handing it to."

With that the dark is split by the ray of a bull's-eye lantern spearing out from the wharf. Jumping across the water, the little spotlight focuses on the bow of a black dory. Standing in the bow, and framed in the circle of light, is a big man wearing a cocked sea cap and a turtle-neck sweater—a man with a carniverous-looking black beard and the build of John L. Sullivan.

"All right," he hails, showing white teeth. "Where's the pay-off?"

"Right here," answers the woman on the wharf. "All three hundred and fifty pounds of it."

The lamp-ray whips around to a snubbing post at the end of the wharf. There, stuck atop the post, all bloody and raw, is an ox-head.

Trained on this pay-off, the bull's-eye lamp was left behind. Clattering and reeling, the springer-wagon departed in the night. It is also told that the dory and its captain departed—after the latter emitted one unholy yell.

True story? No "Pointer" could really say. Next day the ox-head was gone, the black schooner was gone, the man called Ox was nowhere in evidence. Indeed, who could say that anyone or anything had been there in the first place?

But the story got around, as stories do. And there were one or two known facts that loaned it substantiation.

Late that summer Abby Bridewell reported a missing ox. She said she presumed the animal had wandered off into the marshes and had drowned. No trace of it was ever found.

As for the smuggler called Ox, after that summer he never returned to Quahog Point. Some say the Syndicate was broken up by revenue men. Others say something else put an end to it. If one chose, one could believe in local legend.

Ed Brewster concluded the folktale with his prefatory qualification. "As I say, you can disbelieve it, if you want. Here's a fact, though. All those cheese entries in the old store ledger—they end in the fall of Nineteen Seven. And here's another fact. Quahog Point is a county, see. Even today it's the only county in New England where there's no ordinance making it against the law to drive a vehicle at night without lights."

We drew up in front of the Anchor Saloon. On the face of it, I could quite believe the story.

CHAPTER 7

THE raw rain chased us through the door into a shadowy barroom that was not quite as slatternly as the tavern's exterior.

Typical resort bar out of season. Bare dance floor. Vacant tables. A range of windows overlooking a stretch of desolate beach with miles of whitecaps flanking in from distant horizon.

Wind gnawed at the eaves, and the rumble of breakers vibrated the floor. But the room was reasonably warm; ship's lanterns created a marine atmosphere; and the old-time mahogany bar with brass rail would have been picturesque had someone cleared away the trashy strew of wisecrack placards, tacky calendar art and carved coconut-heads.

The bartender put aside a newspaper and spoke in an asthmatic husk. "Glad to see you, Ed."

"How's things, Dober?"

"Fair to middling. Slow, though."

I was introduced to Dober Davenport—two hundred and fifty pounds in shirtsleeves and apron sorely in need of laundering. He gave me a moony smile and a damp, fat hand. He wheezed: "Your friend was here."

"Mr. Martin?"

"Said to tell you he'd gone back to the Center. Expecting a long-distance. Back'n half hour. Would you wait."

We would.

I ordered a rye.

Ed said, "Ward Eight."

We carried our drinks to the far corner away from the windows. Ed said it would be warmer there. In subsequent reflection, I suspected that Ed's concern was privacy; our retreat was partly screened by the façade of a battered old Wurlitzer piano.

Even in the late 30's it was well to speak of smuggling at Quahog Point with diffident circumspection. Pinguid Dober Davenport was simply a post-Prohibition version of the gaslight blackleg. Only the dialect of the business had changed. We did not call the modern Ox a smuggler; in the new argot he was a hoodlum, mobster or racketeer. Instead of knife and six-shooter he used a Tommy automatic or a sawed-off shotgun.

Still, the game had been sufficiently dangerous in Abby Bridewell's day. You could die as hard from a dagger in the ribs as from a Tommy blast. If any part of the ox-head episode were true, the old lady had an iron nerve as well as an inflexible will. I began to see in her a touch of Ma'arm Mandelbaum and Calamity Jane Canary. Masked, of course, by Down East proprieties and pious Sabbatarianism.

Ed raised his glass. "Here's how."

"How."

I heard a phone ringing. After a minute Dober Davenport called from the bar, "It's that Luke Martin. Wants you to come, Ed, with your car."

Ed said to me, "Stay and finish your drink. I won't be long." He gulped his and headed out. At the door he said something to Dober. Presently Dober came to the table to join me with a Ward Eight. He sat down with a gasp.

I asked him if he usually drank Ward Eights (a New England favorite) and where the name came from.

He said he liked the look of them better than the taste. The name? "Some say it's from an insane asylum, ward for alcoholics. I've heard, too, it came from a political ward."

"The sources blend," I said.

He nodded, and sniffed at his drink. Then, looking up, "Speaking of politics, did Ed Brewster tell you a President once visited here? My grandfather—he was a Robinson—used to run the Seagull. You can see his picture in the lobby. Crusoe Robinson. And up in the cupola, still there, there's a big canvas banner says 'Welcome Grover Cleveland.' "

"No!"

"Fact." Dober sipped, and looked at me reflectively. "Ed says you might write something about State Senator Bridewell. You a political writer?"

"No, but I'm interested in Cleveland coming here."

"I don't know about Cleveland," Dober rubbed his chin. "But I can tell you a story my grandfather told me about how Earnest Bridewell got into politics back then."

And, therein as Victorian novelists used to put it, lay a tale. Another chapter of the Bridewell biography that culminated in a murder case.

Chronologically, this chapter reverts to the early red-plush era of the Bridewell history. The year 1884.

Abby Bridewell is in her vigorous fifties; Earnest, smalltown lawyer, is thirty odd; Lionel, in his Adonis period, is in Boston cultivating his voice. Captain Nathan Bridewell is a paralytic, buried. Well, not exactly buried. Entombed in a third-floor eyrie. Characteristic of Abby, who saves everything, to deposit her husband in the attic with the rest of the household's worn-out effects. When he dies she will store his remains in a new brownstone-front mausoleum that dominates the acreage of Headland Cemetery as an imposing and perdurable bank where he can be held in perpetuity.

Meanwhile, with her husband secured under the eaves, Abby can now devote full time to the Bridewell estate and to Earnest, who has been complaining that his Quahog Point career is in the doldrums. Earnest is restless, dissatisfied. What does he want? Barring a J. P. Morgan clientele, what do many budding lawyers want? So did Earnest Bridewell.

It was typical of the time. And, indeed, in keeping with American tradition. Probably nine-tenths of the gentlemen in Congress and a majority of the Presidents had been lawyers. True, three or four Army generals had ridden into the Presidency on the shoulders of hero worship. But a law career was the standard stepping-stone for success in politics. Perhaps because few other professions endowed the practitioner with similar ability to harangue, to debate, to dissemble, to wangle, to temporize, and to indulge in the incompetent, irrelevant and immaterial.

Anyway, Earnest Bridewell espied an opportunity in the political arena. He had been approached. Had made the appropriate donation. Had promised fealty to the Party platform. Had satisfied the bosses in the smoke-filled room behind the State capital. All he needed were a few hundred dollars and his mother's blessing. And, of course, a sufficient number of votes.

He got his mother's consent and the necessary financial subsidy. The votes were horses of another color.

Researching the story's background (details unknown to Ed's friend Dober) I could see what Earnest Bridewell was up against as a candidate for State Senator in 1884.

National politics in that election year were violent, complicated, and confusing. One might say, as always. But our present-day campaigns are almost rational and gentlemanly compared with those waged in the gaslight decades which immediately followed the Civil War.

This was the epoch characterized by public idols with feet of clay. Grant's sorry administration—the Black Friday crash—the Robber Barons—the Pension Grabs—America had never had it worse. As election year dawned in 1884 angry political cartoons showed fat spoilsmen looting the national treasury and porcine profiteers gloating over plunder. Graft ran rampant.

The Republicans accused Boss Tweed and Tammany Hall. They had something there. The Democrats accused the Republicans. They had more.

Then, as later in Harding's time, the Republican leadership was shot through with graft, the worse because it wore a mask of prudence, patriotism and piety. At least it could be said of the Tammanyites that they were not hypocritical Pharisees. Boss Tweed made few bones about his depredations, and his ward heelers bragged openly of stuffed ballot boxes and purchased votes.

The average voter? At this stage of American history he was much as usual. That is, baffled, bewildered and bamboozled. Too busy raising children and trying to make ends meet to give much study to the issues raised in City Hall and the ends legislated under the Capitol Dome in far-off Washington.

While he waits for Election Day, let us further examine this voter of 1884. Stereoscope views show him riding to work in a horse car. He wears a brown, high-crowned derby with a tight-curled brim, a celluloid collar and detachable cuffs, a woollen suit, the trousers tight, the jacket short with small, high lapels. His high button shoes have little knobs on the toes.

According to fancy, he may wear sideburns or a soup-strainer mustache. He smokes one-seventh of a mile of cigars a year, and he expectorates such quantities of tobacco juice per day that an entire industry is devoted to the manufacture of brass receptacles. He probably imbibes too much lager beer, and (dietary caution being relatively modern) his eating habits are atrociously overloaded with carbohydrates and lards. If he attains the higher income brackets, he develops the massive paunch significantly dubbed in period vernacular an "alderman." He will festoon this tummy with a gold chain and a fob, perhaps an animal's tooth. The mark of true success is a gold toothpick and a snap-lid watch.

His wife (who does not enjoy the right of suffrage, but votes through her husband more or less by proxy) wears one of the weirdest costumes in all the history of feminine fashion. Foundation is an hourglass corset that has to be laced by an assistant and is guaranteed to wreck the posture and anatomy of the wearer. Once corseted in this wasp-waisted straightjacket, the lady dons a tight little tunic with choker collar, huge leg-o-mutton sleeves, and a regimental file of some thirty or forty tiny silk-covered buttons. After a twenty-minute struggle with the buttons, she may be ready to step into a tight-waisted skirt that falls to the heels of her shoes and is just the right length for sweeping the streets.

This fashionable garb is topped by a dumpy plumed hat, the same being pinned to the coif by a brace of murderous hatpins. But the crowning glory, if one may use the term in this particular, is the bustle—an enormous pillow affixed to the lady's derrière. To the present day no one knows why she consented to be thus disfigured; if she thought the silhouette defended modesty and turned men's thoughts toward spiritual channels, the joke, like the bustle, was on her. If she supposed the style an improvement on her form, the assumption was certainly assinine. As someone once said of the camel, the costume looked like something put together by a committee.

To politics, then. The voter seen in our 1884 stereoscope may not know much about the major political issues, but he will certainly vote. Aside from the arrival of P. T. Barnum's Circus and the occasional revival meetings staged by itinerant evangelists, nothing excites him so much as an election campaign.

Early in June the Republican National Committee met in Chicago and on the fourth ballot nominated James G. Blaine of Maine for President.

Convening in Chicago in July, the Democrats nominated Grover Cleveland, former Sheriff of Buffalo, for President.

There were two other candidates for the Presidency. The National Greenback Party put up General Benjamin F. Butler. The Prohibition Party nominated John P. St. John. Both Butler and St. John could best be forgotten. And generally were. The big contest lay between Elephant and Donkey.

At the outset both Parties experienced internal trouble. Although clever and occasionally brilliant, James G. Blaine was a political hack whose every move was guided by a wet finger in the wind. He was ingratiating and plausible, but he had slipped on the banana peel of a tricky railroad swindle, and was known to be thoroughly unscrupulous.

Disliking Blaine, the intelligent liberals of the Republican Party broke away to support Grover Cleveland. They weren't called liberals or do-gooders in those days. They were called "Mugwumps." And they were called a lot of other things by the Old Guard leaders who staunchly stood by Blaine.

The campaign soon degenerated into a mud-slinging match that outdid any previous imbroglio in the political arena. It must be conceded that Blaine's record made a ready target. His involvement in the Western railroad swindle was exposed, and great was the smell thereof. Behind front-men he had palmed off a lot of worthless stock on his constituents in Maine. When the Democrats unearthed this skullduggery, the Old Guard leaders panicked. As Maine went so could go the nation.

Desperately searching for a counter-charge, the Republican leaders came across a bonanza. One can only appreciate it against the background of gaslight *tempores* and *mores* in the heyday of prudery and snob Victorianism. Grover Cleveland, when a young man in Buffalo, had fathered an illegitimate child. And now, with forthright honesty, he admitted it.

Well!

Jubilance danced and capered in Elephant headquarters while the Donkey brayed in dismay. No matter that the child's mother, a widow named Maria Halpin, had put a hammerlock on young Cleveland. No matter that the unfortunate offspring had been placed in a good private home. Cleveland was traduced as a philanderer and a seducer of virtuous maidenhood.

Against Cleveland's wishes, the frantic Democrats sought a

breach in the armor of Blaine's private life. Tamely they came up with the charge that he was tattooed. This was much like denouncing a crook for a bad taste in neckties.

The Old Guard had the big mudball, and they threw it for all it was worth. To advertise Cleveland's assumed perfidy, the Republican Club staged a giant rally in New York City. Marchers garbed as "Blaine's Knights"— plumed tophat and gaudy breast-ribbon—paraded down Broadway carrying baby dolls. As they passed under the street lamps they emitted a joyous chant.

Ma! Ma! Where's my Pa!
Going to the White House?
Ha! Ha! Ha!

It made history as the most scurrilous campaign slogan on record. It also made the front page of the contemporary papers and illustrated periodicals. Old Guard leaders, who cared nothing about history, loved the advertising. One can imagine them in their smoke-filled room in Washington when a runner dashes in with the morning edition.

"Boys, we're saved!"

And I could imagine Earnest Bridewell showing his mother the story in the *Illustrated Weekly*. His eyes bright. His cheekbones flushed. His finger trembling as it points to the parade picture.

"Ma, we're saved!"

For the microcosm of Quahog Point was a tiny mirror of the national scene. Earnest Bridewell, like James G. Blaine, had come up against a tough opponent who seemed assured of the election. But now—

"Look, Ma! They're carrying baby dolls. See it? Don't you *see?*"

Dober Davenport did not know whether Earnest Bridewell made a good showing on the stump. Nor was he conversant with the local issues which engaged the State campaigners in that bygone day. Probably area politics inclined the local bigwigs to James G. Blaine because Blaine was a Down Easter. On the other hand, General Benjamin Butler, the Greenback Party candidate, was from Massachusetts. So far as Quahog Point was concerned, Massachusetts was as close to home as Maine.

In the long view of history, Blaine was six of one, Butler half a dozen of the other. A slippery politician and a general who had come out of the Civil War with the reputation of a thief. Butler had also come out of the Civil War with the famous racing yacht *America*, so he may have been personally known at Quahog Point.

Quite possible, then, that Earnest Bridewell ran on the Greenback ticket. His opponent seems to have been a Mugwump.

To complicate matters, Earnest's opponent, Stephen Foster Alden, was a cousin. Only vaguely related, as were most of the "Pointers," but still related—son of Abby Bridewell's cousin-in-law, Sybil Bridewell.

To further complicate matters—at least for Earnest—Stephen F. Alden was an accomplished lawyer, an intelligent speaker, and a man known throughout the countryside for his competence and integrity.

He was two years younger than Earnest. Had been born in Boston where his mother, Nathan Bridewell's second or third cousin, had gone to teach school. Quahog Point learned nothing of the father, save that he was a Back Bay Bostonian named William Alden. It seemed he died before Stephen Foster was born.

Sybil, the young widow, had endured a hard time. Unable to afford Back Bay life, she had returned to Quahog Point to be principal of the little red school. She called herself Mrs. Alden, but the natives knew her as Sybil Bridewell. Eventually she confided to the town that Alden had left her, and she assumed her maiden name. Stephen Foster kept the Back Bay name.

I could picture him as a mannerly lad, lively and alert, doing well in the classroom thanks to his mother's tutelage. Perhaps this was putting too much construction on Dober Davenport's comment that he was "brighter than Earnest."

However, his mother was a bookish person with a respect for

scholarship, and such mothers usually transfer these virtues to their sons. Davenport said he'd heard that Stephen Alden had outstripped Earnest Bridewell in the County Academy, had gained two years on Earnest in college, and was away out in front with a law degree. Davenport figured this situation nettled Earnest and was "gall and wormwood" to ambitious Abby Bridewell.

"An old-timer once told me Abby and Sybil never got along. Sybil lived in this little cottage below the hill, poor as a church mouse compared with Abby. But she had her pride, and wouldn't take aye, yes or no from Abby and Nathan. Then to have Stephen out-do Earnest like that. Why, a big lawyer in New Haven once offered Sybil's son a partnership in his city firm."

It seemed that Stephen Alden had remained at Quahog Point to be close to his lonely mother. Even so, his law office prospered. His services were sought by some of the more prominent persons in New England, and he conducted a number of litigations that won mention in national law journals.

"Earnest's practice was small apples," Dober said. "He might have made a good justice of the peace. He didn't have half the brains of Stephen Foster Alden."

But Earnest's mother had ambitions. And money. And influence. She used these to back Earnest's Greenback candidacy for State Senator in 1884. As Dober expressed it, her "soul must have curdled" when the Mugwumps in July nominated Cousin Stephen.

What a to-do around Town Hall. What excitement at the Center. What a fog of cigar smoke in Local Lodge No. 46. Earnest Bridewell on the stump at one end of the square. His cousin Stephen on the stump at the other.

Political issues were forgotten in this contest of family rivalry. The campaign became a feud which split the Point right down the middle. The Knights of the Local Lodge backed their "fraternal brother" Earnest Bridewell. The United Fishermen sided with Stephen Alden. The Sabbatarian Church supported Earnest; the Unitarian supported Stephen; and the Methodist community broke in two, with the Center congregation for Bridewell, the Shoreside for Alden.

All in the good American, the sound democratic, tradition. There must be two sides to an election, and no populace can vote for both at once. Still, elections are presumed to decide political issues, and personalities are hardly Party platforms. But, of course, we Americans vote for "images"—that goes without saying. And by an odd trick of mirage, the images which loomed largest in the Quahog Point contest were those of Abby Bridewell and her cousin-in-law Sybil.

Yet it was not entirely strange that Abby Bridewell's personality should tower as a shadow behind the torch-lit figure of sallow Earnest. Everyone knew who put him on the campaign stump, and whose policies he would espouse.

Nor was it incomprehensible that the Quahog Pointers should have seen in Stephen Alden the image of Sybil Bridewell, the patient, devoted schoolma'arm who had nursed so many of them along the thorny road to learning.

Two kinds of public indebtedness were personalized by Abby and Sybil. Many townsmen owed Abby for rents and mortgages. Nearly all owed their education to Sybil Bridewell. Which debt was to be paid at the voting booth? The choice could not have been easy.

Since money usually talks, the majority might have decided to play it safe with Abby and vote for Earnest on the Greenback ticket. But even those deepest in vassalage found it difficult to swallow the unsavory record of that Party's national leadership. Ben Butler? Ugh! Cleveland was derided, but Cleveland had never stolen public funds nor appropriated a war-prize racing yacht. (I looked it up. Yacht *America*, winner of the classic Cup. Sold by Lord Decie to the Confederates in 1862 for $60,000. Captured as blockade-runner in 1863. Sold at Annapolis, 1873, to B. F. Butler, political general extraordinary, for $5,000. A steal for one of the queenliest racers on the Atlantic.)

So the grapevine passed the word that even the rocky Sabbatarians were swinging over to the Alden, or Sybil Bridewell, side. Some of them were sensible enough to see the light—instead of the torchlight.

Alden doubtless appealed to reason. If he followed the liberal banner, he advocated higher wages for workingmen, a reduction of the twelve-hour day, a merit system for State employees, and better public schools.

I could almost hear Earnest Bridewell. "A vote for the Mugwumps is a vote for national bankruptcy. My friends, they would spend us out of house and home. Cherishing that great flag as I do—Old Glory furling in the breeze—I say to you, do not be misled by my opponent with his extravagant dream of Utopia. In the words of Daniel Webster: Fellow citizens, the hour is late—!"

I do not know that Earnest used those words; nor Webster, either, for that matter. But Davenport described Earnest as "windy"—the term in the 80's was "gasbag"—and if he ran true to average politician, he "spoketh a deal of nothing." (They had them even in Shakespeare's day.) And the hour was late for Earnest, certainly. For all their provincialism, he was talking to crusty, hardheaded people who were as sharp as fishhooks when it came to deals and nothing.

Earnest Bridewell knew his neighbors. He must have known he was going to lose. In the Bridewell parlor the temperature doubtless matched the heat depicted in one of the Doré etchings of Inferno.

Abby: You've got to win. I've put a lot of money into your campaign.

Earnest: Can I help it? How could I know in June the Mugwumps would nominate Stephen Alden in July?

Abby: That clambake I gave your lodge cost over two hundred dollars.

Earnest (glaring at the Eye): Yes, and some of them *been* talking as though they might just favor *him!* It's a secret ballot, you know.

Abby: Keep them in line.

Earnest: Easy to say. Stephen pumps them full of talk about a shorter work day and free schoolbooks. It's Sybil, I tell you. She's got him to run just to show us up. You! Me!

Abby: We've got to stop Sybil and him.

Earnest: How?

Abby: Somehow. You're the politician. Use your head, if you've got one. Find a way!

Was it coincident with this stage of affairs in the Bridewell, and American, history that Ambrose Bierce wrote in *The Devil's Dictionary: POLITICS—A strife of interests masquerading as a contest of principles?* Next word: *POLITICIAN—An eel in the fundamental mud upon which the superstructure of organized society is reared.*

Bierce began his best-selling *Dictionary* in 1881, and its writing spanned a period of years. It would seem he reached the "P's" before the election campaign of 1884, which called for a stronger word than "eel." The traducing of Grover Cleveland suggests "snake."

However, in the "fundamental mud" Candidate Earnest evidently found his way. Which brings us back to the scene where he rushes into his mother's parlor with the weekly periodical in trembling hands.

"Look, Ma! They're carrying baby dolls! Cleveland had a child out of wedlock! We're saved!"

No one knows what actually occurred at that juncture in the Bridewell parlor. No one could possibly know. But one could conjecture.

For instance, Abby Bridewell could have said, "That's wonderful, but you're not running against Grover Cleveland."

Or she might have put it this way: "What's Cleveland's private life got to do with your Aunt Sybil and your cousin Stephen?"

Or she might have exclaimed: "An illicit affair! Earnest, that does it! We must get in touch with those people in Boston at once."

All pure hypothesis. But based on the account given me by Davenport and on the historical background of 1884. Plus the fact that Lionel Bridewell was studying opera in Boston at the time, and the origin of this story's denouement could have had its source in Boston.

The localities drew their own conclusions, putting two and two together. They knew Abby and they knew Earnest, and they knew that Lionel, circulating in Back Bay society, may have heard certain things and written them to his mother.

In Quahog Point the news about Grover Cleveland had come as a bombshell. The local Mugwumps were stunned. They had neither posed nor campaigned as Puritan Crusaders. But the obloquy now attached to their Party's national leader would certainly cost them some local votes. Thank God the County opposition had nothing against the private life of Stephen Foster Alden.

But then—

Something was up at Local Lodge No. 46. Two or three nights before the election, the Lodge Brothers gathered in secret conclave in their Hall. Excitement electrified the cigar smoke. Big doings.

The meeting, of course, was delightfully clandestine. And quite in keeping with that day and time when Americans everywhere adhered in dense "togetherness" in such fraternal organizations as the Loyal Order of Eagles, the Woodcutters of the World, the Ancient Society of This, the Benevolent Brotherhood of That, and the Knights of So and So. The nation never did a bigger business in Grand Caverns, Grottoes and Mystic Dens. Nor in bloomers, sashes, badges, swords, plumed hats and other items of abracadabra costumery. All of these clans and brotherhoods were up to the hilt in politics, and no candidate for public office could ignore them.

So the Mugwumps of Quahog Point must have been uneasy about the meeting at Lodge Hall. Especially when they saw Earnest Bridewell drive up hell-for-leather in a gig, and enter the Hall in his Ancient Knight, Lodge 46, regalia.

Rumors flew. Somebody told somebody that Earnest Bridewell was offering the Lodge members political jobs. Others averred that a cash payoff was in the deal. Everyone opined that a sensation was brewing. They knew it when, later that evening, Abby Bridewell's carriage dashed across Center Square, and Abby herself, skirts hoisted for speed, ran up the steps to the Hall. Onlookers heard excited palaver at the door. Then Abby Bridewell went in. Glory be! First time in history a woman had been admitted to a Lodge meeting.

Relating the episode, Davenport said that Old Doc Hatfield had told him about it. Dober's words:

"The doc, he was pretty well along, back then, but his memory hadn't dimmed. He could tell you who had the measles in the first year he practiced, and just who had the typhoid when the town first put in a reservoir and the wrong water mains were connected. He knew every Pointer from head to toe, and maybe that's why they were kind of afraid of him. He was a free-thinker. Didn't belong to any Party or to the Lodge. But they let him alone."

Dr. Hatfield saw Abby Bridewell enter Lodge Hall. And there were other witnesses. No outsider knew what went on in there, but everyone knew what happened afterward; the town talked about it for years.

On Election Day eve both Parties climaxed their campaigns with mass meetings. Candidate Bridewell spoke from the steps of Lodge Hall. The Mugwumps staged a rally in front of the schoolhouse on the other side of town, with Candidate Alden speaking from a platform.

In the tangy autumn night the torchlights flared in the offshore breeze like agitated storm signals. Man and boy—yes, and woman and maid—the whole town had turned out for the occasion. Excited leaves blew across the curbstones. Dogs and youngsters raced underfoot. Everyone was keyed up. Fireworks, literal and figurative, were expected.

Doc Hatfield joined the throng at Lodge Hall, and listened to Earnest Bridewell for a time. Then, misanthropic, he walked four blocks across town to listen to Stephen Foster Alden.

He heard Alden appeal for common sense in the State capital. For an end to the privilege and patronage. For a school system worthy of the name. In closing, Alden quoted the Cleveland slogan. "A public office is a public trust." And then it happened.

A blare of band music in the night. A distant outburst of pandemonium and cheering. The uproar swelled and loudened, coming across town with a parade. And then the marchers came in sight. First the brass band blazing out an incongruous rendition of *Marching Through Georgia.* Then a regiment of boys and men bearing torchflares. And finally the Ancient Knights of Local Lodge No. 46, all fifty of them, in full regalia—Zouave bloomers, opera capes, and tophats caparisoned with ostrich plumes.

With a crash of tympani the parade wheeled into the street before the schoolhouse. The crowd, there, fell back gaping. For the band, passing the speaker's platform (as though Alden were on a reviewing stand) burst into a new tune—*Bye Baby Bunting!* Then everyone was staring at the torch bearers—at the little white flags fluttering on the poles beneath the flares. Lettered on each flag was the name, ALDEN.

And now the Knights were passing in review, each Knight cradling in his arms a toy baby doll. Someone yelled, "Eyes right!" and as they passed Alden's stand, the Knights shouted a chant.

"Ma! Ma! Where's my Pa?
"Ask Sybil Alden!
"Ha! Ha! Ha!"

Everyone saw Stephen Foster Alden go rigid, his face as white as bone. His supporters were too stunned to move, to lift a hand. It was all over before they could realize what had happened. The paraders swept around a corner, broke ranks and melted off in the dark. Doc Hatfield, who saw it all, could not say whether Earnest Bridewell had been in line of march or not. The doctor found himself staring, numbstruck, at Stephen Foster Alden. The doctor did not understand.

At that juncture of Davenport's story, I did not understand, either. I admitted, "I don't quite get it. The little white flags with Alden's name—"

"Diapers," Dober said.

"Do you mean to say that Alden had an illegitimate—?"

"No," Dober said. "Not Alden. That wasn't the chant. They chanted, 'Ask Sybil Alden!' "

"His mother."

"You can imagine what a stunner that was," Dober wheezed. "In a town the size of Quahog Point. The story got around. See, there hadn't been any marriage when she was a schoolteacher in Boston. There wasn't any Mr. Alden who deserted her. She'd made it all up. Seemed like Stephen Foster was what they called a child of sin."

"Rotten term for it."

Davenport agreed. "The way my grandfather told it, the town never suspected. But the Bridewell family must have suspicioned something. Specially with Sybil first calling herself Mrs. Alden, then changing back to Bridewell. Probably Abby got to wondering about her cousin-in-law."

"So they investigated."

"My grandfather always figured it was Lionel. Sashaying around Boston in Back Bay society, he could have stumbled on the fact there wasn't a William Alden. So he wrote the news to Abby. Then when it looked like Earnest might lose the election, Abby had a check made up in Boston. There were some people who'd known Sybil. She'd been deserted all right. By a sailor on a Baltimore clipper."

"That was what the big Lodge meeting was about?"

"The way my grandpa figured it. Abby brought the official word. Even Doc Hatfield hadn't known about it. Worst of it was, Stephen Foster Alden hadn't known about his mother, neither. That he was illegitimate, I mean."

The parade. The scurrilous doggerel. One could almost groan for the man struck in the face by this wallop of fundamental mud.

Bad enough for a stalwart Grover Cleveland, who had only his own reputation at stake and could shame his detractors by uttering an honorable admission of the truth. What could a Stephen Foster Alden say from the platform? What word could he utter to down the forces of smalltown prejudice? How could he ever clear his mother? As for his own good name—

"Never call a man a bastard," Dober Davenport said. "He may be one."

I glared at the fat man. "And that's the story of how Earnest Bridewell got elected to the State Senate?"

"How he got into politics," Davenport corrected. "He didn't win that particular election, no."

None of the major County candidates did. Dober did not say so, but I could well imagine that Ben Butler's yacht wrecked the election chances of Earnest Bridewell and the Greenback faction. The Greenback ticket was snowed. The Republican candidate, a straw man, never had a chance. The Mugwump-Democrats had no time to find a winning replacement, and the Point election went to the Temperance candidate. On the national level, Cleveland won.

"And while he was President he visited Quahog Point," Dober said proudly.

"And I suppose they gave *him* a great big hand."

"Well, my grandfather said he never seen such fireworks."

"When did Earnest Bridewell finally get elected?"

"Four or six years later. Then a lot of times."

"What happened to Stephen Foster Alden?"

"Well," Davenport observed, "if I'd been him, I'd have blown my brains out. Losing a 'lection like that. Old Doc Hatfield always claimed that Alden was assassinated."

Apparently Stephen Foster Alden had made no answer from the public platform. No doubt Quahog Point was disappointed. He should have prevented his foes from enjoying the satisfaction of adding insult to the injury done him and his mother. According to Victorian tradition, he should have gone down to his law office that election eve and shot himself.

Instead, he behaved sensibly. He stayed around Quahog Point for a time. Then he quietly "wound up his affairs" and went to Texas or Australia or somewhere. Or so Dober Davenport believed.

Dober apologized for not being certain about the details. He reminded me that it had happened many years ago—"practically back to the Civil War"—and he had heard the story from his grandfather.

"Quahog Point is full of stories," he assured me. He stood up wheezily. "Excuse me, here's a customer. . . . Oh, it's Ed."

As Dober Davenport retired to his post behind the bar, Ed came to the table and plumped down.

Ed said, "Luke Martin is still on the phone. Thought I'd better come back for you, case you got bored."

"Far from it. I've been hearing some local history."

A cautious expression curtained his countenance. "About who?"

"Someone named Stephen Foster Alden."

Ed shook his head to indicate he did not know the name.

I inquired, "And a Sybil Bridewell?"

"Oh, her," Ed said. "Used to live here at the Point. Used to teach school, they say."

"Did she go away?"

"Manner of speaking," Ed said. "She shut herself away. Never heard why. But I recollect she lived in this cottage—the little place down the hill from the Bridewell house. Shutters always closed and the door locked. Nobody in the village ever saw her. Recluse. They say she was crazy."

"How did she manage to exist?"

"Never did know. She must've had some money. They used to deliver groceries to her back door—she'd come out at night, I guess, to get them. Methodist minister tried to call, I've heard, but she wouldn't let anyone in. They say the only Pointer who ever saw her was Doc Hatfield, and he wouldn't open his mouth about her. . . . Sybil Bridewell. . . . I used to go by the cottage."

"How long did Sybil Bridewell live?"

Ed frowned off. "Nineteen Sixteen? No, it was during the World War. . . . What'd Dober tell you about her?"

"Quite a tale. He said he got it from his grandfather, Crusoe Robinson."

Ed said from the corner of his mouth, "The biggest liar since America was discovered. Dober's just as bad. He'll read something in a magazine, then tell you six months later it happened."

"But there really was this recluse? A Bridewell cousin?"

"Like I said," Ed affirmed. "She outlived Old Abby for some years. The Pointers used to call her Spooky Sybil."

Buried alive. The victim of a character assassination that had also finished her son? I could not help wondering if the murder of Abby Bridewell had not actually been payment deferred.

Ed asked, "Do you want to try a Ward Eight?"

"No thanks," I said.

We said goodbye to obese Dober Davenport, and I was glad to walk out into the gentle rain from heaven.

CHAPTER 8

For supper that night we had planked swordfish smothered in a sauce that almost reestablished my faith in the brotherhood of man. During a meal devoted to eating and short on conversation, the rain stopped and the watery gloaming at the window became suffused with a spectacular amber light. Before darkness set in, Luke Martin was off with Ed Brewster, bent on surf-casting at a beach called Shipwreck Fathom. Ed was to taxi him and come back.

I did not go. Ed had an extra pair of hip boots and Abercrombie gear, but I lacked the requisite skill with rod and reel. Nothing frustrates an expert so much as a blundering tyro who continually tangles his line and hooks nothing but rocks. And nothing frustrates a tyro so much as an expert who can cast beyond the farthest breaker with fluid and tireless ease. I told Luke to go ahead and bring in a whale.

Annette Brewster went out to play bridge somewhere with the Ladies Aid. Left to my own devices, I wandered (perhaps gravitated would be the better word) into the Victorian parlor. I could not let the Bridewell story alone. Postman's holiday.

The furnishings of the pentagonal chamber had become familiar, if not exactly friendly. The lithographed orb overlooking the mantel had acquired significance. With its optic, pseudo-mystical stare, the Eye had witnessed in that room something more than acrimonious squabbles over money. It had stared at countenances that were cold masks of secrecy. At faces flushed and bright-eyed, joyously vengeful. Had it seen a conference between Abby and Earnest wherein mother and son planned the character assassination of the two relatives who stood in their way?

I had rather admired Old Abby after Ed's recital of the ox-head incident. The election campaign story altered grudging respect to a conviction of lefthanded justice. The old woman in her rocker must have been a cross between Mrs. Jeffray and Dickens' Madame Dufarge. True, notorious Mrs. Jeffray disposed of her victims by poison, and the fictional Dufarge sent hers to the guillotine. It appeared that Abby Bridewell, equally ruthless, perhaps employed devices beyond the reach of the Law's reprisal —indeed, that she had borrowed the lethal technique from certain political leaders on the national Currier and Ives scene. Stab your rival's reputation. Murder his good name. But was the Alden story truth or fable? Even if true, it had occurred long before the murder of Abby Bridewell. Twenty-seven years had intervened. America had paced from a horse-and-buggy civilization into the era of the automobile. The bustle had been replaced by the hobble skirt. There'd been a Hot Time in the Old Town Tonight. Abby, in her eighties, wore lavender and old lace.

Sweeter as the years go by? Somebody did not think so. Lionel Bridewell had been trying to relieve his mother of her money by means of a law suit. State Senator Earnest wanted her incarcerated in an asylum. Cornelia Ord, the stubborn niece, cherished a resentment against the old woman as massive as a grand piano.

And then the cousin-in-law entombed in the cottage down the hill. Did she abide there in a desolation of self-reproach and despair, excruciated by a masochistic conscience? Had she, in her bitter isolation, nursed a cancer of hatred for relatives responsible for her son's ruin? What of Spooky Sybil?

But I was to learn that Abby, in the prime of old age, had by no means exhausted the potential in local enemies. When she herself did not make them, it seemed her sons cultivated the field. Apparently at this type of horticulture Lionel was as adept as Earnest. Cornelia and Sybil were not the only Ophelias in the Bridewell drama.

The subject of women in general was introduced by an overture from the gramophone. Ed returned from the beach to find me in the parlor musing over the relic. I observed that it was a marvelous machine and asked him if it played. It did. Ed cranked it up, placed a cylinder on the rotary, adjusted the needle. Out of the morning glory came a nasal tenor, thin and tinny. "Daisy, Daisy. . . ." A second random selection entertained us with a quartet. *I Want a Girl Just Like the Girl that Married Dear Old Dad.*

I had a fleeting mental view of Lionel, Earnest and Abby listening to this vocalized sentiment. Three faces as expressionless as cement.

Ed said when the machine stopped, "That song's a laugh, isn't it? Ever notice how it's bachelors are always singing it? Get a few of them at a convention, or only down at the men's bar, and the next thing they're all packed together like a bunch of bananas harmonizing that chestnut. But catch them meaning a word of it."

"About wanting a girl?"

"Like the one that married dear old Dad," Ed amended. "Seen it a thousand times. Back in the Navy. Clambakes here at the Point. Veterans of Foreign Wars. Heck! Half those old goats wouldn't want any way, shape or form of a wife whatsoever. That's why they stay bachelors."

"And the other half?"

"*They* stay bachelors so they can chase girls in any way, shape or form. But want one like the one that married Dad? They'd run a mile nothing flat to get away from the marrying kind." Ed held out a palm at the room, and apostrophized, "For example."

"I take it, you refer to Earnest and Lionel Bridewell."

"Just the types," Ed said. "Here they play it on their gramophone. But marry a girl like dear old mother? Huh! Beats me why one of them would buy that record."

"Maybe to flatter dear old mother," I suggested.

"You got something there. It must've tickled her, knowing those two. Earnest was the typical bachelor type. Men's clubs. Lodge night. Not much use for females."

"What about Lionel Bridewell?" I asked.

"All lady's man and a yard wide," Ed made a sweeping gesture. "Brunettes, blondes, redheads—shoulders up didn't matter to Lionel. That is, if you could believe what they said around town."

What they said around town (if you could believe it) was that Lionel Bridewell in his salad days had been the Don Juan of Quahog Point. The Newport set. The croquet contingent. The bathing beauties in bloomers. The lassies who arrived on the excursion boats. According to local legend, Lionel had played the field from top to bottom. Or, as Quahog Point phrased it, "from shoulders to bottom."

Of course, like most overheated philogynists (see Dictionary for great lovers) our seaside Lothario had favored the spectacular.

"Like the soprano they say he got running with up in Boston," Ed described. "When his mother found out and made him come home from opera school."

"Soprano?"

Ed held up a flirty hand. "But not the la-de-dah type. According to Old Doc Hatfield, she sang in a troupe called Commodore Tooker's Garter Girls. Down at the Scenic Palace—that's the movie theater here—there's a big old-time poster, backstage, advertises that show. Commodore Tooker's Garter Girls. . . . Thirty Beautiful Babes. . . . Thirty."

"You mean Lionel's coloratura followed him here?"

Ed considered it, pulling at his underlip. "If you wonder did the soprano chase him to Quahog Point, I never thought of it in that connection. It's a real old poster, at that. . . . Tell you one thing. If she did, I bet Old Abby chased her back to Boston. Not that Lionel would have needed to worry. One girl isn't the only pebble on the beach at a beach resort."

I thought: *If seven maids with seven mops swept for a half a year. . . .*

I said, "Quahog Point must have been a happy hunting ground for girls."

Ed nodded, "Even now the shooting is pretty good. Back in the old days, they say, it was real gamey. I don't know about Lionel. But if some of the stories is true, he must have done some fast sashaying in open season."

I could imagine. A regular ding-dong-daddy. Especially from June to September when the summer colony was at the Point. He'd have put a carnation in his buttonhole and gone dashing around, all sparks and smoke, like the four-horse fire engine Ed had described. But under cover, of course.

The mental metaphors were becoming somewhat tangled, but the picture that came to mind was clear. I asked what Lionel did in the winter when Quahog Point was frozen in and his fire engine was snowbound, so to speak.

Ed grunted, "Maybe he was a picture collector."

"A what?"

"Well, somebody around this house collected pictures," Ed said. "I found some dandies in a cigar box out in the barn. Annette made me burn them. But there were some others." He pointed to the old papers and magazines heaped on the drumhead table at the end of the sofa. "Did you get a chance to go through this stuff?"

I told Ed I hadn't.

Sorting through the stack, Ed absently hummed, "I Want a Girl, Just Like the Girl. . . ." Then he turned with, "Here's some old-timers. Look at these."

With that preamble the curtain rose on another act of the Bridewell melodrama. A Quahog Point version of *Peck's Bad Boy* blended with *They Knew What They Wanted.* I confess I enjoyed it. How was I to know that the next performance might be as grim as *Titus Andronicus?*

Police Gazettes. Or, to give the periodical its official name, *The National Police Gazette.* Anyone old enough to recall Jack Johnson and Jesse Willard, anyone ancient enough to remember Cannonball Baker, Honus Wagner or Willie Hoppe would instantly recognize the once-famous pink sheet. In the day when a haircut cost a quarter and a shave cost a dime, what barbershop was without the *Police Gazette?* House organ of the billiard hall, favorite of the fireman's dormitory and the Turkish Bath, the Broadway boy's companion, the sporting man's almanac—this journal was as much a part of the American scene, and as influential on national thought, as the little red schoolhouse, Bull Moose Progressivism, the five-cent cigar and Fourth of July.

Leafing through the pink pages, I could almost smell Lucky Tiger Hair Tonic and Sweet Caporal Cigarettes. As through a haze of panatela fog (or was it the dusk of a waiting room on the Third Avenue El?), the old familiar format reappeared. America's first best-seller pictorial. Photographs.

Of prizefighters in black tights. Wrestlers bulging the seams of brown tights. Dancing girls in pink tights. Female fencing champions in white tights. Burlesque stars in flesh-colored tights. True, there were baseball players in striped stockings, motorcycle racers in puttees, Floradora Girls in flouncy petticoats, bathing beauties in bloomers, and policemen wearing brogans. But the warmly clad were, for the most part, relegated to the inside pages. Rare was the issue of the *Police Gazette* that lacked a cover displaying the human form, preferably female, encased in leotards.

Because of its consistent appeal to the male animal, its emphasis on sports associated with gambling, and its news coverage of colorful trainwrecks, fires, crimes and personages, the *Gazette* was considered racy and sensational. Conscientious parents banned it from the library table, and if the Little Boy in the Buster Brown suit wanted to read it, he had to trail his uncle (the one in the Navy) down to the barber's. As I started to turn the pages that evening, the Buster Brown somewhere inside me felt a faint and exciting tingle of guilt.

Then I wanted to laugh. How innocent the America of grandfather's time. How ingenuous the moralists of the early 1900's. Compared with the literature of the 1930's, the Sunday supplements, the Daddy Browning tabloids—yes, even the stories in the conservative morning papers—the *National Police Gazette* was as tame as Mother Goose. The muscular athletes in black tights, the burlesque soubrettes with the powerful thighs and calfs clad in slightly wrinkled leotards—theirs were as comedy costumes to the day of nudist colonies and George White's Scandals.

Sensational news coverage? The *Gazette* of February 24, 1900, contained a truly flamboyant feature story. Anna Held was opening in a new play—"Papa's Wife."

Police Gazette feature story, April 14, 1900:

> The Boer Women who can shoot a bit and who have nerve, are organizing to make a last stand at Pretoria to defend that town against the British Army. In the Modder River Battle, where Cronje made his last desperate resistance, many girls and women were found dead and wounded in the Boer trenches where they had fallen while fighting with their countrymen. The women have undoubtedly taken no little part in the hostilities.

Another blood-curdler appeared in the issue of July 21, 1900. W. Reyman, the "Lone Cycler," had just completed a bicycle tour around the world. He had pedaled across Siberia to Vladivostok—and was only prevented from pedaling back to 'Frisco by the Pacific Ocean. In the course of his global wheeling he had been arrested in England as a Jack-the-Ripper suspect, had been held in France as a spy, and had been chased through Peking as a "foreign devil."

Several earlier issues of the *Gazette* I found to be equally exciting. One contained the story of a raid on Canfield's "gambling hell." Another reported the Broadway opening of a show starring Louise Heppener, "the Flatbush Brunehilde." There was a column devoted to Chuck Connors, the Mayor of China Town. The police had arrested an Irishman for wrecking a Bowery saloon.

Why on earth had this pink sheet been tabooed in America's middle-class homes and in the respectable mansions on the avenue? I found two or three patent medicine ads that were surprisingly clinical, but similar ads appeared in the conventional news journals of that day. Indeed, one of the hypocrisies of the time frowned on the mention of certain diseases in news reports, yet permitted the publication of paid advertisements which candidly named these woeful maladies and fraudulently guaranteed their cure.

But the *Gazette* (like the forementioned ills to which mankind was heir) remained socially *de trop.* Recalling its rowdy reputation, I was surprised to find it on hand in the Bridewell mansion among the formal furnishings of period respectability.

I said to Ed Brewster, "Wasn't this pretty risqué reading for a roué in a family of front-pew Sabbatarians?"

Ed humphed. "Know where I found those magazines?"

"Behind the barn?"

"Closer to home. I found them up in that bedroom next to yours. Back cupboard. I was fixing a shelf, and noticed a couple of loose boards in the wall. Pulled them out, and behind the boards were these magazines. I was sort of hoping I'd find some hidden bonds or money in there. Wouldn't have put it past Lionel."

"It was Lionel's room?"

Ed chuckled and nodded.

Handsome Lionel, I thought, with his treasure trove of racy reading. Sneaking home with the latest issue under his coat. Tiptoeing upstairs to add "the Flatbush Brunehilde" to his private collection.

"Look at this ad," Ed said.

It was in an early issue of the year 1894. A full-page spread.

DR. SANDEN'S ELECTRIC BELT.

The illustration showed a paunchy middle-ager in under-drawers. Around his midriff he wore a contraption that resembled a champion strong man's victory belt attached to a truss. Instead of the usual American-eagle belt buckle, there was a device that resembled a fancy doorbell.

The trusting reader was advised that Dr. Sanden's Electric Belt was "not a cure-all." It was, however, "invented solely for the cure of all weaknesses of men." Wars? Speculative investments? Their neighbors' wives? No, but the belt was "guaranteed to cure all forms of nervous debility, impotency, spermatorrhea, shrunken parts, nervousness, forgetfulness, confusion, languor, dyspepsia, rheumatism, and the many evils resulting from bad habits in youth and the excesses of later years." Dr. Sanden stated (in quotes) that the belt was "an absolutely positive cure." Electricity "which is nerve force" was the secret. The doctor added —it would seem rather daringly—that five thousand dollars would be forfeited if the wearer failed "to feel the electricity."

I was interested to note that someone, presumably Lionel, had scissored the little order blank from the bottom corner of the page. I showed the excision to Ed.

"Do you suppose he suffered from confusion, or was he troubled with rheumatism?"

"I don't know," Ed said, veering suddenly toward the front window. "But here's someone who might."

The front door slammed. In from the vestibule walked a "Pointer" who might have stepped from the script of a soap opera about Down East Yankees. He gangled in rubber boots. Wore a blue knitted hockey cap on the back of his head. Carried a basket of lobsters. The stereotype caricature complete with jib nose, nasal twang and a week's growth of beard.

Ed introduced, "Like you to meet Fishbait Fred Fox."

I said hello.

Fishbait grinned. "Your servant," he said quaintly. With a mocking bow he handed Ed the basket. "And yours."

Smiling, Ed said to me, "Fishbait, here, runs the Shoreside Inn, used to belong to the Babcocks."

"Still does," Fishbait said. "I'm a Babcock. My Aunt Nellie's side by a miscarriage, in case you want the genealogy."

"He doesn't look it," Ed informed me, "but he's really a college graduate."

"Sure," Fishbait gave me a wink. "Summa cum laudanum."

Then he sighted the *Police Gazettes,* cocked an eyebrow, and started to turn away. "Don't let me interrupt *your* homework," he told Ed.

"Sit down," Ed urged. "Have a drink."

"Scotch," Fishbait said, instantly sitting down.

Ed departed with the lobsters. Grinning at the *Gazettes,* Fishbait Fred Fox drew a pair of black hornrimmed reading glasses from his vest, and put them on. The effect was extraordinarily salacious. He looked like some sort of rapscallion scholar.

He was reaching for a *Gazette* when Ed returned with bottle and glasses. Fishbait's reach swerved to a glass.

Ed handed him the bottle. Fishbait filled his tumbler to the rim. "High tide," he said, lifting the glass. The tide ebbed immediately.

Fishbait drew a long wrist across his mouth. "And now what's all this highbrow literature?" he asked. "I don't suppose you're looking over those old female hams in an effort to find out if Shakespeare was Bacon."

"Not hardly," Ed said. "Look. You recollect Lionel Bridewell."

"Now you're talking about Francis X. Bushman."

Ed showed Fishbait the Electric Belt advertisement with the coupon excised. "We was wondering if it was him who sent away for the thing."

"I don't know why he'd have wanted any more electricity," Fishbait observed. "As I recall, he would light up every time he saw anything go by in skirts."

The recollection illuminated Fishbait's glasses. He drained his tumbler, and turned to me. "Remember Sliding Billy Watson's Beef Trust?"

The name immediately called to mind a backstreet theater in my old home town. The Casino. You could hardly see the stage for the cigar smoke. Gargling comedians in slapstick shoes, and a pony line of cavorting females who could never quite keep in step.

"Well," Fishbait narrated, "Peter Ross once had a bull named Sliding Billy Watson. Had the initials S. B.—for Sliding Billy—branded on its rump. One night just before the County Fair—this was a long time ago—some of the boys sneaked into Ross's pasture and changed the initials S. B. to L. B. Nobody noticed it until the animal went on show at the fairground. Didn't that raise Hail Columbia!"

I asked, "Did Abby Bridewell know about the bull?"

"She was one of the judges at the cattle show. Mad as a wet hen. Seems she bought the bull and had it slaughtered. Doc Hatfield used to say she should have kept the bull and slaughtered Lionel."

"So Lionel continued to speculate in the Beef Trust."

Fishbait filled his glass reflectively. He took a long drink. Held it in his mouth. Puffed his cheeks, and sloshed the Scotch through his teeth as though it were a dental wash. Then he swallowed the drink and said, "I'd say Lionel just about cornered the market."

"Romance at the Surf and Sand," I ventured.

"That's right," Fishbait said with a grin. "You know how women are at summer resorts. Away from home for a couple of weeks. Sea air. The beach. A big round moon. Mash? Managing a resort hotel, you get it hot and steaming on a platter."

"Don't forget he could sing," Ed put in. "Or so they say, don't they, Fishbait?"

"Heard my father tell," Fishbait nodded. "They'd flock around Lionel at the piano there at the Surf and Sand. He'd put on a one-man concert. Songs like *The Last Rose of Summer*—that kind. Besides, they thought he owned the place. Anyway, he was in charge of the room keys."

"So if his throat couldn't find the right key, at least his hand could."

Fishbait laughed at my sally. "That's a good one. But of course he had a pass key. It was a standing joke around there—see, my father worked there for a couple of seasons—that a cutup who used a pass key as often as Lionel should have realized there's such a thing as a keyhole."

"Especially with a Fox in the house," Ed jibed.

"Well, the help doesn't miss much in a resort hotel," Fishbait admitted. "Say, Ed, do you remember the one they used to tell about Lionel and Sophie?"

"No," Ed said as Fishbait reached for the bottle. "Look," he turned to me. "I got just time to get to the liquor store before it closes. You tend the Scotch here with Fishbait. He's got a story on the line. . . . Tell it, Fishbait."

Ed hurried off to replenish the famine-threatened Scotch supply.

While Ed was gone, Fishbait Fred Fox, stretched full length in a chair, his rubber boots crossed on a footstool, regaled me with the story of Lionel and Sophie.

Sophie St. Clair. The "Pointers" thought her right name was Sowalski—something like that—and that she probably hailed from a mill town, perhaps Fall River. Anyway, she was Polish. Nothing against her. Nothing at all. Except she didn't quite mix with the New York and Boston types that patronized the Surf and Sand.

A haystack blonde with an I've-got-it figure and a come-and-get-it walk. She wore a French sailor tam with a red pompom, a middy blouse with a notably daring "V" and a hobble skirt slit at the ankle. That was her seaside costume. For evening promenade she appeared in sailor straw with black ribbons, white blouse with even more expansive "V," shiny patent leather belt four inches wide, and black skirt slit half-way up the calf. Fishbait recalled her as the first woman he ever saw smoking a cigarette. *Violet Milos*. She wasn't a small woman, neither was she Junoesque. Her build was just right. In the vernacular, a lulu.

She arrived fresh off the boat in the midsummer of 1904, and her advent at the Surf and Sand created a stir that animated the rocking chairs the entire length of the seaboard's longest hotel verandah. By day's end wives were counting their husbands, Yale boys were planning to stay another week, and spinsters were talking about "that woman."

We are a people fearfully and wonderfully made. Gentlemen, we wear our clothes as suits of armor (by day, at least) pretending we are a highly civilized, upright, courageous, down-to-brass-tacks group of officers, professionals and businessmen. We like our women, to be sure. But with a manly tolerance that thinks they don't know how to drive their cars, a patronization that mistrusts their bridge, a cunning avarice that underpays them in factory or office, and a conviction that no woman could ever be President.

Gentlemen, we are a pack of frauds. Not one general among us could outsmart a Sophie Sowalski if marooned with her three months on a desert island. Not a single judge in our Supreme Court could concentrate on law if locked in a closed chamber with such a female for one month. And any Venus who cares to break up a State of the Nation address to Congress could do so in an instant by sauntering down the center aisle in her altogether. You could resist her on that desert island? You wouldn't look? You'd go right on talking? Come now, General—Your Honor—Mr. President— You can fool some of the public none of the time. Her. She knows your little pretense, your petty secret. She has known it since the day of Adam.

As for you, Dear Lady, in your Mother Hubbard, your housewife's apron, your party smock or evening gown—you are quite content to let His Highness think he is Master of the Castle and King of the Sea. This small boy with his uniforms and paper hats and cap pistols, his toy trains and skyrockets—you've resigned the world to him because it keeps him happy and out of your hair, and he'd have a tantrum if you took his candy away. He wants the Moon with a Little Red Fence around it? Let him reach for it. Let him pretend. Let him alone and he'll come home, wagging his tail behind him.

But civilized? Not you, Dear Miss or Madam. Underneath the corset on all of you there is this Cave Woman. You are playing whist at a card table, or knitting at a get-together, or dining under a crystal chandelier, or chatting small talk on a hotel verandah. Along comes one of your kind in a tam with a red pompom, a blouse with an expansive "V," and you reach for your stone-age club. The higher the cut of your formality, the thinner your veneer. Your pet Small Boy with his toy trains and big cigars must be protected from the Amazonian invader.

In the rocking-chair jungle of the Surf and Sand they hated Sophie (Mrs. St. Clair) Sowalski. The female primates in the jungle, that is. The males beat their cardboard shirtfronts and privately dreamed, or schemed, some sort of ambush.

The cynosure of all this primordial commotion and emotion strolled the scene at her leisure, coolly selecting her prey. Her methods were not without sophistication. For her first few days on locale she struck a posture of studied indifference as she sauntered into the dining room or promenaded the verandah. When she paused to tap a cigarette on a manicured thumbnail, and an assortment of eager gallants would step forward with matches alight, she would smile wordless thanks, strike her own match, and walk on. Determinedly (and designingly) she walked alone.

Several of the older Jim Bradies—gentlemen posing as widowers and so on—maneuvered to intercept her on the staircase or to speak to her at tea. Their invitations were graciously declined by a husky-throated, "No, thank you," and a politely extended third finger exhibiting the diamond of a wedding ring.

Mrs. St. Clair dined by herself at a centrally located table. Walked by herself on the beach. Took her cocktail by herself in the sun parlor. Sat by herself at evening in a secluded corner of the verandah. A conspicuous display of decorum that fooled nobody—least of all the management in the person of Lionel Bridewell.

Searching his memory, my informant could not recall any witness accounts of the initial meeting between Lionel and Sophie. But the encounter was easily imagined. The after-dinner concert hour. Enter Lionel (who usually dined in his private office), his hair pomaded, his features slightly blooded, his jaw handsomely profiled—in his tailcoat, waistcoat and trousers composing a pen-and-ink sketch by Charles Dana Gibson. He smiles and bows to the right, smiles and bows to the left. Then, centerpiece in a bouquet of young ladies, he moves to the grand piano.

A twirl of the stool, and he is seated. He flips his tails and adjusts his cuffs. And he is just bursting into song, his lips forming pear-shaped tones, when Sophie appears in the rear doorway which frames an alcove of the sun room.

Eyes meet for an instant. Lionel's baritone skids a shade off-key. Smiling disinterestedly, Sophie advances, passes the group at the piano, and is gone. A whiff of Violet Milo lingers in her wake. Thus *The Last Rose of Summer* sheds its petals in the gusty breeze from *Ta Ra Ra Boom-de-Yay.*

"I'm not in voice tonight, ladies. I'm sorry."

And Lionel is off and gone as though drawn through the outer doors by suction.

If Sophie were as artful as she seems to have been, she must have fended off Lionel's opening advances with the skill of a lady matador evading a charging bull. No, thank you, there's nothing you can do for me, Mr. Bridewell. My room is very comfortable, thank you. Yes, the service is excellent. Thank you, no, I don't think I'll go down to the Center this evening. I've had rather a tiring day. Thank you, and good night.

She would have been similarly cool toward the offerings of table flowers, pressed duck and free champagne that soon followed. Would have stared in dismayed surprise when he pressed her hand as he paused to speak to her on the verandah—"Is everything all right, Mrs. St. Clair?" And if she played her gambit with the wiliness attributed to her type, she would have insinuated once or twice that his attentions were unwelcome, and would have resisted his first upper hall embrace with the reminder, "Please, Mr. Bridewell; I'm married."

By that stage her victim's surface suavity must have peeled away to reveal the buffalo underneath. Another week, and she would have the ring in his nose and the rope in her hand.

"My friends call me Soph. You know. For sophisticated."

"Call me Lion."

"Lion!"

"Soph!"

So the age-old traps were baited; the age-old game was played. But this time with the difference that the age-old question of which was hunter, which was victim (who can say when Nimrod and Diana are the principals?)—this time the question was definitely answered. There could be no doubt concerning who caught whom.

I think Lionel Bridewell was one of those putty sportsmen who fancied himself a big-game hunter and never bagged a trophy larger than quail. Mrs. St. Clair was his first tigress, so to speak, and she ate him alive just as he thought he had her in the bag.

It was an evening late in August. Warm. With the transoms open. Sophie had vanished from the verandah. Lionel had disappeared from the lobby desk.

Sophie's room was on the second floor—a corner room with windows giving view on moon-silvered sea. The room was dark, and had been so for some time. Then suddenly a flash of radiant light burst blindingly at the transom. Ensued shouting, loud banging at the door. "Open up! We know you're in there! We've got the picture!"

Sophie, her hair down, opens the door. In rushes the irate man in the straw skimmer, followed by the leering photographer with the Graflex.

"Come on, you!" orders the irate man. "We know you're in the wardrobe!"

Out of the tall wardrobe, his features as sickly as those of Dr. Caligari, steps Lionel.

Hearing about it, I asked Fishbait Fred, "Was he wearing Dr. Sanden's Electric Belt?"

He snorted. "If he was, he must've blown a fuse. He swore he'd never even had his necktie off. He said Mrs. St. Clair had rung for ice water, the bellboys were all busy, so he'd taken her some. Trouble was, the pitcher in the room was lukewarm, and the lights had been out. Lionel was caught cold."

Sophie weeping. "My reputation! My good name!"

The man in the straw hat cursing. "You'll answer for this, you scoundrel. I'm her husband!"

Lionel—a stag at bay. "Please! We can settle this!"

In New England? Where the seduction of a married woman is high crime—a serious felony termed "criminal conversations" in most of the statutes; a capital crime in one of the Puritan States!

"I'll have your head for this, mister! Hotel manager preying on innocent female guests! You'll pay for this!"

"Wait! Can't we talk it over?"

"What's there to talk about?"

"How much—? I mean—if a hundred dollars!"

"Hundred dollars? Aren't you the geezer! Look, Bridewell, if you really want to stay out of jail . . ."

A ridiculous burlesque, surely. Played in skit after skit in the Broadway musicals of the Roaring Twenties. But not so comic in its gaslight heyday. The "Old Army" routine. The badger game. If the story were true, Sophie (Mrs. St. Clair) Sowalski took Lionel Bridewell with a swindle as characteristic of the period American scene as the *Police Gazette*.

Indeed, the old *Gazette* contained many an account of the badger game as popularly played in that button-hook decade. It struck me as indicative of a low intelligence quotient that an avid reader of the barbershop journal could have been trapped by so stale a contrivance. Humpty Dumpties are usually simple souls like brigadier generals and mid-West industrialists.

"I suppose it cost Lionel—or, rather, his mother—a lot of money," I said.

Fishbait chuckled. "You can wager it was an expensive squeeze."

Naturally. Old Abby would have had to pay through the nose. Not only to rescue Lionel, but to save the Surf and Sand. Easy to imagine how polite society would have eschewed the hotel had that transom photograph been published.

"Oh, well," Fishbait said, limbering to his feet. "The Bridewells could afford it. They were richer than fertilizer."

Scratching the growth on his cheek, he eyed the empty bottle on the tabouret by his chair. Abruptly he extended his hand to me. "My dear sir. Please convey to our host my apologies for not awaiting his return. And thank you for listening. Who was it said a friend is an ear?"

"You're not going?"

"Sorry, but I must. Besides, Brewster must have gone to Edinburgh for that Scotch."

He tipped his hockey cap over an eyebrow, and clomped out.

Ed laughed when I told him about Fishbait's abrupt departure. "You know, Pointers are like that. When they want to drop in, they drop in. Mind to go, they go."

But the cautious curtain once more descended over Ed's expression when I briefed him on the Sophie St. Clair story.

"Fishbait," Ed said with a headshake, "is a champion drinker and a champion fabricator. You wouldn't know he was cooked to the gills tonight, now would you?"

"He didn't look cooked."

"It's the same with his stories. You never know whether they're on the level, or made up as he goes along. He's a character," Ed said. "Giving out that his father worked there at the Surf and Sand."

"Didn't he?"

"I've seen the stone up in the cemetery. Eli Fox—Fishbait's father. He died around the year Fishbait was born. So he couldn't have told Fishbait— Wait a minute!" Ed broke off. He snapped his fingers. "What do you know?"

"What?"

"Fishbait was nine or ten years old in Nineteen Four. *He* worked at the Surf and Sand. Bellhop. . . . Mackerel!" Ed glared around the parlor. "Maybe it *did* happen. I wouldn't put it past Fishbait to have been in on the thing with the photographer."

"So there *was* a Sophie Sowalski?" I asked, amused by Ed's reaction.

"Damn, yes. At least, there was this blonde peacherino ran a beauty parlor named Madame Sophie. Henna rinses and manicures for the hotel set and summer people. Her shop was smack in the middle of the Center. She drove a big red Winton. I remember hearing some of the villagers wonder where she got the dough."

"She must have had a carload of gall," I observed. "If she set up shop on the Bridewell money."

"Come to think of it, there *was* talk of some kind of rumpus between her and Old Abby. Leastwise, that Old Abby never went there for a hair-do. Love of mike! Being a kid, I never thought much of it."

I could follow Ed's thinking processes on his mobile face. Why had Old Abby put up with the woman? But what else could she have done? Either pay up, or Lionel went to jail and they closed the Surf and Sand.

Madame Sophie had the Bridewells hogtied.

Of course. And every adult native of Quahog Point was party to the affair. But the Pointer fathers were content to let the matter ride. Each would have asserted he was all for minding his own business. Smeizers handled their own affairs. Bryces handled theirs. Let the Bridewells take care of their'n.

Too, there must have been some lip-smacking, some amused satisfaction at the situation. Here was the Point's first family taken hook, line and sinker by this Jezebel. Pride goeth before a fall. Old Abby could run the town, but she couldn't run this female bandit *out* of town. What if the old lady did have to pay up a few thousand dollars? Bridewells could afford it. And hadn't *they* put the squeeze on other people? Now they were getting it from this blonde. Tit for tat, in a way.

"It's odd," Ed said, knocking out his pipe and sitting up. "A thing like that can make a ruction for a while in a place like this. And then it all dies down and it's—well, not forgotten, but sort of accepted. You know, like getting used to the smell of squid. First time I went on a fishing boat, the smell almost killed me. Now I don't even know it's there, and I expect I'd miss it if it wasn't. See what I mean? About someone like this Sophie?"

Ed was telling me that perverse men and nations at first endure what they think they cannot cure. In time the endurance becomes resignation; resignation becomes social acceptance (the abnormal becoming the norm); and in the *reductio ad absurdum* of human nature and rationale, acceptance generally leads to indulgence.

Sophie was like war. Everyone knows that war means killing, and killing is a crime. One of the basic Thou Shalt Nots. A cardinal sin. But man has learned to endure war; has become resigned to war; indeed, has rationalized it as a necessity to the point of glorifying its indulgence.

Similarly Sophie was eventually indulged. Once you begin to compromise—?

Well, Absalom Purdy took to dropping in, and nobody could believe he went there for a manicure. Neill Smeizer went there, too. Finally Horace Ross stood up in Town Council, one weathery night when Abby Bridewell wasn't there, and made a motion to permit the removal of a watering trough which blocked the curb in front of Madame Sophie's beauty parlor. Everyone knew who sponsored Horace's proposal. But Madame Sophie, by that time, was well to do. Like war, she made money, and money has a way of inviting tolerance. The watering trough was removed.

"Matter of fact," Ed said wryly, "this Sophie added tone to the Center. She was smart as new paint, and her shop smartened up the old Center a lot."

I could picture it. The red Winton at the curb and a boy in a monkey jacket to escort in the customers. I said, "I don't suppose there was a Mister St. Clair around."

"A good question," Ed nodded. "It seems, as I recall, she called herself a divorcee."

But naturally. The confederate invariably disappears. Sophie would have blamed the "divorce" on Lionel Bridewell.

"What finally became of Madame Sophie?"

"She left the Point, bag and baggage, directly after Abby Bridewell was murdered."

"I see. The blackmail payments were cut off."

Ed frowned reflectively. "Look. If there was any blackmail—and I don't say there was—I'd guess it was cut off before that. Maybe in the summer of 1910—the bad season after the P. and Q. crash. I remember some petermen visited the Point. They got into Sophie's beauty parlor and burgled her safe."

Petermen. Another expression as dated as the *Police Gazette*. The gaslight safe-blower with his sack of tools and his hotwater bottle loaded with nitroglycerine. They "milked" it out of stolen dynamite, and they carried the "soup" in a rubber bag because a jolt might smash a glass bottle or blow a metal container sky high.

I once interviewed a veteran peterman. A quaint little character with mild blue eyes and a gentle, apologetic smile. He had spent two-thirds of his adult life in prison—he was just out of Oklahoma State—and with great humility he admitted that he hadn't been tops in his profession. The best, he said, were known as "Johnsons," after a wizard whose name was Johnson.

This master peterman, Johnson, was a wonderful operator—a former Army officer (West Point graduate) who had concluded that he could make more money blowing "cans" than he could blowing up Indians in Arizona or Spaniards in Cuba. A really good man could peter a safe so the explosion would scarcely be heard. You muffled the box with an old bedquilt, and applied just exactly the right amount of "soup." A bad job might blast the safe door clean into the street, and you with it, along with a tornado of coins and currency. You could always tell an inferior peterman when he showed up with a sackful of bent silver dollars. The old-timer of the interview ruefully showed me a bent silver dollar. Sad old fellow—his left wrist ended in a stump. He had not been an expert "Johnson."

Apparently the petermen who burgled Madame Sophie's safe were in the "Johnson" class. Nobody saw them come or go. Nobody heard the blast. Daylight revealed a jimmied window and the safe in the corner wide open with its laminated iron door hanging askew on one hinge. The miniature vault had been picked clean.

Ed recalled: "She—Sophie—raised all kinds of hullabaloo. Wanted the State Police. Vowed she would hire Pinkerton men to track down the criminals. Isn't it odd how a pirate will scream to high heaven when they themselves have been looted?"

I could not help remarking that the reaction was basic. The barracuda cries "Outrage!" when caught by the shark. The shark wails "Vandalism!" when chawed by the killer whale. What nation has not done the same thing—plundered some weaker nation or people and then bellowed for law and order when threatened, in turn. (What? *We* never plundered anybody? Ask the American Indians.)

"Funny thing," Ed said. "Right after that robbery, somebody stood up in Town Council and sponsored a motion to order Madame Sophie out of town. I remember hearing talk about it. They threatened to lock her up if she didn't go."

"On what charge?"

"Selling her favors," Ed said delicately, "without a license. My old man said Sophie was wild and called the charge a slander. But it seemed like somebody had procured a warrant."

I had been waiting for Abby Bridewell to strike some sort of retaliatory blow. But why, at that particular date, would the old lady have chosen to strike? What unleashed the counter-attack hitherto held in check by the Damoclean sword over Lionel?

Then I saw it. The robbers who had cleaned out Sophie's safe! Would talented petermen have bothered to burgle a beauty parlor? Not unless they were after something, and—

"Ed!" I exclaimed. "Do you suppose Abby Bridewell could have hired those burglars?"

"You couldn't prove it by me," he said. "Remember, all that was a long time ago. Coming from Fishbait Fred Fox, you got to take that badger-game story with a grain of salt."

There *was* a hole in the end of it, and I remarked it to Ed. If Abby did lay hands on the alleged blackmail photograph, she would hardly have delayed in abolishing Madame Sophie along with the picture. A legal ouster of Lionel's Nemesis seemed too mild. And Sophie, it seemed, had taken her time about going, if she did not leave Quahog Point until after Abby's demise.

"Of course," I noted, "Sophie may have threatened to kick up a scandal, anyway. Or something else may have held Old Abby's hand."

"I don't know," Ed said. "Tell you what. There's an old fella in town—Needles Thorn—once worked for the Bridewells. He might give you some dope." Ed consulted his watch. "Nine-twenty. Luke wanted me to pick him up at ten. I'll drop you at Needles' while I go pick up Luke."

It was Needles Thorn who told me of the episode which could have held Old Abby's hand. The story of Magdalena Gero.

CHAPTER 9

NEEDLES THORN sat on a barrel under a dim electric light. Behind him a decayed frame building leaned in gray dissolution against an equally shabby boathouse. The lighted scene included a glimpse of oily water, a tethered dory, and the squat bow of a trawler named *Milly O.* A faded sign on the building said: *Thorn's.* A scrap of fishnet dangled from the sign.

Needles was reading a newspaper when I walked up. Holding the paper about two inches in front of his face. When he lowered the paper I saw he was as old and dilapidated as the building. A little man in dungarees. Wizened. He wore a countenance of brown clay which had shriveled and cracked into a million cracks while undergoing Time's ceramic process.

He spat brown juice. "So you're writin' something on Quahog Point? Local lore and such. Ed Brewster tell you about Ghostly Mary?"

He cupped hand to ear. Speaking up, I told him I was interested in Senator Bridewell.

"No," he shook his head. "She wasn't a bride. Little girl, she was. Got drownded by the ship-wreckers back in the old time. Come ashore with a May basket, and you see her out on the headland, moonless nights. Lots of folks has seen her. Ghostly Mary."

"The Bridewells," I said into his cupped hand. "Senator Bridewell."

"Oh, yes," he nodded. "So Ed told you about Sitting Bull."

I shouted into his ear that the only bull I had heard about was one named Sliding Billy Watson.

"Hee, hee," the old man giggled. "But this here Sitting Bull was a cigar-store Indian. A *jumping* cigar-store Indian. Sensation at

Quahog Point for years . . . Pull up a lobster pot. Pull up a lobster pot."

I found one of the wooden cages in the shadows, and I drew it forward and sat on it. Presuming I might as well let the old man on the barrel warm up.

He took his time about it. And the cigar-store Indian legend is worth briefing only as one which manifests the fireside credulity of the Gaslight Era. Today we phenomena-lovers have Flying Saucers and goblin crockery that soars around the house. Sixty years ago Quahog Point had this jumping cigar-store Indian.

It seemed that Chester Goodbody owned the cigar store. And early in the 80's, he acquired the phenomenal Indian. He purchased it out on the West Coast where he'd gone to visit his sister in San Francisco. The wooden Indian, man-size, proved a transport problem. To avoid the high cost of Wells Fargo Express, Mr. Goodbody boxed the Indian and brought it East by ship, keeping the big box in his stateroom as a piece of luggage.

The point is that the Indian traveled by ocean steamer. And going around the Horn, the steamer bucked through hell and high water. The entire voyage was stormy. Gale after gale. When at last he reached New England, Mr. Goodbody was groggy. So, it appeared, was the cigar-store Indian.

Proud as punch of the splendid figure—Sitting Bull standing on a pedestal with a fistful of stogies—Goodbody unveiled (or unboxed) it at Quahog Point with great ceremony. Well! If Tobaccanist Goodbody thought this Chief was going to stand in the doorway of his cigar store—or anywhere else—he was in for a surprise. First of all, the entry was too small to accommodate the Red Man on the pedestal. Nor could the Indian be gotten through the door. So Goodbody placed the figure in the side yard, facing Main Street.

Next morning the wooden Indian was not in the side yard, facing Main Street. During the night, it seemed, he had wobbled about-face. A prank, of course. Some of the villagers had turned him around.

But, no, the following night Sitting Bull had about-faced again. What's more, he had jumped into a bed of marigolds at the side of the cigar store. Goodbody was furious. He put up a no trespassing sign, and warned the village boys to leave the wooden Indian alone. Three mornings later the Red Man was discovered half-way down the yard. Tracks? Yes, there were tracks. A series of blotches in the grass where the pedestal had jumped. But that was all.

From there on out, the legend follows the usual formula. Goodbody sitting up all night. Installing a watchdog which hears nothing. The Indian settles down for a time. Then, sure enough, at dark of the moon (and of course when no one is looking) it goes jumping again.

It jumps into a manure pile. It jumps to the end of the yard. It jumps the back fence and is found lying flat on its face. Doubtless it would have jumped over the moon had the gaslighters come as far as the mid-Twentieth Century.

Nevertheless, the phenomenon did all right. It made the contemporary press. It won mention in at least one history of the area (I looked it up). People flocked to Quahog Point in wide-eyed wonder. After several seasons of jumping, the Indian was sent to Brown or Yale or somewhere. To go on the track team? Not a bit of it. To go into a laboratory where grave Professors made elaborate studies of weights and balances which might be swayed by laws of gravity.

And finally comes the pseudo-erudite pronouncement, wrapped in the vaporous wordage of "official explanation." The sea voyage. Weeks on the rolling ocean must have imparted some mysterious pulsation to the wooden figure's center of gravity. The kind of wood—high tide and low tide—the location of Quahog Point—these are doubtless contributory factors. In time the impulse will probably evaporate, and Sitting Bull will come to a standstill. End of phenomenon. End of legend.

Of course, the legend is funny. But behind it, something isn't. The trouble with that kind of mishmash is that it emanates from the minds of seemingly reasonable men. Listening to Needles Thorn, I had to ask myself: If Ph.D's could indulge such nonsense, what chance had light and reason in a place like Quahog Point?

Then I heard the Gero story.

Needles got around to it after I trumpeted some leading questions in his ear. Yes, he said, he had once worked for a spell for Senator Bridewell. At the Bridewell house? No, at the Kelp Company. The hired help at the Bridewell house was a couple named Gero. Who were they? A man and his daughter who worked there for a time. Man was maybe a Portuguee. Something happened (seemed like) to the daughter. What happened? "Well, nobody knows for sure, *but* . . ."

The story did not emerge in continuity. I had to clear it of digressive deadwood, tangled colloquialisms and much tobacco juice. Some of Needles' pauses and shrugs I may have misinterpreted. I am certain his deaf ear missed some of my queries—in particular, those he did not care to hear.

But here is the substance as best I could put it together.

The Gero story is not a long one. I am glad to make it brief.

The man's name was Joe. Joe Gero. Maybe he was a Portuguee. Maybe he wasn't. But the "Pointers" took him for a foreigner. There were numerous Portuguese drifters in the area, so it seems consistent with the background to make of him a surly peasant in corduroy whose Old World name was Joao.

The girl was called Lena. Joao's daughter, she had probably been christened Magdalena. Needles said he could not recall what she looked like—just a girl. A young girl? Well, youngish. Fifteen? Maybe. Sixteen or seventeen? Needles couldn't say. Trying to visualize her, I saw Lena as a shy, thin, pathetic little slavey with enormous eyes under a straggle of hair.

It would not be overdoing it to picture a Cinderella in the Bridewell household. Joao would have been the hired man, tending the garden and stable yard. Lena, the hired girl in the kitchen. Old Abby needed servitors, what with Captain Nathan a paralytic to be waited on hand and foot, and the Bridewell boys no less demanding.

So Magdalena is up with the chickens. She goes to bed when the last dish is done. In addition to the routine daily tasks, she does the Monday washing and the Tuesday ironing, the Wednesday baking and the Thursday canning, the Friday sewing, the Saturday housecleaning and the Sunday dinner. She is paid three dollars a week, and she dutifully hands the money over to her Old World father.

It is not to be supposed that Lena's probable lot as a household drudge would have been abnormally Bridewellian or unusual. We have forgotten that fifty years ago many of our sovereign States were without humane child labor laws.

> Little orphant Annie's come
> To our house to stay,
> To wash the cups and saucers up,
> And put the things away. . . .

An entire generation of schoolchildren recited James Whitcomb Riley to fond parents who, at graduation exercises, felt a twinge of sympathy for Orphan Annie. Yet never gave a thought to eight-year-old urchins in coal mines and little girls in pigtails slaving in sweat shops.

> The golf links lie so near the mill
> That nearly every day,
> The laboring children can look out
> And see the men at play.

The lady humanist who wrote those lines early in the present century was considered an agitator. Nevertheless, I was surprised to learn that in New England, in the year 1910, children were still "bound out"—a condition I had always associated with servitude in the day of Nicholas Nickleby and Oliver Twist. So, to give Abby Bridewell her due, she was no worse than the contemporary pork-barrel politicians and tycoon industrialists who did their best to scuttle child labor legislation. Besides, work was considered good for children. Kept them out of mischief.

If the Bridewell establishment ran true to custom, Joao probably slept on a straw tick in the loft of the Bridewell barn. He would have smelled too much like a horse blanket to be permitted the house.

Indoors, Lena doubtless had the cubby off the washroom behind the kitchen. Not a bedroom (I inspected it), but a store room with space for a cot. From this nook a back stairway, narrow as a secret passage, went up to the second floor. I believe such recessed covert-ways used to be called the "servants' stair." But Needles Thorn seemed to know nothing of the quartering arrangements, and that detail concerning Lena derives from deduction. If she lived in the house, as was probable, those were the servants' quarters.

And so, in the autumn of 1909, Abby Bridewell finds the girl weeping over the laundry tubs, and discovers she is pregnant. That, too, derives from deduction. Not mine, so much as the town's. As Needles Thorn told it, "something happened." What? He was not sure. How would he know, he asked, blinking watery eyes. *He* wasn't there.

"It was just that Gero and his daughter up and left Quahog Point. All the sudden like."

"Did Old Abby fire them?" I had to shout it twice.

Needles' manner became evasive. "Don't ask *me*. Maybe they quit. Young fella named Cudworth—Hobart Cudworth—got the job as hired man. Next year Earnest fetched a lad, just a kid, down from Marblehead or somewhere. Had him bound out. Orphan boy name of Walter Jones." Needles squinted at the light bulb over his head. "Seems like the Bridewells didn't want another girl around the place."

"Why not?"

"Eh?"

"*Why?*"

"Don't know." Needles paused to ruminate. Then he arched a thoughtful squirt of tobacco juice at the water. He said with a headshake, "Unless it had somethin' to do with a rumor about rape."

"Rape? Who got raped?"

He looked at me, innocent-eyed. "Maybe nobody did. But it was funny, Gero and the girl leaving all the sudden like that. Someone said there was a baby born in Boston or somewheres. And Lionel leaving town."

"Lionel!" I exclaimed. "Did *he* leave Quahog Point?"

"Yessir, he sure did. Right around that time. Packed up and

went to an inland town north of Newport to live. . . . You can see how it might have been."

I certainly could. Magdalena weeping at the tubs one autumn day, and Old Abby standing over her like the wrath of God in black alpaca.

Old Abby (pointing a condemning finger): When did it happen? Tell me!

Lena (sobbing): Last summer.

Abby: Wicked child! Your father shall hear of this. Right now!

Enter Joao Gero, bowing over an obsequious hat to the chatelaine of the manor. He stands stunned as Abby tells him the news. Then, as realization sweeps over him, he rages at the daughter who has now deprived him of her weekly stipend.

Gero: *Cachorra!* You are a bad, bad girl!

Lena: No, Papa! No!

Gero: Mother of Heaven! That you should bring such disgrace upon the name of Gero! God will punish you!

They played it heavily in those days. Striding and gesturing. Bellowing about Sin and Hell's Fire and Judgment. Storming, of course, at the girl, the descendant of Eve, originator of man's downfall. Until someone—in this case presumably Gero—remembers that Adam was held partly responsible.

Gero: Who did it? Name the man! He must [in good Old World tradition] marry you immediately!

In spite of her desperate plight, Magdalena refuses to tell. Blows, buffets and promises of Purgatorio cannot force the name from her.

Gero: Who was he? Tell me, girl!

Lena: He made me do it! He made me swear by the Blessed Virgin never to speak!

Gero: Speak, or I will beat it out of you!

Lena: No, Papa! No! I couldn't stop him! I couldn't help it! He caught me on the stairs, and—

The terrorized girl goes into hysteria.

Conjecture that far, and it is easy to imagine a subsequent scene in the Bridewell parlor. Poor Cinderella has refused to name the man who victimized her, but the possibilities are strictly limited. It could hardly have been an outsider, for the girl would have told the invader's name. An insider, then . . . and the possibilities narrow down to two.

There must have been a stormy interview between Abby Bridewell and the sons. I could almost hear the dignified shouts of wrathful denial from the outraged State Senator. "What? That common girl?" And the desperate disclaimers from Brother Lionel. "Girl in trouble? I swear to God I don't know anything about it!"

Conjecture. Entirely conjecture. Naturally the Bridewells would not have advertised it; Old Abby would have done her best to keep it quiet. In the end, it would have been necessary to hustle the girl, and her father with her, out of the picture. Everything must be swept under the rug. Nevertheless, such a business would take some doing. One can squelch a possible blackmailer, but you cannot hush a rape case if pregnancy is the consequence.

So rumor whispered around Quahog Point with the speed of mercury. Rumor that an infant was born in Boston "or somewhere" early in 1910. Rumor that the mother died in childbirth. Rumor that one of the Bridewells had been forced to pay. And if one of the Bridewells was a rapist, it wasn't hard to recognize the one. Earnest had his faults, perhaps, but he was, after all, a State Senator. And it was Lionel who moved to another town.

"Mr. Thorn," I queried, "do you think this rape actually occurred? Or was it just backfence gossip?"

He did not hear me.

One cannot shout the word "rape" across a waterfront, but I tried again.

The old man on the barrel gave me his final answer.

"Can't prove it by me. Wasn't there."

At which juncture Luke Martin burst in from the outer darkness. His face was crimson with cold and elation. He shouted, "Hey, I caught a beaut! Striper! Where's the scales?" Without waiting for an answer, he charged off down the wharf to weigh his fish.

On the drive back to the Bridewell house, I saw the road ahead of the carlights without seeing it. I was visualizing a scene in that mean cubby behind the washroom back of the kitchen. A Prince of Darkness clutching white-faced Cinderella by the wrists, and no Guardian Angel to come to her rescue.

When we got back to the house, Ed Brewster handed me a drink. "Feeling all right?" he asked. "You look kind of bleak."

I did not tell him the story I had heard. But I could not repress the opinion that Lionel Bridewell must have been an unmitigated rat. It gave me pleasure to say so in his mother's parlor.

CHAPTER 10

THAT night sleep eluded me. I'm no insomniac—the infernal Bridewells kept me awake. A wind was up, so I could hear them moving around in the house, creaking the floorboards, trying the doors. Then, wakeful in the dark, I could see their faces. On the ceiling, on the wall, and under my eyelids.

I decided that I detested Abby. Earnest I had come to despise. As for Lionel, had he been downstairs, I am sure I could have joined any lynching party that gathered in the moonlight outside.

So far as crime writing is concerned, this was over-identification with the subject matter. It's not good. You lose your objectivity (or what story men used to call the "omniscient observer's angle").

A reporter should never lose his objectivity. He should remain as aloof as a camera. If he doesn't, he becomes an editorial writer or a propagandist. The one expresses opinion, and the other doctors the facts to suit opinions.

But the omniscient observer must never observe too closely. The absolute truth could be entirely too distressing.

And the writer of case histories should retain a sense of humor about crime. Such atrocities as the Bridewell case ought to be handled with the kid gloves of literary savoir-faire. Treated in the light and almost whimsical style of an Edmund Pearson, or with the mordant detachment of a Roughead. Or in the scholarly manner of Rebecca West, who can discuss the most sordid homicide in such marvelously impeccable English that the reader forgets the crime in his admiration for the prose.

No, the true-crime story, like the Hollywood fairy tale—or for that matter, like so-called history—must be made palatable. Something we can swallow with large chasers of chocolate and popcorn. Much of published history is a euphemism, and for peace of mind it is probably better to serve it up with candy and cereal. . . .

Good Lord! All this because of a villainous rape that may never have occurred. It had me wound up like the alarm clock Luke had set for some 5:00 A.M. surfcasting.

I groped to a bedside chair for my trousers. I found my lighter, and snapped the flare. The clock on the bureau said 2:18. I had been asleep for twenty minutes, and—

Someone *was* moving around downstairs.

Was that a faint smell of smoke?

I put on my trousers, found my bathrobe and went down.

Ed Brewster sat in his undershirt on the parlor sofa. He was dangling a poker between his knees, and staring dully at the fireplace. I noticed smoke reeling from a mound of charred papers—the smell I had detected upstairs.

Only the table lamp was lighted. With his face half in shadow Ed looked a little drunk. A pint of Old Taylor rested at his elbow. It was down a scant three inches, so I saw I was wrong.

"Ed."

He started as I spoke, then eyed me somberly.

"Hi. Come on in. Hope my fussing around down here didn't wake you."

"I was awake. I smelled smoke and thought I might have left a cigarette around."

"Damn draft." He glared at the fireplace. "When the wind's turned south it don't draw . . . Come in." He offered the bottle. "Nightcap."

"No, thanks. But I'll have a cigarette."

I lit one, and walked to the hearth to drop the match into the ashes. I couldn't help wondering why Ed was burning papers at that hour. I suppose my curiosity showed.

"It's Nan," he grumbled, as I glanced at the smouldering carbon. He took a drink, ran a wrist across his mouth, and eyed the fireplace ruefully. "My wife's been giving me what for."

Sympathetically I asked, "What for?"

"Well, she objects to all this stuff." He indicated the stack of papers we had left on the end table. "And this." He shifted position to show me a cardboard carton beside him on the sofa. "Old letters. Bills. Notes. Bridewell stuff. I been burning it."

"Not that old store ledger, I hope."

"No. Just bills and things. The attic is full of a lot of crap. Never had time to go through it."

He added that his wife thought the attic a rat's nest. Was always after him to clean it out. "When she come in tonight and saw it down here, she was off again."

I could not help being amused. It was a quaint hour to start your husband on a spring housecleaning.

Ed frowned at the poker. "Nan's tired of all this old stuff, I expect. Besides, she thinks the Pointers—me, for one—are hard on the Bridewells. To her, it's gossip." He looked up. "Well, maybe I have been a little strong on the old lady. I'm sorry about the carbolic acid."

Remembering, I had to laugh.

Ed shook his head. "Annette calls it speaking ill of the dead. She's French Canadian, you know. They're superstitious."

"She's very kindly, Ed."

"Nan? Best-hearted woman ever lived. It's just . . . well, take this parlor." He aimed the poker around the pentagon. "I don't blame her for not wanting to go down cellar. Can't say I like that dark stairway, either. But just because there was once a casket over in that corner—! Holy mackerel! It was back in Nineteen Eleven. Women are queer."

"They have a different skin than we do."

"What she says. She can *feel* things in this room." He looked around glumly. "Half a mind to get rid of some of this junk, myself."

He pointed at the stuffed owl. The Eye over the mantel. With poker raised, he pantomimed a blow at the Parian statuette of Chief Massasoit. Then his glance went to the gramophone. Abruptly he rose and walked over to it. He wheeled to face me, and stood with an arm around the morning glory.

"I wouldn't junk this," Ed said in a tone of defiance. "Dealer last summer offered me a hundred dollars for this talking machine. I wouldn't take five hundred for it. This was the first phonograph I ever heard."

What is it about antiques? I had seen curio collectors wear the same expression. The protective arm. The eyes shiny, intense. The pride of ownership.

Then Ed was talking about it, and I realized he meant it literally. About the five hundred dollars. About that particular Edison gramophone being the first he'd ever heard.

It was when he was peddling papers. And as he came up the path to the Bridewell house, he thought he heard a band playing. One was. He didn't know it at that moment, but it was Sousa's Band. *The Stars and Stripes Forever.* Cymbals, drums, brasses, trilling fifes—as though it was somewhere close, but still far away. Wonderful.

The boy halted his bike to listen. The front door of the house was open to the summer afternoon. And the boy's wonder grew when he realized the sound was coming from somewhere in the house. A brass band at the Bridewells. What in the world!

As reprisal for the two-cent scolding he had once received from Old Abby, the paper boy would usually throw the news at the Bridewell door to let wind or weather take it from there. Now he stood transfixed, listening. Then he carefully folded the paper in the approved fashion. Dismounting, he propped his bike against the hedge. He carried the paper to the doorstep, placed it carefully just inside the door. Big-eyed, he peered into the dim, cool vestibule.

The band music came marching out of the parlor. The boy leaned and craned. But he couldn't see around the inner door into the parlor, and he had to know where that thrilling music was coming from.

He ran back to his bike. Keeping it under cover of the hedge, he wheeled it up to the house and around to the nearest parlor window. He leaned the bike against the clapboards under the window, and climbed up to kneel on the crossbar. With cupped hands, he peered through the windowpane. He found himself looking across the room right into the mouth of the gramophone's morning glory.

He had never seen into the Bridewell parlor before. He had known it would be rich and plushy like the sitting room at the Surf and Sand. But he'd never expected any marvel like that brand new phonograph. Why, there was nobody in the room at the time, and here was this thing going like a hurdy-gurdy with no one turning the crank. Only the music was fifty times better than any hurdy-gurdy.

The boy pressed his nose against the windowpane, and listened with his pulses thumping. Holy gee! What a swell machine. The painted morning glory. The spinning rotary. The varnished box. He supposed it played just that one tune, but that was enough. He almost put his face through the window glass when he heard the morning glory speak. A man's voice—

"This is an Eddy-son reckord."

The thing had talked—actually talked!

With arm around the gramophone, Ed Brewster stared at me, hard-eyed.

"You know what? I vowed I'd one day own one of these machines." He returned to the sofa. He sat down and weighed the poker thoughtfully. A smile formed. "Kids get some odd hankerings, don't they? I wanted a talking machine more than I ever wanted anything. One just like that. With a big bell mouth and a brass crank. Like the Bridewells had, see? Like the Bridewells."

He patted his big palm with the poker, and smiled at the gramophone.

"Kids are nutty, aren't they? Finally, I must have been about eleven years old, my dad came home one night. He asked me what I wanted for my next birthday. You know what I said. And my father, by God, said if I'd save enough for half he would get me one." Ed thwacked his palm.

"What happened, Ed?"

"The P. and Q. Rapid Transit Company happened."

Apparently his father had not been a stockholder. But when the transit company crashed the whole Point suffered.

The year was 1909. Tracks were coming across the dunes. An engineering company had started the long trestle over the marshes. State Senator Bridewell told the town that the trolley trestle was a rainbow that would turn the Point into a pot of gold. Everybody knew that Earnest spoke in the voice of Old Abby.

She told friends that the transit corporation had decided on a special stock issue. The shares were to be offered at par—a real bargain!—but the issue was limited, and she urged those who could afford it to buy in. Keep the trolley a local business—that was the idea. They were all one big family, and the Bridewells wanted to share the wealth with neighbors.

Ed Brewster groped into the cardboard carton at his thigh. He found and extended to me a certificate the size of a high school diploma or a Naval Reserve officer's commission.

"This was in the stuff up in the attic. Here's that stock."

Interested, I examined the certificate. Aloud I read: "Number twenty-nine. Ten shares. The Peninsular and Quahog Rapid Transit Corporation. Incorporated under State Law. Authorized capital: five hundred thousand dollars. Par value of shares: ten dollars. This certifies that the holder is the owner of ten shares of the Common Capital Stock of the P. and Q. Rapid Transit Company, Incorporated, transferable only on the books of said company . . . etcetera . . . etcetera."

The fringework was dark green. The face was emblazoned with a steel engraving of a trolley car flying the American flag between an airborne Goddess of Liberty and the winged horse Pegasus. Posed recklessly on the track in front of the speeding trolley, a motorman shook hands with a conductor. A gold seal was splashed on the lower lefthand corner of the certificate. It looked gaudy, official, and valuable.

Ed said, "It's not worth a sheet out of a Sears and Roebuck catalog."

He took the certificate from me. Lit a match. When the paper caught, he dropped it into the fireplace.

The brief flame-glow reddened his features as he stood looking down. His jawline hardened. Then he shrugged.

"My old man maybe was luckier than some. The Smeizers got stuck. So did the Robinsons, Thorns and Purdys. John Y. Gillion lost his shirt. Grimes family, too." He turned to the end table, picked up a yellowed newspaper. "Here's the story."

Quickly I scanned the column. *Rapid Transit Corporation Goes Into Receivership. Stockholders Suffer Heavy Loss. It is believed that some of the charter shareholders sold out in time to rescue their investments. Morgan interests deny manipulation. State's Attorney General may demand investigation.*

"Was there an investigation, Ed?"

He grunted. "With Earnest Bridewell a State Senator on the Attorney General's side? Anyhow, I guess the deal was legal enough. How does it go? Caveat empty?"

Let the buyer beware, of course. The slogan of the Barnums, the James G. Blaines, and, I was given to suppose, the Bridewells. But small consolation coming from the trader who's just rooked you with a spavined horse.

"What finally became of the Transit Corporation?"

"Out of business. Few cents on the dollar, or something like that. Bingo!" He shied another stock certificate into the fireplace.

But the Bridewells would have pulled out of it before the crash. They always do. And I could just see Old Abby keeping a few shares of worthless common around the house to create the impression that she and her precious sons had been as hard hit as anybody.

Ed said, "Well, it seems Earnest and Lionel went around complaining hard times and crying poor. I don't know about Old Abby. Whether she wailed around in public or not."

It did not seem likely. As I conceived it, hers would have been the public role that combines Spartan fortitude with Pollyanna optimism. Now, now, we must all keep our chins up. Practice frugality. Eat less. Things will soon be better if we labor in the vineyard, make of necessity a virtue, keep our powder dry, and trust in the Lord. Back to work, everybody!

Yes, that was probably the role. Borrowed from the threadbare nobility down to its last Cadillac. From the tattered philanthropist who urges community austerity before he (or she) departs for the racing season at Saratoga. From the political demagogue who promises soup kitchens to the very constituents who have been diddled. And everyone is fooled except the canny peasantry, the angered community and the sullen constituents in the bread line. The trolley crash must have left Quahog Point in an ugly mood.

"But here's something," Ed said, fishing a crumpled sheet of paper out of the rubbish box. He smoothed it on a knee, and handed it to me. "Notice of a cattle sale. October Nineteen Ten. Old Abby's selling off a stable of prize oxen."

That was interesting. The block-lettered handbill announced that the animals could be had for a bargain. A second handbill, dated January 1911, read:

TEAM OF MATCHED BAYS AND 1 SORREL MARE. . . .

ANY REASONABLE OFFER CONSIDERED. . . .

October 1910. January 1911. I thought I knew the why behind these operations.

"Ed," I said, "old Needles told me that Lionel Bridewell pulled out of Quahog Point."

"Why, so he did."

"When?"

Ed stared into space. Then counted on his fingers. Then shook his head. "Seems he went to an inland town—place called Lookout Hill. Folks said he went into tea for a time. Peddled orange pekoe. You know. Drove one of those wagons."

It was an entertaining thought. Handsome Lionel, the orange pekoe man. Like the one who used to stop at my childhood home, bowing in with his suitcase display of teas, condiments and spices. Just the thing for a Lionel Bridewell. If you're in hot water, go into tea.

But Ed could not "rightly remember" when Lionel left the Point. "Old Captain Nathan—Abby's husband—died early in Nineteen Ten. Big funeral. Abby stowed him in that mausoleum—only one in the cemetery back then. I disremember if Lionel went away before or after."

However, Lionel frequently returned to Quahog Point. Weekends. To keep an eye on the estate?

"Well, maybe," Ed said, frowning. "Folks did say there was a hell of a wrangle over the old man's legacy. Shouted so loud in this parlor that Mrs. Smeizer heard it up the hill."

"Lionel's being out of town gave Earnest the edge with the old lady," I supposed.

Ed surprised me by saying, "But Earnest wasn't here with his mother *all* the time. He had to spend some of the time with his wife."

So it goes with story research. This was the first word I'd had of Earnest's wife. The first time I heard of a daughter-in-law in the Old Homestead background.

"I'd like to get the cast straight," I told Ed. "All this time I've been seeing Senator Earnest as a bachelor. The kind who sang *I Want a Girl* but didn't mean it."

"He kind of was," Ed explained. "Like I said, the bachelor type."

"But he did get married?"

"I thought you'd see it from these old news accounts. Married to a woman, Floss Grimes. They had a farm way over on the south side of the Point. Set up housekeeping there."

"I didn't see her picture in the album."

"There you are," Ed said. "She was as different from Old Abby as a mouse from a cat. Quiet. Kept in the background. She was out of it. She didn't figure."

Ed went on to say he could barely recall Earnest's wife. And I began to see the situation. You didn't marry into a family like the Bridewells. Or, if you did, they kept you off the reservation. So Floss remained on the south side, an outsider.

Too, it seemed that Earnest's wife was not a Sabbatarian. And as the Sabbatarians were not on speaking terms with the congregation she belonged to, this placed her further outside the Bridewell fold. Finally, the Grimes clan did not "care much" for the Bridewell clan, and vice versa. No shooting feud or overt antagonism. Just a lack of recognition when clansman passed clansman on Center Square. Apprised of this state of affairs, I could understand why the Bridewell family album lacked a photograph of the old lady's daughter-in-law.

"Earnest spent a lot of time home here with his mother," Ed recalled. "Him and Lionel kept their bedrooms here. Usually they'd be on hand over the weekend to have Sunday dinner with Old Abby. Don't recollect seeing Earnest at his place on the south side much."

"It sounds to me as though he married a farm instead of a woman."

"Like I told you," Ed reminded. "Appears he didn't care much for women. They say he used to campaign all out against the suffragettes."

Evidently domesticity galled the Senator. To elude his mother, he married. To elude his wife, he came back home to mother. To elude them both, he went to the State capital and voted against woman's suffrage. But his only chance to escape distaff domination lay in money? I could imagine. So long as Abby's apron strings were, in reality, purse strings, Earnest Bridewell, like Brother Lionel, was compelled to linger by the maternal fireside.

Glancing about the Victorian parlor, I perceived that the Bridewell picture had changed a little from my earlier conception. It contained more complexities than a mother and two adult sons bound in the close proximity of an uncongenial togetherness. Still, Earnest's marriage to a woman on the south side and Lionel's departure to a county in the hinterland, did not drastically alter the family portrait. Old Abby continued to rule her sons' fortunes.

Need, mistrust and greed kept them fixed in the matriarchal orbit. The Old Homestead remained an inferno.

"Five hundred, mother. Cash. I've got to have it this week!" That would be Lionel.

And Earnest: "Goddam it, mother, you know I need money. You say you're out of ready cash; what the devil did you do with the money from that livestock sale?"

The pressures must have heightened during the winter of 1910–11. Some unremitting stress or strain had forced Old Abby to sell her blue-ribbon oxen and three of her carriage horses. Mrs. Smeizer was not the only neighbor who heard unusually loud shouts of contention echo from the Bridewell parlor. Norman Purdy, delivering charcoal, walked in on a thundering row one Saturday morning. Asa Goodbody, another neighbor, heard a tempestuous quarrel one Sunday after church. Earnest was seen shaking a fist at his mother. Lionel was seen slamming out of the kitchen door. Town talk reported that the sons were going to contest their father's will.

Home sweet home.

I stared at Old Abby's rocker. There she had sat like iron with her sons beating at her hammer and tongs. An anvil in a lace cap. Grim. Holding out. But after the sons departed, she was alone in the house—now that Captain Nathan had gone to the cemetery. Monarch of all she surveyed, but with night closing in on her matriarchal realm. Earnest at her for her money. Lionel at her for her money. Other enemies in the background—fellow townsmen—relatives—perhaps a daughter-in-law—possibly a blackmailer—perhaps the father of a wronged girl. And she was a widow, solitary. Alone, there. Alone.

"Ed," I asked, "did anyone stay here in the house with Abby Bridewell? After Captain Nathan died and the sons partially moved out?"

"Well, there was the hired help."

"A man named Cudworth and an orphan boy?"

"That's right. Hobe Cudworth, he was about twenty-two. And the orphan—a kid in kneepants—Walter Jones. They slept out in back."

"Just Old Abby alone here with those two?"

"Alone here with those two."

I said without thinking, "It's a wonder somebody didn't kill her."

Ed yawned, "Somebody did."

He sighed to his feet. Stood absently clutching the poker. His gaze settled on the gramophone. He said in a drowzy tone, "Damn odd how things work out."

Then crossing to the fireplace, he carefully placed the poker in the coal scuttle. He smiled at me sleepily. "Know it's almost four A.M.?"

"My Lord!" It was like the lights coming on at the climax of a seance. "Will you give me the murder details after breakfast, Ed?"

"Noontime," he promised. "When Annette's gone to church. As I said, she don't like to hear anyone speak ill . . ."

CHAPTER 11

So Abby had it coming.

And it came for her at the end of a beautiful April day—a shining April day not unlike the one wherein I learned the details.

The air warm with the promise of spring at last fulfilled. A breeze as gentle as silk from the sea. The sky cerulian, the sunlight buttercup yellow, the good earth garbed in shades of delicate green.

One of those days when houses opened their windows for a long-needed inhale of fresh air. When you thought about taking down the shutters, but got out the hammock instead. When your wife pinned on her new hat. When the boy with the squeaky voice called to take your giggling daughter for a walk. When the kids took to the yard to knuckle "mibs."

Yes, you could almost see the garden growing. You could hear a hum in the air like the sap rising in the trees. The first houseflies buzz around—where the devil do they come from?—and from way across lots comes the sharp bark of a dog or the grinding sound of someone cranking a car.

The mackerel fishing ought to be good this year.

Cherry blossoms will soon be out.

One of those days— Balm of Gilead to a Quahog Point coming out of hibernation after a long, hard winter.

But tricky in a way. You can't quite be sure. Better keep your coat. The sun still sets early, and late afternoon shadows can turn chill. Seventy at noon can go to forty at night.

You can't trust the weather around a place like Quahog Point. At least you couldn't on the evening of Tuesday, April 11, 1911.

On the evening of Tuesday, April 11, 1911, Cornelia Ord decided to pay a call on Abby Bridewell. Occasionally she went to her aunt's house for Sunday dinner, but a Tuesday evening call was out of the ordinary. The fact that such a visit was unique eventually brought it to the notice of the County Coroner who invited Cornelia to explain the matter at an inquest held in the basement of Town Hall.

Unfortunately the records of that inquest did not remain available for the inspection of literary antique dealers and such rummagers into archives as myself. Upon inquiry, I was given to understand that fire and water had obliterated some fifty years of the history of Quahog Point—an obliteration which included the old Town Hall itself and the particular records in mention.

By dint of research in contemporary newspapers and local memory, and by usage of imagination, I reconstructed some of the missing data. It covers the territory explored by the Coroner's inquest, and must be taken as a simulation only. However, I assure the possible reader that the spirit is there, if not the letter.

As stated, Cornelia went to call on her aunt that Tuesday evening. She went on Tuesday because she had not felt well enough to visit her aunt the previous Sunday. Cold in the nose. Nothing more than that, but she had feared it might be a starter.

Anyway, she had taken a good Saturday night dose of sulphur and molasses. And it had given her a touch of indigestion. At Sunday morning service she had told her aunt, Abby Bridewell, about it. To quote from the simulated record:

Q. You went to church that morning, you say?

A. Of course. I go every Sunday.

Q. You sat in your aunt's pew?

A. It was mine as much as hers.

Q. But it was your habit to sit with your aunt and the other Bridewells?

A. Or theirs to sit with me.

Q. What we're getting at, Mrs. Ord, wasn't it also your usual custom to have Sunday dinner at your aunt's house?

A. I did. When I was invited.

Q. Didn't she invite you that Sunday?

A. Yes, but I told her I wasn't feeling well.

Q. You felt well enough to go to church.

A. I didn't expect to eat a full-course dinner during church service.

Q. But you were really not very much indisposed.

A. I didn't feel up to a big dinner.

Q. Did you tell your aunt that?

A. Yes.

Q. That you were sick?

A. Not sick. If you've got to know, it was gas. I felt hiccupy. I told my aunt about the sulphur and molasses. It had made me feel voluptuous all night.

Cornelia dined at home with her cats that Sunday. A bowl of fish chowder and a cup of camomile tea. Her nose continued runny, but the "voluptuousness" subsided on Monday. By Tuesday she had perked up.

About seven o'clock she felt well enough to go over to the

Bridewells' house. She put a couple of blow handkerchiefs (*sic*) in her reticule, and pinned on her hat. She decided to walk.

From the Coroner's record:

Q. How far was it to your aunt's house?
A. It's still the same distance—about three miles.
Q. You must have been feeling a lot better.
A. Well, my digestion had settled down.
Q. But you were too late for Tuesday supper.
A. I didn't go there for that.
Q. Why did you go?
A. I had an errand. I wanted to see my aunt.
Q. What about?
A. It was private business.
Q. Mrs. Ord, under the circumstances I think you ought to state what it was.
A. I don't know what it was.
Q. You mean to say you don't remember?
A. I didn't say that. I said I didn't know what it was.
Q. How could you go to see your aunt on private business and not know what it was?
A. She said it was private, that's how. She had told me at church she wanted to see me on a personal matter. Would I call on her as soon as convenient.
Q. She didn't tell you what the matter was?
A. One thing about my aunt—she'd never discuss business in church.

Cornelia Ord reached the Bridewell house at just a little after eight. She recalled the time, because the Center Methodist had a bell tower, and it played a hymn every evening at eight. *Throw Out the Lifeline, Throw Out the Lifeline, Someone is Sinking Today.* The last clong echoed into silence and "someone had sunk" just as she reached the roadbend that gave view to the Bridewell place.

Cornelia stopped at the foot of the path to adjust her hat and tidy her nose. Then, squaring her shoulders a little, she strode up to the front door. She had a feeling something was wrong at the house—her aunt asking her to call like that.

Just as she started to go in, the front door opened. Lizzie Robinson marched out.

Q. Who is Lizzie Robinson?
A. The dressmaker.
Q. Your aunt's dressmaker?
A. Abby Bridewell didn't own her. She sewed for a lot of people.
Q. You say she marched out?
A. Yes. Good and mad.
Q. Did you speak to her?
A. She to me. Something about being underpaid and sick of working her fingers to the bone for nothing.

Cornelia stated that she had made no comment to Lizzie—none of her business, come down to it. But expecting trouble, she had braced herself for an unpleasant interview. She found her aunt waiting for her in the sewing room. Her aunt looked all upset.

Q. How do you mean, all upset?
A. I mean all upset. Excited and shaky. She took me into the front parlor. Said she wanted to talk in there. I asked her what was wrong. She said she would tell me as soon as the ears were out of the house.
Q. What did she mean by that?
A. She meant the hired man and the boy. Hobart Cudworth, and the orphan Walter Jones. They were working around the kitchen. She said she'd tell me as soon as they went to the picture show.
Q. They soon left the house?
A. About a quarter after eight. Cudworth stopped on the way out, and she gave him fifty cents.
Q. Then what did your aunt tell you?
A. It seems she was frightened.
Q. She told you that?

A. Not in so many words. Her manner. I'd never seen her like that. She said a lot of things had gone wrong. That everyone was against her.

Q. Did she name anyone?

A. I gathered she meant her sons, for two. After saying everybody, she told me she'd had a hard time with Earnest and Lionel. The past Sunday they'd had an awful fight.

Q. Over what?

A. The money Captain Nathan had willed her. Her sons were trying to get it away from her. She told me she was going to leave the homestead, too. Sell out. Pack up and go away from Quahog Point.

Q. You say Abby Bridewell planned to leave her home?

A. As soon as she felt well enough to travel, she said. When she said that, she almost cried. She rolled up a sleeve and showed me a bad bruise on her arm. She showed me another on her knee. I asked her had she fallen down. She shook her head.

Q. You imply, Mrs. Ord, that these bruises were from blows?

A. She didn't say. She just showed them to me.

Q. And that was the business your aunt wanted to discuss with you?

A. I don't think so. She said she got the bruises on Sunday afternoon—after she'd seen me at church, that would have been. And she said that was when she made up her mind to go live somewhere else.

Q. Then what *was* the business she wanted to see you about?

A. She didn't say.

Q. Didn't say?

A. No, she didn't. She got more and more distracted. Then all at once she stiffened up. She said something to herself like, "This will never do." Then she asked me would I join her in a cup of tea and some spiced pears.

Q. Tea? Spiced pears?

A. She loved spiced pears and tea. But the thought made me hiccup. When I said no, she thanked me for stopping in, and would I now excuse her. She said she would fix herself a snack, and go do some more packing.

Q. Then you left?

A. I did. When my aunt asked you to excuse her, it was time for you to go.

Q. What time was that?

A. Minute of nine o'clock, according to the clock on the parlor mantel.

That was Cornelia Ord's story, and she stuck to it. She could not have picked a worse evening to spend an hour in unwitnessed privacy with her aunt. The only person who could have verified her story was Abby Bridewell. And at the Coroner's inquest Old Abby was not talking.

Statement of Lizzie Robinson, spinster, age twenty-one plus, to County Coroner and Jury; Special Inquest Session, Town Hall, Quahog Point, April 1911:

My name is Lizzie Zenobia Robinson. I am a dressmaker as well as a seamstress. What the French call a modest. I ain't—aren't—paid half enough for my work. Wasn't by Mrs. Bridewell or any of them. This village don't appreciate style.

No, I did not have a quarrel with Old Abby—Mrs. Abby Bridewell—on the evening of April 11. Yes, was there fitting a dress from six-thirty to close on eight. It was a taffeta with a lace collar and beadwork on the bodice. We did not exchange sharp words then, or any time. She was exacting and particular, but no more so than most.

What I said to Mrs. Ord when I met her as I was leaving was generalities. I'd lost a thimble and pricked my finger, and I was tired out. With dressmaking in general. I didn't mean it personal about Mrs. Abby Bridewell. I liked her well enough.

No, I did not notice any bruises on Mrs. Bridewell. She did not mention bruises to me. Did not seem upset to me. She said she wanted the dress quick as she could get it . . . they all do.

Should think I would have noticed bruises when she tried on the dress, yes. Well, mostly I was pinning up the hem. She did not say anything to me about leaving Quahog Point. She seemed all right when I left the house.

That was when Mrs. Ord went in.

Statement of Walter Jones, age thirteen:

My name is Walter Jones. I am an orphan. I was bound out to Senator Bridewell by the Milk Street Orphans' Home, Boston, October 1910. He placed me in his mother's home to help with the chores. I worked in the stables, fetched wood, tended the yard, shoveled snow, and helped in the kitchen.

They sent me to the Quahog School. I was put back a year . . . the sixth grade. I did not like the school. Senator Bridewell promised me a new corduroy suit, but I did not get it. I had the back room behind the washroom . . . me and Cudworth had it. He's the hired man. He was good to me. He would take me with him to the motion picture show when the old lady let us go.

She promised us we could go Monday night, but we had to stay in on account of Senator Bridewell was there and we had to help in the kitchen at suppertime and after. Cudworth didn't want to, but she said we could go Tuesday.

We went Tuesday night. The dressmaker had been there right after supper, and then Mrs. Ord came to call. Mrs. Ord was there chatting with the old lady when we left the house. Didn't hear what they said. I was with Cudworth in the kitchen.

Went to the Scenic Palace. It was a two-reeler and we laughed. About this cowboy named Alkalai Ike. There was another two-reeler about a man who came home and found his wife sitting on the knee of a salesman. They had a big fight and he hit him with a chair. After that they had Lamont's Cockatoos, which was a bird act with white parrots. Then we went to the Center Ice Cream Parlor, and walked home.

I didn't see what time it was. There was a light in the parlor window. Cudworth and me thought the old lady was waiting up for us to give us some chore. We went around back and in by the kitchen door. Didn't make a light. Didn't want her to see us. It had gone cold and windy, and Cudworth didn't want to get called to build a fire. We went quietly to our room in the back so as she wouldn't hear us.

I went straight to bed.

I think Cudworth went straight to bed.

In reconstructing Cudworth's inquest statement, the present writer had some difficulty in visualizing the deponent. Nowhere could I dredge up a description of the witness, who was delineated simply by age and by occupation as "hired man."

He was from somewhere "up coast." Had been some months in the Bridewell employ. Who pays much attention, after all, to a plodding figure in overalls as common to the rural scene as a pitch-fork and a manure shovel? I finally settled on a cloddish young man with a sheaf of hair over one eye and a bandana slouching from hip pocket. Unless addressed, he wears the vacant expression one sees on the aimless idler who can spend an afternoon whittling a stick.

However, from Cudworth's subsequent statements in court and elsewhere—statements which remain on available record—one can construe the substance of what he must have said at the Coroner's inquest.

Q. State your name and occupation.

A. Name's Cudworth. Hobart Cudworth. I'm the old lady's hired man. . . . Or I was.

Q. On the evening of April 11 you went to the moving pictures with Walter Jones?

A. To the Scenic Palace.

Q. Was anyone there at the Bridewell house when you left to go to the pictures?

A. A woman was there. Mrs. Ord.

Q. And earlier in the evening?

A. The dressmaker.

Q. Tell us if you noticed any trouble between Mrs. Abby Bridewell and either of those ladies.

A. Trouble? Didn't notice any. I was with Walter in the kitchen. Since supper. . . .

The old lady had not wanted much supper, so they'd had oatmeal. He, Cudworth, was fed up to the scuppers with oatmeal at the Bridewell place. They ate all right when Earnest or Lionel Bridewell were at the house, but half the rest of the time it was oats. Cudworth had finally told the old lady he wasn't a horse. No, they hadn't quarreled about it. But because of the grub, he had several times offered to quit.

Well, she wasn't too hard to work for. Now and then she'd come through with time off. Like the evening of April 11 when she let him and Walter go to the Scenic Palace. It seemed as though she wanted them to go. She gave him, Cudworth, fifty cents. He went to the parlor to get it.

Yes, she was in the parlor talking to Mrs. Cornelia Ord. He didn't hear what they'd been talking about. Just heard the voices after Mrs. Ord came in. He didn't know anything about the old lady being upset that night. Did know she'd started to pack some things. Day before, she'd asked him to fetch a trunk down from the attic. Didn't tell him she was going away anywheres. Thought she was packing stuff he'd have to carry back up to the attic.

Well, there had been kind of a row on Sunday. Heard Senator Earnest Bridewell yelling at his mother. Goddaming and the like. Lionel Bridewell had been there for the weekend. They were both cussing each other. Something about a will.

No, it wasn't unusual. All winter, every time they were at the house, it was like that. Senator Earnest stayed over till Monday after Lionel Bridewell left on the evening boat. Monday noon there'd been another row. The Senator wanted to know why she had sold three carriage horses a while back. She wouldn't tell him. They really had it out.

Nobody at the house with the old lady all day Tuesday, so far as he, Cudworth, knew. He spent most of the day in the barn. Grooming the black mare and such.

What time did he and Walter Jones leave for the pictures that evening? Well, they left the house at eight-fifteen. Looked at the time because the show began at eight-thirty; they had just time to get there if they ran part way.

As it was, they were late. Got there when a sign was on the screen: Ladies Please Remove Your Hats. They saw a comedy Western and a Nestor Picture. Stayed till it was over. Went down the square for sundaes and a malted milk. Walked home. Hurried. Windy and turning cold. Must have got there about eleven. . . .

Q. Did you see Mrs. Abby Bridewell when you got there?

A. Didn't see her. Saw a light in the parlor, so we went around to the back. Thought she had company, maybe.

Q. Did you hear anyone in the parlor? Any voices?

A. Didn't hear nothing but wind whooping around the house. . . .

Had tiptoed into the dark kitchen with Walter Jones. Had gone straight to bed—the cot next to Walter's. Had set the alarm for five-thirty. Didn't hear it. Overslept. Woke up at five of six. . . .

So much for the hired man's deposition concerning his knowledge of events just prior to, and on, the evening of April 11. Hobart Cudworth, age 22, was not the brightest witness in the Bridewell case.

But Cudworth was certainly one of the more important. As will be seen, he allegedly found and reported what the Coroner would have referred to as the "corpus delicti."

If the testimony Cudworth eventually uttered under oath was reliable, he roused from his cot at six A.M. This was the morning of April 12, 1911. A day beginning like all days. Gray mist silhouetting the window shutters, and the cubby in semi-darkness.

Cudworth did not provide the detail, but one can imagine him sitting there in the chill gloom, half awake, bitterly resenting the forces which have boosted him out of the quiltings of warm slumber. Perhaps subconscious habit. Perhaps a distant rooster. He wouldn't know. He sits there, chin on chest, somnambulistic, while sleep flows from him. He groans. Scratches under an arm. Then, opening an eye, sees the tin alarm clock. Do Jesus! The old lady will be up and give him what for. He grabs for his denim overalls.

Tucking in a shirttail, he hikes for the kitchen. Good—it's still dark and the house is asleep. He pauses to put a kettle on the oil stove beside the range. Then, quietly opening and closing the kitchen door, he slips out to the porch. He notices that the wind expired sometime during the night. The morning is deathly quiet —so absolutely still that he can hear the faint, far hornblowing of fishing boats off the harbor. The garden is cobwebbed in mist, the house wrapped in a cocoon of vapor.

Cudworth hastens to the facility at the end of the yard. After answering what he will describe in public as a "call of nature," he tangents to the pump near the grape arbor. There he pats icewater on his eyes, rubs his hands in his hair, wipes them on his shirt. Ablutions thus completed, he hustles back indoors to escape the chill fog.

The kitchen is cold, gray-dark. Cudworth concentrates on the range. He places kindling in the firebox, douses kerosene on the kindling. Then, as gently as possible, he dumps in the coal. He is still "trying not to wake up the old lady."

He had the fire reddening the iron lacework of the draft and the kettle steaming briskly by 6:15 A.M. He lit an oil lamp in a bracket by the stove. And he was warming his hands at the range when his glance happened to wander to the other end of the kitchen.

"That," he said, "was when I noticed the cellar door standing open."

Q. Was it wide open?
A. No, only part open.
Q. What you'd call standing ajar?
A. I guess you'd call it that.

Q. What did you do then?
A. I went to close it.
Q. And—?
A. That's when I seen the old lady. She was lying down there at the foot of the steps.
Q. What did you do when you saw her down there?
A. I called out her name. *Mrs. Bridewell!* It occurred to me she might've had some sort of accident.

Cudworth's was a pretty good guess. In fact, it verged on the clairvoyant. Clinging to the door-handle, he peered down into the fusty gloom. When he could summon the wit to do so, he called out to the old lady a second time.

"Mrs. Bridewell!"

Abby Bridewell made no reply. At the foot of the steps she remained as inert as a bundle of laundry. She wore the black dress Cudworth had seen on her the previous evening. She lay stomach down, her hands pressed under her bosom, her feet together, toes pointing earthward—her body positioned like a barrel which had rolled down the steps and stopped, kerplunk, at the bottom. Her head almost touched the sidewall, and was askew, so that her right cheek pressed the basement floor and her face was toward the steps. Cudworth could see the left eye. He could also see the bloody smear on the left temple. And the leakage of blood from the nose.

Broken glass gleamed on the third or fourth step down. Halfway down lay an object which, at first glance, looked like a dead rat. Actually it was a rat—beauty-parlor colloquial for a pad of false hair.

Hobart Cudworth uttered something which was never officially reported, but was probably the equivalent of "Christamighty!" He backed away from the cellar door. Wheeled about-face. Ran. Or, to quote his testimony, "went for help."

Q. You did not touch the body?
A. Nossir. I didn't go down the steps.

Q. You say you went for help.
A. And that's the truth.
Q. Where did you go?
A. I went to fetch State Senator Bridewell.

I was unable to locate any account of what State Senator Bridewell was doing at the moment when Cudworth reached "the south side" with the news. Apparently Earnest was up and about, but had not yet breakfasted. Let us say, for the sake of visualization, that he was in an upstairs bedroom of his wife's farmhouse, stropping a razor.

On the washstand waits an ironstone bowl and a pitcher of hot water. In his pet shaving mug, a creamy fluff of lather. The Senator stops stropping, reaches for the mug, and applies a beard of cream to his chin and jaws. He then places a thin finger under his horseshoe mustache, delicately raises the mustache from his upper lip, and is leaning toward a mirror, with razor poised, when he hears the front gate slam. Rounding to a window, he sees Cudworth, sweaty, gasping, jogging toward the side porch. If that was by chance the situation, the Senator may very well have nicked his chin in his hurry to finish shaving.

Cudworth did not at once deliver the news to Earnest Bridewell. In scanning the press accounts, I discovered a new character on the scene. This was Alvin Bridewell, either a foster son or a stepson—available records and local memories were not clear about the relationship. The matter is of no consequence. Neither was Alvin Bridewell. A youth in his late 'teens, he was a cipher who lived at the "south side place" with Earnest's vague wife. However, Cudworth summoned Alvin to the porch, and through this indirect medium the alarm was conveyed to the State Senator.

Of course, the word brought Earnest galloping to the door in a figurative, if not a literal, lather. "What is it? What's this about my mother?"

Cudworth gurgles and makes frantic gestures, pointing north. The long cross-country run—uphill over back roads and downdale through the neighboring orchard—has left him winded. But at last he blurts it out. "She's lying in the cellar. She's all blood!"

"Get the roan out of the stable! Hitch the buggy! You, too, Alvin. Damn it, don't stand there!"

Earnest rushes back into the house to get his coat. He shouts to his wife, "I got to go! It's ma!" He may have had a hangover that morning, for it would seem that he collided with a chair or something near the door. Then he slipped on the buggy step and bruised his knee. Cudworth would say he could not remember Earnest barking his kneecap. But Cudworth was holding the horse's head at that moment and he may have been too excited to notice anything. Later that morning, however, someone noticed that Earnest had a slight limp. And the same sharp pair of eyes noticed scratches (razor cuts?) on the Senator's chin.

Earnest poured on the whip, and they careened down the road heading northward.

From our simulated Coroner's record:

Q. Now, Senator, how long did it take you to get to your mother's house that morning?

A. We got there lickety split.

Q. Five minutes by the road? Ten?

A. Ten at most. We'd have got there faster, except I missed the turn in the fog, and had to turn around and come back.

Q. It was a little after seven when you reached the house?

A. Yes, a little after seven.

Bursting into the kitchen, Earnest made straight for the cellar door. It was standing ajar as Cudworth had left it. Earnest glared down the cellarway. Then he rushed to the kitchen door and shouted to Cudworth: "Go fetch Doc Hatfield! Quick!"

Q. You say you sent the hired man off for the doctor before you went down cellar?

A. I sent him at once.

Q. Before you looked to see if your mother needed medical help?

A. Certainly. Why wouldn't I?

Q. She may have merely fainted down there. How did you know she hadn't just fainted?

A. My mother, sir, did not fall in faints. I had never known her to swoon. Besides, I could see she was badly hurt.

Q. Go on, Senator.

A. Then I went down to look at my mother.

He almost fell down the steep flight of steps. The third step down was coated with a fruity sirup, and there was a scatter of broken glass. He noticed blood on the sidewall, and he got blood on his hand lower down when he caught the bannister.

He tried to move his mother, but he couldn't do it without stepping over her body, and he was afraid he would slip and fall on her. He dabbed at her bleeding forehead with a handkerchief. Then he mounted the steps to the kitchen, and ran for help.

Q. You left the house, and your mother down there?

A. There was nothing I could do. I couldn't get her up that steep flight of steps alone.

Q. Where did you go for help?

A. I went down the road to a neighbor's. To Asa Goodbody's.

Q. How far was that.

A. About three minutes down the road. I ran all the way. Or most of it.

Earnest Bridewell broke through the front gate at Goodbody's, sprinted up to the porch and yanked the bell-pull. After a moment the door opened a crack, giving view to Mrs. Goodbody in night-cap and wrapper. She told Earnest that Asa was "out back."

Earnest hurried around to the barnyard. He found Asa sitting on a bench mending a fishnet. Beside Asa on the bench sat a bottle of Duffy's Malt. Asa suffered from arthritis. Duffy's Pure Malt Whiskey, advertised as "a beverage and medicine combined," was guaranteed to relieve that complaint and almost anything else that ailed one, including a sudden emergency. Accepting an offer, Earnest downed a gulp of the 100-proof restorative. This may have been the source of a subsequent rumor that he was somewhat "in liquor" that morning.

Asa accompanied Earnest back to the Bridewell house. Their progress on the road was slowed to a walk by Asa's arthritic condition. The fog cleared away as they walked. Bands of early sunlight were slanting through the trees by the time they reached the Bridewell gate. It must have been about a quarter to eight.

They found Doc Hatfield's buggy standing in the dooryard. Down the yard, Cudworth was frantically pumping a bucket of water. Walter Jones stood on the kitchen porch, looking scared. Earnest told the boy to wait on the porch. The Senator and Asa entered the kitchen.

Cornelia Ord sat at the kitchen table, her features stony. Her nose was red, and she blew it violently as the men entered. But the blow was not lachrymose. Cornelia was not the crying kind. In fact, it was remarked afterward that there wasn't a wet eye among the members of the Bridewell family.

The remark was made by Mrs. Bertha Smeizer, who was standing at the stove as supervisor of the kettle. She was the wife of "Smudge" Smeizer, a lobsterman. She looked a little like George Washington might have looked if he had been a woman. Unfortunately she lacked Washington's alleged reputation for veracity. Or it might be more charitable to say, as some of the "Pointers" did, that she was as honest as the next person.

Mrs. Smeizer had seen the doctor's buggy from her window. The Smeizer dwelling occupied a slope overlooking the Bridewell grounds. She had covered the distance in no time, motivated by the usual blend of kindliness and curiosity. Emphasis on the curiosity.

Ignoring Mrs. Smeizer, Earnest Bridewell demanded of Cornelia, "How did *you* get here?" The explanation was simple enough. Her voluptuousness had returned during the night. About six A.M. (her normal rising time) she had decided to try some pepsin. Since the drugstore would not open until eight, she had driven over to see the doctor. She had just hitched her team to the Hatfield hitching post when Cudworth drove up with the news about Abby Bridewell. So she had come with Dr. Hatfield.

Earnest said "Humph!" or something to that effect. Went to the table. Pulled an envelope from his pocket. Found a pencil in another pocket. And hurriedly scribbled a note. Slamming out to the porch, he handed the envelope to young Walter.

"Run that down to the Center fast as you can go. Telegraph Office. It goes to Lionel Bridewell, Lookout Hill."

The message read: *Come at once. Ma's hurt bad.*

A decided understatement.

As Earnest Bridewell reentered the kitchen, Doc Hatfield emerged from the cellarway. The doctor was in his shirtsleeves, with the cuffs turned back. A stethoscope dangled around his neck. He was wiping his hands on a towel.

The doctor was a leisurely man. He wiped his hands thoroughly. He hung the towel on the latch of the cellar door. He fished a packet of Bull Durham from his vest pocket, rolled a cigarette, put it between tobacco-stained teeth. He wore rimless, expressionless glasses pinched to the bridge of a Roman nose that was etched with a fine tracery of red pen-lines. He said as he lit the cigarette, "She's gone."

Earnest Bridewell stood glaring at the doctor.

A few days later he would stand glaring at the County Coroner. And that official would question him along the following curtain line:

Q. Senator, would you care at this hearing to tell us where you were on the night of Tuesday, April 11? Between the supper hour, say, and six o'clock the next morning?

A. I would prefer to enter a full and formal deposition and have it notarized. But I can safely say for your record that I did not see my mother, nor was I anywhere near her house, on the night of Tuesday, April 11. Between the supper hour and six the next morning, I was with my wife at our place on the south side. I was there the entire time. This inquest can put that in its pipe and smoke it.

Statement of Asa P. Goodbody, retired cooper, fisherman:

I'm Asa Goodbody. Friends call me Ace. Live down the road a piece from the Bridewell place. Used to be a cooper. Quit it to take up fishing. No money in coopering any more. Not much in fishing, neither.

Didn't go out on the boat, morning of Wednesday, April 12. Misery in the joints. Was mending a net right after breakfast when the Senator—that's Earnest Bridewell—pops into the barnyard. He looks right peaked. Pale as the belly side of a flounder.

Earnest waves at me like an accident, would I come? I said accident to who? He grabs a drink—some spirits I had there—and then hustles me by the arm out to the road. We start for the Bridewell place, me on a cane. Out on the road, he says to me, "Ace," he says, "I'm in trouble and need your help."

Yessir, that was the first thing Earnest says to me. That he was in trouble, and would I help him. I went with him to his mother's house. Didn't know what trouble he meant at the time. Soon as I seen the doctor's buggy at the door, I guessed. Later he told me that he wanted me to say, if anybody asked, that he was always kind to his mother.

Statement of Bertha Smeizer, wife of Harold "Smudge" Smeizer:

My name is Bertha Smeizer, born Ross. On the morning of Wednesday, April 12, my husband got up early and went lobstering. I was up at six. About six-thirty I'm on the front porch feeding chickens. Porch looks down toward the Bridewell place, other side of the road.

It's a quiet morning. Misty. I hear the Bridewell kitchen door slam. I can always hear it slam when it's slammed, and I once complained about it. Then a minute later, the Bridewell hired man breaks out of the fog, and I see him go loping up the road. He cuts off to a path through the orchard below our place, and disappears running.

Half hour or so later, I hear a carriage coming hell bent. It's the

Senator's buggy. Earnest larruping the horse, and Cudworth with him. They go like crazy into the Bridewell drive, and slam into the house.

Then Cudworth comes out and drives away, hell bent. I hear Earnest shout after him Doc Hatfield's name. Couple of minutes later, Earnest runs from their yard and goes top speed down the road toward the Goodbodys'. I know something's happened when I see Doc Hatfield's buggy racing up a few minutes after that, Cornelia Ord in it, too. So I went down and across to see if I could help.

Walter Jones, the orphan, came out of the house as I got there. Said he just woke up, didn't know what had happened. Cornelia Ord told me straight off I saw her: It was Abby. The doctor had gone down cellar. When I looked down, he told me to please get away from the door, he needed the light, would I get more hot water.

Then the Senator came in with Mr. Goodbody. I noticed scratches or cuts on his chin, but I didn't think anything of it. Still don't. I noticed Earnest limped a trifle like he had a sore leg. Didn't think anything of that, either. He had a breath. But I don't think he was much in liquor. Not that morning, anyway.

Well, he had taken to drinking some that spring, although I don't imagine a great deal. When he was in liquor his voice was pretty loud. Well, I could hear it on nice days when the windows were open. Like the Sunday afternoon previous to April 11. Then late in the afternoon of Tuesday, April 11—say about five-thirty.

He drove up to the house at that time Tuesday, yes. He had a bottle on him. I saw him stop the buggy just before he turned in, and take a drink. He went in the back. But I could hear him shouting in the parlor where the windows were open. He was swearing at his mother. Something about three thousand dollars.

They'd had the same argument Sunday afternoon when Lionel was there. I heard something about three thousand dollars. Both of them could sound pretty violent. I guess drink made Earnest violent sometimes, like last winter when he struck his mother and knocked her down. I wasn't there, but I heard about it. Think Cudworth may have told me. I don't remember.

Yes, I saw Earnest come out of the house Tuesday, before suppertime. I'd say quarter to six. He drove away. Whipping the horse. Then after supper Lizzie Robinson went in. When she came out, Cornelia Ord was going in. No, I didn't notice for an hour or two after that. In my kitchen doing dishes.

Couldn't see much after that. It was dark. I would say about a little after nine P.M., Tuesday evening, I did see the front door open and close. Saw the light. Later I heard the kitchen door slam. Don't know the time. Saw a figure on the Bridewell side porch. In the dark. I couldn't say if it was a man's or a woman's. It seemed tallish, though. I remember wondering if Earnest Bridewell had gone back to the house to see his mother.

When I saw him there next morning, I meant to ask him. Then I told myself it was none of my business. Besides he seemed awful distracted. I shouldn't blame him with his poor mother lying down there dead.

No, I never had trouble with the Senator as a neighbor. I always liked Earnest, even if I never voted for him. He could be mean at times, but what man isn't? If the family was stingy, I'd say they got it from the mother. Or perhaps poor Abby Bridewell was just thrifty. She probably had her reasons.

I felt real sorry when the doctor came up from the cellar and told us she was dead. I recall thinking maybe if she hadn't hung onto her money so hard, she might be still alive. I was going to say as much to Cornelia: What's the good of money if you're liable to get killed for it? There aren't any pockets in a shroud.

But I didn't. There were too many people in the room, and besides Doctor Hatfield did not say at the time that she had been murdered.

▲

Earnest Bridewell demanded, "What happened?"

Dr. Hatfield said flatly, "Looks like a fractured skull. Her neck seems broken. There's some contusions on her knees, and a bad cut on her right cheek. I expect she died from shock."

From the subsequent Coroner's record (simulated):

Q. Did she die while you were tending her, Doctor?

A. She was dead when I got there.

Q. What time would you say you got there?

A. Fast as I could. Mrs. Ord was just coming to my place. This hired man, Cudworth or whoever, was with her. I had the buggy already hitched. Was going over to see Delia Bryce about her goiter. Mrs. Ord told me to come at once. Cudworth said there'd been an accident. It's only a quarter mile up the road to the Bridewell's.

Q. Mrs. Abby Bridewell was dead on arrival?

A. I'd say she'd been dead for some time.

Q. Approximately how long?

A. I couldn't rightly say.

Q. Had rigor mortis set in?

A. As you gentlemen must be aware, there's a lot of horse—excuse me, I mean controversy—in the profession about rigor mortis. It's like the weather. May set in earlier or later. All depends. Physical condition of the subject. Fat or lean. One hour? Two hours? Room temperature? You know.

Q. Doctor, we are not conducting a class in morbid anatomy. You could make a guess on how long she had been dead.

A. I did. It looked to me like she'd been dead maybe hours. At least eight or nine.

The spare-boned doctor had been unable to hoist the body up the steps. That office was finally performed by Earnest and Cudworth, with advice from Mrs. Smeizer. They carried Abby Bridewell into the sewing room at the side. Cornelia hurried upstairs to fetch a cover. The body was placed on a wicker settee. A candlewick bedspread was draped over the body. Earnest and Cornelia followed the doctor out to his buggy. The doctor halted, put down his little black bag, and carefully made another cigarette.

He drew a deep lungful of smoke and expelled it thoughtfully. He said to Earnest, "Your mother was a strong woman. For all her age she was in vigorous condition. Never knew her to have dizzy spells, did you?"

"I did not."

Cornelia said, "My aunt was never dizzy."

Dr. Hatfield said, "She went down those steps hard."

Earnest Bridewell seemed very positive about it. He said, "Doctor, wouldn't you say that my mother dropped a jar of preserves as she was coming up the steps, then slipped in the sirup and fell, fatally striking her head against the sidewall?"

Dr. Hatfield squinted thoughtfully through the smoke of a short cigarette. He moved the cigarette around between practiced lips. Then he said, holding the cigarette between his teeth, "Well, Earnest, I don't know. Maybe she had a heart attack. Maybe she just slipped like you say. Maybe she didn't. Seems to me—a man in your position, there ought to be an autopsy."

Earnest was firm about it. He wanted no autopsy. Neither would Lionel. Wasn't that right, Cornelia?

When she remained mute, Earnest flatly declared that he didn't want some veterinarian cutting up his mother out of scientific curiosity.

Dr. Hatfield took the jibe without comment. He had long ago become inured to Bridewell insolence.

"Very well," he said. "It's your mother, and I suppose it'll be your funeral."

Earnest said, "You'll issue a certificate of death by accident?"

"Yes."

"Then if you'll drive over and tell Undertaker Meck. And send me your bill."

I patched and threaded together the foregoing memorabilia from newspaper items, correspondence and similar source materials which Ed brought down from the Bridewell attic. He himself provided recollective bits and pieces for filler here and there.

We went over Old Abby's death while Annette Brewster attended church. Annette was a Catholic. As the Point lacked a Catholic church, she drove twenty miles inland, weather and road permitting, to attend late Mass—a devotional effort that cost half a day. And sometimes longer, depending on what Ed called the mood of his Protestant Kissel. As the roads were bad at that particular time of year, and Ed's Kissel proved more left-footed than usual, I had ample time for research into the details of Abby Bridewell's demise.

When my shorthand notes reached the point of the doctor's departure to summon the undertaker, I asked Ed about the town's reaction to Abby's death.

"It created a whale of a ruction," he recalled. "Neighbors running from house to house. Carriages dashing from farm to farm. Seems to me a crowd gathered at the Post Office, all excited. But the big thing, of course, was the funeral."

"Did you go?"

"Probably the only kid in town who didn't. Laid up with a cold or something. See if you can't find a story about it in that old copy of the *Quahog Weekly Pointer.*"

The local obituary contributed little. It did offer the statement that Mrs. Abby Bridewell had passed away as the result of "an unfortunate accident." The rest of the obit was devoted to an encomium of the deceased. The encomium would have convinced a reader unacquainted with Abby Bridewell that she had embodied the virtues and graces of Boadicea, Good Queen Bess, Molly Pitcher, Mrs. Astor, Nancy Hanks, the Empress Eugenie and Mother Machree.

> And now on high in Beulah Land
> She abideth up above.
> Our mortal loss is heaven's gain.
> We miss someone we love.

The flowery phrases and tearful verse were open stock. The wise printer kept a block of type for use in emergency. Nothing personal. The *Quahog Pointer* would have run the same obituary paragraph for Cornelia Ord, Mrs. Bertha Smeizer or Delia Bryce, or, on the national level, Mrs. Mary Baker Glover Patterson Eddy. In fact, the obit might have been run for Madame Sophie. It was strictly a matter of first come, first served.

"This obituary, dated April 13, attributes the death to accident."

"Yes," Ed said. "From what Doc Hatfield spoke later, it would be interesting to know what he wrote on the death certificate. Too bad all those old files went up in smoke when the Town Hall burned. People around here were still arguing about the old lady's death ten years afterward."

I could find nothing more in print by way of an original obituary notice. But I did have another original referent that was first hand, and to hand. The cellar stairway. When I completed my obit notes, I asked Ed if I could look into the cellar again.

"Go on down if you want. Here, I'll get a flashlight."

To add to authenticity, the day had suddenly darkened under a rush of thunderheads. Gray shadows engloomed the kitchen, and with a little imagination I could turn back the calendar to a certain evening or early morning of 1911.

Ed opened the cellar door and shot the light down the steps. Holding gingerly to the wooden handrail, I went down. I counted twelve steps. They were made for a steep and painful fall. The lumpy sidewall offered protuberant cobblestone for a head-cracking. I could imagine the steps glazed with glutinous sirup—treacherously slippery. Add jagged glass, and bodily anguish was assured.

"The old lady was coming up, not going down," Ed reminded from above. "They knew that because she was bringing up a jar or jug of something. I recall Doc Hatfield saying the steps were a mess, so was she, and he'd never be able to enjoy fruit sirup again."

I observed, "She must have been holding to this handrail, then, with her left hand. Cradling the jar in her right arm."

"That's it," Ed said. "She was defenseless. Come up the steps like that, and you'll see how defenseless she was."

I liked Ed's term for it—defenseless—and as I started up the steep, stone steps, I could see how vulnerable she had been. I went up with left hand holding the skinny wooden rail, right elbow curved in simulation of carrying a heavy jar. Even in pretense I had to be careful. It was almost like climbing a ladder one-handed.

As I neared the top, Ed stopped me with, "That's where she got it."

I confess it made me feel uncomfortable.

"See, from where you are," Ed pointed, "if you had a jar in your arm and dropped it, it would smash on that third step from the top. Notice, too. Where you're standing, your head and shoulders are coming up through the door-frame. Anyone waiting here at the side, could step around quick and let you have it."

Anyone waiting there at the side. Although I had anticipated the development, the simplicity of it gave me a mouse-run through the hair.

I could imagine the motionless shadow there on the floor—back a little from the doorsill—waiting. Coming up the steps, the victim would not see it.

I could imagine the killer standing with indrawn breath. The victim, puffing a little, would not hear the flexing of tightened muscle, the faint, secret sounds emitted by any tensing human body—a controlled swallow, the stretch of a sinew, the tiny pop in some excited digestive organ.

Abby looked up and saw—?

Ed's smile seemed to spread across the doorway. "It kind of gets you, doesn't it? To this day it sort of gives me a creep. Whoever figured it out sure had the old lady set up for a kill."

Stepping up into the kitchen, I expelled a breath.

Ed closed the heavy hand-hewn door and turned the hoop handle to fasten the latch.

We went into the parlor to attend Old Abby's funeral.

CHAPTER 12

HORATIO A. MECK, Undertaker and Embalmer. From what Ed told me about him, I deduced the "A" could only have stood for Alger.

"Like his father, Eustace Meck, before him," Ed described, "Horatio was a go-getter. Ever hear of an undertaker who'd rather die than miss a funeral? Both Mecks were like that. Doubled in spades."

Because the "Pointers" were notoriously hardy, the Mecks ran the local meat market on the side. It seemed the ice vault at the rear of the butcher shop made a dual-purpose chamber for cold storage. And in the old days the meat wagon was subject to conversion. That is, the "customer" would be brought to the shop in this delivery cart because Old Eustace liked to save the hearse "for the big parade." Some of the villagers, squeamish, objected to having their chops and roasts delivered in the same market wagon. To objectors, Eustace Meck would quote: "From the funeral baked meats, let the wedding feast be served." Old Eustace was a Shakespeare fan. He had once seen Edwin Booth in *Hamlet*, and the Boston performance lasted him a lifetime.

"You should have seen that old hearse," Ed said. "It was a real fancy job with a driver's seat up top, like a circus wagon, and with cut-glass windows. Old Eustace would drive in a frock coat and tophat almost as tall as Abraham Lincoln's. You got two horses with plumes for the fifty-dollar service, four horses with plumes for the hundred-dollar, and six horses for a real big go-down."

Even a two-horse funeral was an event in a community the size of Quahog Point. What Ed termed a "six-horser" generated almost as much civic emotion as the Fourth of July or Hallowe'en. When Eustace cracked the whip to start a big procession on the way to Headland Cemetery, it was his proudest moment. It was the same with Horatio when he took over.

Horatio Meck was, in local idiom, a chip off the old block. Ed's use of the phrase went nicely with a depiction of the two Mecks as smallish men with sandy side-whiskers and buck teeth, dapper and quick in movement, like a pair of chipmunks.

But Horatio had one specialty. "He had this trick of mourning." He had trained under his father as a hired mourner—a thespian seldom seen today, but a popular performer at mid-Victorian funerals where demonstrations of grief were considered mandatory. If you couldn't cry over the demise of Uncle Albert, at least you could procure a substitute to do it for you. Horatio Meck was so adept at shedding specious tears that they sometimes sent for him at Boston, Providence and other dry-eyed metropolises. If the legend were true, at instant's notice he could weep like a willow.

Of course, the habitués of the Anchor Saloon would get Horatio to put on his performance. "Mourn for us, Horatio," they'd pester him. "Okay," he'd agree, "say something sad." They'd say something sad like, "Garfield just passed away," and Horatio would go into a crying jag. Or they'd sing, "Go tell Aunt Rhoda the old gray goose is dead," and he would literally bawl. He could stop any time, and grin like anything.

This was not to say that Horatio was incapable of genuine grief. Let a client talk about economizing, and he would become as mournful as a tombstone. "What?" he would dolefully protest. "You think my price too high for a lot in Headland Cemetery? Why, people are dying to get in!" And if anyone from Quahog Point were lost at sea, he would be absolutely inconsolable.

"Here's the thing," Ed said. "Neither of the Mecks could bear to lose a customer. Horatio was worse than his father. Why, one freezing winter night when you couldn't get a horse or wagon up the hill at land's end, he went after the customer with a wheelbarrow."

The customer in mention was Grampa Bryce, an ancient mariner who lived in a hermit shanty way out near the lighthouse. Nobody knew how old Grampa was. Some said he had served as a powder monkey on the frigate *Constitution.* That he must have been a nipper when Nelson's flag captain, Sir Thomas Hardy, tacked in to bombard Stonington, Connecticut, during the War of 1812 (and got his bottom scorched, Hardy did, for his pains!). Anyway, it was on record that Jonathan Bryce had been with Calbraith Perry at Vera Cruz in 1848. Grampa Bryce was so old that he had forgotten all these things.

He was so old that he had outlived all the members of his lineal family (the other Bryces at Quahog Point were of another branch) except a female descendant who resided in Newport. As a pillar of the D.A.R., this lady preferred to think of her distinguished ancestor as a marble monument rather than a filthy old man who swore dreadful oaths and spat tobacco juice and wet his pants. Accordingly, she had not seen her great-great-grandfather for a number of years. She had, however, arranged with the Mecks for a noble monument, and had ordered a six-horse funeral for Grampa, if, as, and when.

Of course, Grampa chose the coldest week in that December of '95—or was it '96?—to pass away. Because of the blistering freeze, Horatio Meck wired the Newport relative to see if the obsequies could be delayed. Nothing doing. She wanted the ceremony that weekend, because she was going to Europe. If Meck could not bury the ancient, she would send a Newport undertaker. Lose a six-horse funeral? That was what sent Horatio barrowing out to land's end.

"The story was, he went at night," Ed narrated. "They say he darn near froze to death getting out there. And he was almost as stiff as the customer, time they got back to town. It must have been a sight, Horatio wheeling that barrow with Grampa in it sitting upright, staring straight ahead. But the worst was when they got back to the shop and he couldn't thaw out Grampa."

The Mecks sat the customer near the stove and built a roaring fire. They put hotwater bottles in his lap and placed his feet on a footwarmer. As with King David in the Old Testament: "They covered him with covers and he gat no heat." It appeared that

Grampa Bryce had been sitting dead and frozen in his hermitage rocking chair for several days. The boreal ride to town in a wheel barrow had definitely fixed him in jackknife posture. This stumped the undertakers with a problem in solid geometry. Posed like an angle-iron, the customer refused to fit a longbox. As neither circular nor L-shaped coffins were in vogue, the problem seemed insoluble. As the funeral hour approached, the Mecks became desperate.

"What did they do?" I asked Ed.

"Well, there were versions."

According to one, Horatio procured a sledge-hammer and . . . but I preferred the more heroic version. In this, Horatio offers to go to the service as a substitute. He dons the ancient mariner's jacket and cravat. Puts on the old man's spectacles. Whitens his hair, hands and face with flour. What'll they use for a beard? "We'll bob Old Fanny!" And Horatio is laid out in the coffin ready to go when—just at the last second—the true customer "snaps out of it."

"The point is," Ed concluded the vignette, "Horatio Meck would have gone to the grave himself before he'd lose a six-horse job. Or a two-horser, for that matter. Once he had you scheduled, there was just one thing in the world that could stop him from burying you."

"What was that?"

"The sort of thing that happened at Abby Bridewell's funeral."

But I did not learn of the Abby Bridewell obsequies from Ed Brewster. Having baited my hook with the Meck preamble, he left me to fish in a fresh stack of yellowed newspapers and note papers from the attic reliquary. After directing my attention to these waters, he told me he had to go down to the Center and pick up a brace of guinea hen for six o'clock dinner.

"The service for Abby was here in the parlor," he said, and walked out.

At four o'clock I pushed aside the faded copies of the *Weekly Pointer*, the *State Capital Clarion-Journal* and other contemporary journals. So far as press accounts were concerned, I had the skeletal framework of the story.

Here, then, are the surface details concerning Abby Bridewell's funeral. I say surface details in deliberate equivocation, because as you know, and I know, the press seldom covers the under-the-surface story of anything.

The *Journal* item was treated to the usual reportorial formula of Who, When, Where, What, and Why. The formula is sound enough for basic story data, but the tag-end "Why" is too often lopped off to make room for a late ad or some special insertion. That is why news stories frequently end with a jolt, or seem to hangfire in incompletion. I recall an unforgettable example which appeared some years ago in a hinterland paper in Pennsylvania. From an item reporting a mine cave-in, the "Why" was amputated to make space for a Christmas poem. The verses must have been composed by the mine-owner's maiden aunt, or submitted by some subscriber as influential, say, as Abby Bridewell. I can still remember the poem's title—*Frankenstein and Myrrh.*

Similarly chopped off, the *Journal* story of Abby Bridewell's funeral was abridged in favor of an ad announcing that the Star Royal Lawn Mower "featuring 11-inch wheels, three pawl ratchets and a minimum of noise" was now on sale at Bryan and Minnisink's at a greatly reduced price. In fact, I almost missed the funeral item because of the ad on the opposite page—an overpowering picture of the smart Dexter Shoe—"cloth top and pearl buttons for $2.00 the pair." The reader had just time to skim over the Bridewell story before he raced downtown to the shoe store.

Then the original account in the *Quahog Weekly Pointer* went to the other extreme. Five columns, with most of the copy reading like the listings of the county census. "In attendance were Mr. and Mrs. Otis Purdy, Mr. and Mrs. Saul Smeizer, Henrietta and Tansy Thorn, Captain Aquarius Robinson of the *Letty and Marge. . . .*" On and on. Evidently the only localites who failed to attend Old Abby's funeral were Ed Brewster, recluse Sybil,

Madame Sophie, and Chester Goodbody's cigar-store Indian. But here was a news story which never got much farther than "Who."

So my own account, based on those in mention, is admittedly superficial.

As will be seen, it was the facts which were buried at that funeral, not Abby Bridewell.

Everyone tried to get there early so as to sit behind the family and not be left in the dining room or stranded out on the front lawn. House funerals usually meant a shortage of space and folding chairs. The ice-cream chairs from the Center Soda Emporium —small with springy back-supports—were uncomfortable when the service was long.

But the early birds found others who were earlier. Mrs. Bertha Smeizer had been there since breakfast time. She had, in fact, come over with an offer to prepare breakfast, hurrying crosslots the moment she saw Cornelia Ord drive up to the house.

Cornelia had left her farm at four A.M. At five she had been in the throes of a dress fitting in the home of seamstress Lizzie Robinson. Now, posted at the Bridewell front door to greet comers, she stood in the vestibule in her black veil and weeds like somber Hecate, Ruler of the Shades of the Departed. She had nothing to say to Mrs. Smeizer, who definitely had no intention of departing. And Mrs. Smeizer had nothing to say to Cornelia.

At seven Horatio Meck arrived. He put on his crying act, saw it made little impression on the bereaved, and briskly got down to last-minute details and instructions.

Horatio (blowing his nose): Now, then, Earnest, it looks a little cloudy out. But I know you'll want Mother laid to rest, rain or shine.

Earnest Bridewell: Why not? We've got umbrellas.

Horatio: I don't like to suggest an extra expense. However, if you'd like a canopy—?

Earnest: A canopy?

Lionel Bridewell (coming forward): Certainly we'll want one if it rains. Hell, I'm not going to ruin a new suit in any downpour.

Earnest: It's not going to rain. Look here, Horatio. Can't we hurry this up an hour? It's a strain, this waiting.

Horatio: Now, Senator, you wouldn't really want that. People are coming from miles around.

Earnest: I suppose so.

Horatio (sotto voce): As it is, some may feel you're a bit previous on the usual three days. You know how people are.

Earnest: I do. And they can shut their . . . never mind. All right. Nine to eleven. Will you tell the minister to time his speech?

Horatio: Glad to, Earnest, glad to. No use prolonging the painful . . . Hmmm . . . I'll go see about the urns.

As Horatio moves off, Earnest grips Lionel's arm and steers his brother into the kitchen.

Lionel (wrenching loose): What do you want?

Earnest (gritting): That bottle on your hip! Lay off, you fool! Do you want these busybodies to see you drunk?

Already the carriages are lining up before the house. Friends and neighbors come trooping in. Old folks, young folks, parents herding their children. For the most part they wear their Sunday-go-to-meeting clothes, and as they approach the Bridewell door they put on their Sunday-go-to-meeting faces.

Cornelia gives each a cold handshake in the vestibule, and says tonelessly: "In there."

At the threshold the visitor stalls a moment with that instinctive hesitation which causes most of us to pause before we enter the presence of the departed. What word of consolation can we offer the next of kin? What consolation can we offer ourselves as we face this reminder that our own sojourn on earth will one day terminate? The presiding clergyman will assure us that the departed is in a Hereafter of golden streets and angelic choirs—a far, far Better World. But catch *him* taking Charon's Ferry! So we hang back, instinctively reluctant to join the one-way traveler. Even the most confirmed immortalist seems to do his best to prolong his mortal stay.

Reconstructing the scene, I could see it there—the coffin under the fixed gaze of the Eye.

Furniture has been shoved back and various nicknacks rearranged to make room for the folding chairs and flowers. In one corner looms a floral donation from the Fire Volunteers—a setup the size of a fireworks display. However, instead of such pyrotechnic ballyhoo as "Hurrah for Teddy" or "Columbia the Gem of the Ocean," the silent flowers spell out "Gates Ajar." Another tripod holds a heavenly harp of black dahlias—contribution of Local Lodge No. 46. Urns of purple gladioluses (from the First Sabbatarian) flank the catafalque. A chrysanthemum "Peace at Last" carries a placard labeled Babcock's Grocery. Other floral displays are from Meck's Market, Jones's Livery, Ross's Blacksmith Shop, The Scenic Palace, and the Beach Hotel Association.

And Abby? We are such stuff as dreams are made of, and her little life was rounded with its sleep. She did *not* look natural. Not with her hair combed in a wing across her forehead to hide the deadly bash on the left temple. Not with her hands folded on her bosom, supine.

Yet even in this condition of repose, the chatelaine manages to hold her final reception with an air. Certainly she dominates the parlor. Her wintry little smile may be as artificial as the cosmetics applied by Horatio Meck, but it is disturbing, none the less. "You may think you've got me down," it seems to say, "but I've not gone yet."

The viewers file in for the last look. Uneasy, shuffling, subdued, women with handkerchief to mouth, men hat in hand.

Now the parlor fills rapidly. Scuffing of chairs. Nervous coughing. Heads turning to see who next comes in.

The air becomes oppressive, drugged with the scent of hothouse plants, of heavy breathing, of woollens, pomade, menthol. Plus a faint but insistent hint of formaldehyde. You could always detect it in the old days, whether you went to Moriarty's or to Campbell's.

Sudden hush. Enter Earnest and Lionel Bridewell, each with black crepe on his sleeve. Then Floss and Alvin Bridewell in black.

Enter Cornelia Ord, from head to toe in midnight. (A small

child wails in fright and is promptly slapped by its parent. "Hush up, Herman, or you'll go straight home.")

Enter the Reverend John Q. Ironquill, parson of the old school. His mien is enough to scare any child. It is supposed to. (And if that statement seems exaggerated, the doubter may refer to the Methodist Doctrine of 1900—a book which advises the aspirant preacher not to smile in public. Stern Ironquill, of course, is a Sabbatarian.)

The Bridewells and Cornelia take reserved seats. The minister strikes a pose by the catafalque. He looks like a statue of Discipline.

The hush deepens.

Ironquill: Brethern and sister'n, we have assembled here to pay our last respects to one we have all revered and loved. That our mood may be appropriate, let us sing. Brother Lionel, would you care to lead?

Lionel (standing up reluctantly): Yes, we'll gather . . . ?

Reverend Ironquill: I think we all know that one.

If we don't, we had better learn it. All of us are going to be there sooner or later.

Yes, We'll Gather at the River.

Out in the dining room the overflow shifts and cranes. Someone bangs the front door and wins a community scowl. Another general frown is evoked by a latecomer who presses in through the vestibule. It is one of the summer people early at the Point to open her sea house. In she comes in a motoring hat and linen duster. Of course, being an "inlander" she doesn't know any better. She is passed hand to hand across the dining room until she is deposited at the threshold of the kitchen.

"I'm terribly sorry," she whispers to a lounger there. "I tried to get here on time, but my car broke down . . . I was fond of Mrs. Bridewell."

Needles Thorn regards her noncommittally. Then, approving the costume, he reassures her gallantly, "It's all right. Have my chair."

Lady (speaking behind her hand): Thank you. Can you tell me . . . when it happened?

Needles: Tuesday.

Lady: What a shame.

Needles: It was expected like.

Lady: Yes . . . her age.

Needles: Not that, exactly. Somebody seen a death baby.

Lady (shocked): A wh-what?

Needles: A death baby. Out in the front yard. I can see you're not a New Englander.

Lady: I—I'm afraid I'm not.

Needles: It's a kind of toadstool. A sort of omen. Them as see one near their house ought to kill it right away. It's bad.

(Authentic Down East folklore: The "death baby"—a fungus of the genus *Ithyphallus*—portended a fatality in the home. The superstition may have stemmed from the growth's confusion with the death-cup, a poisonous mushroom.)

Chorus from the parlor: *The beautiful . . . the beautiful . . . River. . . .*

Lady (to turn the subject): It happened suddenly?

Needles: Right sudden.

Lady: Here at home?

Needles: Right there behind you. Broke her neck on those cellar stairs.

The lady rises silently and beats a retreat out through the kitchen door.

Now from the parlor a monotone drone. Quarter hour. Half hour. The Reverend Ironquill compares Abby Bridewell's life to a river. He begins with the springs of infancy, goes into the tributaries of adolescence, descends into the channel of the prime, and flows unhurriedly on and on to the estuary of old age, the delta of antiquity, and at last the sea. It is a discourse the ministerial geographer seldom covers in two hours. But today he chooses the Jordan Valley instead of the Amazon, and he reaches the sea at eleven o'clock. This is the big moment for Horatio A. Meck.

"This way, please."

The house is cleared. The assemblage is martialled in the dooryard. Hats off. Then a general movement toward the carriages that are lined up as far as the road-bend behind the hearse.

In high hat and frock coat Meck mounts to the driver's seat

with all the pride and dignity of an Admiral boarding a ship. I could not imagine the order that he might have given to start the solemn procession on its way. To six black horses with plumes "Giddyap!" would hardly have sounded appropriate. Nor could I imagine the utterance of a prolonged "Scuddahoo-scuddahay!"

The matter is academic. For, whatever the order, it was of no consequence that day. The horses were just digging in when an automobile swerved into view up the road and came speeding toward the hearse, head-on.

The tandem leaders reared and neighed. Clutching the reins, Horatio Meck reared and neighed with them, glaring in outrage. The car pulled up only in time, and with a shriek of brakes came to a halt athwart the roadway. Heads popped from the caravan of carriages. Someone scolded, "That ain't no Quahog car. They ought to rule these noisy autos off the roads."

They ought to rule out barking dogs, too. A commotion like that at such a time. And now this slamming of car doors as the motorists pile out. This stomping and loud talk at the roadside. The Reverend Ironquill glares from his buggy. What sort of corruption is this?

Advances a heavy-set man with silvery hair and a red face—a beefy stranger in a flapping overcoat with a pugnacious derby in his hand. Behind him, apologetic, comes Pythias Ross, town constable. Behind Pythias comes Wen Tasker with his walrus mustache, his Sheriff's star and his abdominal artillery.

Constable Ross holds up his hand in an appeal for silence.

Ross: I'm sorry, folks. This here funeral is over.

Earnest Bridewell (stepping from his carriage): What the devil is this, Pythias?

Ross: This here is a gentleman from the State's Attorney's Office.

Earnest: What's the meaning?

Gentleman: I have a restraining order.

The Sheriff (moving in): Hate to tell you, Senator, but your mother can't be buried today. Seems like the State wants her held for an autopsy. There's going to be an inquest.

Cornelia Ord (striding up): Inquest! What in heaven's name for?

Sheriff: To determine cause of death.

Lionel Bridewell: Well, hold an autopsy then! Good God!

Gentleman (pugnaciously): We intend to.

Sheriff: I'm afraid we got to hold you, too, Senator.

Earnest: *What!*

Sheriff: At least until this clears up. Sorry to say, Earnest, you're under suspicion. The State's Attorney got this word. Someone here in Quahog Point thinks your mother was murdered. There's this rumor you done the matricide.

Rounding to the hearse, the Sheriff hands a "cease and desist" to Horatio Meck.

According to the story, Meck burst into the only genuine tears shed at Abby Bridewell's funeral.

CHAPTER 13

AT SIX o'clock I drove with Ed in the Kissel out to Shipwreck Fathom Beach, intending to pick up Luke Martin. We had just time to eat and catch the seven-thirty boat back to civilization.

But Luke had himself a sea bass and wanted another. He had joined a party of big-game fishermen—business acquaintances from New York—and he elected to go on surfcasting and dine later with them. The New Yorkers had cars and would drive us to an inland town where we could catch a midnight train to Newport.

Whereby Luke missed a feast of guinea hen with wild rice. And I had another evening on locale, with opportunity to follow the Bridewell case to its historic courtroom conclusion.

After dinner Ed worried, "You sure you don't mind if Annette and I go over to a neighbor's for a while?"

"Not at all, Ed."

So while Ed and his good wife were in the Center paying a social call, I covered the trial of State Senator Earnest Bridewell. Which is to say, I read through the press accounts of what contemporary newspapers called "The Bridewell Murder Mystery." This contemporary press coverage was not up to the best of American journalism in the century's first decade. And any who care to check that standard will soon discern that with the notable exception of Richard Harding Davis and one or two others the best was none too good.

The *Clarion-Journal* tried. So did the *Coastal City News* and the widely read *Seaboard Herald.* None of these dailies had a Davis or the one or two others on its staff. All were more interested in the Mexican situation than in the strange death of an old lady in remote Quahog Point.

Of course, the fact that a State Senator was held under suspicion of matricide most foul did demand a number of frontpage headlines. But as the novelty wore off, the story was quickly relegated to page 6. I had a feeling, too, that the prisoner's Senatorial status somehow restrained the flow of journalistic ink. Soon after Earnest Bridewell went to jail, news editors began to treat the case with diffidence. A use of polite adjectives—a respectful or sympathetic tone—a resort to such qualifying loopholes as "it is said"—one can easily recognize the styling when journalists handle a story with kid gloves. Even before the trial began, the area papers were dealing gently with the accused. Midway through the trial they were treating him as though he were a troublesome but eccentric granny and they were Boy Scouts helping him across the street.

It *was* a mystery. For several weeks it vied for space in the *State Capital Clarion-Journal* with a serial by Anna Katharine Green. With all due respect to that popular story-teller, I could not help but feel that her fiction tale was contrived and conventional in comparison with the Bridewell case.

At least, Miss Green's fictional mystery came to a logical conclusion. The Bridewell case proved the polar opposite. For the trial of Earnest Bridewell, up for willful matricide, came to what must remain on record as one of the more outlandish courtroom conclusions in the annals of New England jurisprudence.

In my own coverage of the case, I had two singular advantages over the contemporary journalists who reported it. They were at the scene of the trial. But I was at the scene of the crime.

True, I was there almost thirty years late. In going to press, the contemporary accounts were only twenty-four hours behind time. I could visualize those mustachioed newsmen with their green eyeshades and pink armbands, pounding their Smith-Premier and Oliver typewriters. But so far as I could determine from their stories (and I subsequently checked through newspaper after newspaper in various city libraries) not a single out-of-town reporter visited the Bridewell homestead.

Skimpy press coverage notwithstanding, Quahog Point must have seethed with the news on that day when Earnest Bridewell was carted off to the County Jail. First Old Abby's death. Then the funeral brought to a dead end. Then the inquest finding—murder! Then the elder son charged with the slaying. Sensation after sensation. But no reporters, local or out-of-town, were on hand to interview the accused when the jail door clanged on his person. At that date (April 18, 1911) readers of the *State Capital Clarion-Journal* had to satisfy a taste for thrills with the early installments of "The House in the Whispering Pines" by Anna Katharine Green. Most of the space in the *Weekly Pointer* went to social items and ads for such commodities as Holman's Fever and Ague Poultice, Columbia Bicycles and Castoria.

Here I enjoyed my second advantage over the contemporary reporters. I was possessed of an informative dossier which would not have been at their disposal even had they made an effort to interview the prisoner.

This dossier was placed on my knee by Ed Brewster before he left the house that evening. "Scrapbook," he told me. "Found it in the attic under a lot of junk. The Senator maintained it while he was in jail waiting trial."

Earnest Bridewell's prison scrapbook offered an interesting close-up of the accused. Evidently while incarcerated, he had subscribed to most of the area dailies. These he had perused with picky care. Every column, every paragraph devoted to his case he had torn from the page and painstakingly pasted into the folio.

Then he had carefully studied and analyzed the news accounts. With pencil he had checked or underlined various statements. He had made numerous marginal notes—little side-remarks and comments such as "Bah!" and "Not true!"

To be sure, the book was not as revelatory as a diary. But the analecta and accompanying notations did furnish an insight into the writer's mental attitude and character. I saw that Earnest had followed the case with engrossed self-interest to the very end of the trial. Cryptically he had circled the name of every witness who had testified against him. Or perhaps the encirclements were not so cryptic. They were made with red pencil, and I could not believe the maker was compiling a Christmas-card list.

The scrapbook also contained numerous items of correspondence. Most of these were from well-wishers offering sympathy. But a letter addressed to the orphan boy, Walter Jones, caught and held my attention. Wondering how the boy's letter came to be in Earnest's private scrapbook, I examined the smudged envelope.

It was postmarked Boston, April 3, 1911. Which meant it should have been delivered to the boy during the week prior to Abby Bridewell's death. The stationery bore the letterhead of the Milk Street Orphans' Home, Boston. The missive was signed by a Miss Adelaide Fitzgibbon, Orphanage Secretary. An excerpt:

"We hope that you will now have a perfect attendance at school—we are sure your resolutions about this are very good. We are sorry to disappoint you about the corduroy suit. The reason that we do not send you one is that it was understood between the Orphans' Home and Mr. Bridewell when you were taken to Quahog Point that Mr. Bridewell should buy all of your clothing and pay whatever other bills were necessary for your support and welfare. If Mr. Bridewell wishes to order a corduroy suit, and will pay for it himself, we will be glad to have one sent from here C.O.D."

Of course. The Senator had picked up this letter at the Post Office. And for reasons of his own had never given it to the boy. Another glimpse into the Earnest Bridewell personality. The man who intercepts an orphan's mail, reads it and then withholds it from the youngster—such a character has a mean streak all wool and a yard wide. Or, as in this instance, all corduroy and a yard wide.

The scrapbook divulged a second letter which had never been delivered to young Walter Jones. This too had been dispatched from the Milk Street Orphans' Home. Dated April 22, 1911, the letter read as follows:

Master Walter Jones
Quahog Point
My dear Walter:

Because of the recent happenings at Quahog Point, we do not feel that you should stay there any longer. We have written to your patron saying that you must come to Boston on the Plymouth Line steamer which leaves Quahog Point on Wednesday, April 26. We want you to come that day without fail. Someone will be at the South Boston dock to meet you.

Sincerely yours,
Adelaide Fitzgibbon,
Orphanage Sec'y.

The above letter was followed by one from the Milk Street Orphans' Home to Earnest Bridewell, Esq. "It is over a week since we wrote requesting Walter Jones' return to our orphanage. . . . As we have heard nothing further from you, we write now to ask exactly when we may expect him. The Childrens' Aid Society will be happy to refund you the amount of his passage, if you will forward the bill."

To this peremptory note was pinned the carbon copy of a typewritten reply, probably dictated by Earnest Bridewell in the office of his defense attorneys. It was dated May 8, 1911—two weeks after the orphanage had directed Walter to return to Boston. Earnest advised the orphanage secretary:

"In reply to your recent letter, will say I have been under arrest for several weeks but am now released on bail. I am the victim of a plot of which you know nothing and I will prove my innocence at the first hearing which will probably be May 23rd.

*"Walter Jones knows positively of my innocence and for that reason the guilty parties are anxious for him to get as far away from this town as possible before the hearing.**

"Walter gave his testimony at the inquest in a manner which everyone gives him credit for, as the inquest was entirely one sided and I was under detention and not allowed a representative. Walter being a boy, the opposite side tried very hard to rattle him but I understand that he was as cool and level headed as a man. Now in justice to myself Walter should be allowed to remain with us until this unfortunate affair is over and the facts of the case exposed. He is a very important witness. . . . Therefore I request that he be allowed to remain here for the time being."

Naturally the foregoing correspondence never reached the public eye. And the good secretary of the Milk Street Orphans' Home must have wondered (as did I) just how a thirteen-year-old boy, who had spent the crucial evening at a moving picture show and then gone straight home to bed, could possibly "know positively" that the accused Senator was innocent. Even the Senator seems to have cherished a private doubt about the matter. In the scrapbook he had drawn a circle around Walter's name where it first appeared in newsprint. And in the margin opposite he had pencilled a question mark.

No, the currently serialized "House in the Whispering Pines" contained no mystery as mysterious as that one little notation.

With the Walter Jones enigma in mind, I turned eagerly to the press accounts of the trial of Earnest Bridewell, State Senator charged with matricide.

Counsel for the defense consisted of Vernon Bibbs, Esq., and Erasmus T. G. Coulter—an astute, and therefore expensive, team. Bibbs had pleaded a number of frontpage cases, and apparently was on his way up as a criminal lawyer. From his tactics I deduced

* Emphasis supplied.

that Coulter was a pleader of the older gaslight school which produced more gas than light. But sharp. A smalltown Joseph Choate. (And lest some nostalgic alumnus of Harvard Law protest the implication that Choate had a sharp side, be it remembered that the famous Choate as a young man was sharp enough to escape the Civil War draft by hiring a substitute to fight in his stead. It was Choate, too, who later wangled a whitewash for Captain Bowman McCalla, a martinet who touched off one of the relatively few mutinies in the U.S. Navy.)

That Bibbs and Coulter were adept was evidenced by the publicity immediately generated in their client's behalf. Less than two weeks after Earnest Bridewell's arrest, the *Coastal City News* published an opinion which flatly stated that the charges against the Senator were groundless.

"Considerable mystery enshrouds the case, and there is a report in court circles that he [Earnest Bridewell] may never be tried. . . . It is understood that the Attorney General's office has failed to produce a shred of incriminating evidence."

The prosecution, as embodied in the Office of the State's Attorney General, apparently did not protest this effort to suborn public opinion. Either the Attorney General was asleep, or he felt confident that the State had an open-and-shut case and he could therefore ignore such hokey-pokey defense tactics. There remains one other possibility—one having to do with politics. But the Attorney General himself had pushed the case against the defendant; he would hardly call off his dogs immediately after unleashing them.

The prosecution was entrusted to State's Attorney Bolivar Dodd. Dodd seems to have been determined enough. The day after Earnest Bridewell's arrest, State officers and police detectives were dispatched to Quahog Point to procure evidence and round up witnesses. Of this latter there was no lack, especially in the anti-character category. Scores of depositions were taken. Evidently most of them were freely offered.

Bibbs and Coulter scored a preliminary victory for the defense by maneuvering the case into District Court. Those who know the area informed me that this maneuver gave the defense a decided gambit advantage. At that date (1911) the District Court would have been awed to its bootstraps by a capital case.*

I do not know that Judge Mather P. Cottonwood, the jurist who sat on the Bridewell case, wore bootstraps (whatever they might be). He does seem to have been awed by some of the courtroom developments. Practically all of Quahog Point arrived by excursion steamer to cram the little down-coast courthouse. Lured by the rumor that a State Senator might possibly hang, rubberneckers came from such distant points as Woods Hole and Sag Harbor. "It was said" that some of the rich Van Cleafs might be in attendance. "It was said" that the Governor planned to send an observer. On opening day the courtroom would be stuffed chock-a-block, with windowsills and standing room at a premium.

Eleven witnesses were assembled by the defense. Prosecution mustered a total of seventeen.

If Messrs. Bibbs and Coulter for the accused had won a tactical victory in bringing the case to District Court, State's Attorney Bolivar Dodd did not undertake the prosecution empty-handed. Moreover—opposition publicity to the contrary—he entered court with a trump card up his sleeve. To wit:

Shortly after the inquest findings which had led to a murder charge against State Senator Bridewell, inspectors from the State's Attorney's office had visited the old Bridewell homestead. There another finding was found. The find was made when the detectives, accompanied by Sheriff Wen Tasker, searched Earnest's upstairs bedroom.

On a tip-off? Or by sheer chance? The finger of the secret informant, or the finger of Fate? Both are denominators common to police work. But it struck me as beyond the probable operating of mere chance that detectives should have walked upstairs in Abby's house and looked under the mattress of Earnest's bed. What per-

* In this area [anonymous] the District Courts of the period, in dealing with a capital case, conducted what amounted to a preliminary trial or judicial hearing. The Judge could not pronounce a capital sentence but, if convinced the case warranted, would order its ultimate proceeding in a superior court. He could, however, dismiss the case.

chance could they have expected to find? . . . It seems they found what purported to be the murder weapon.

So the stage was set, the cast summoned, the props assembled for the courtroom drama.

Hear ye! Hear ye!

The Court is now open for the trial of State Senator Bridewell, charged with the willful murder of his mother, Abby Bridewell, said matricide allegedly occurring on the eleventh day of April at Quahog Point in the County of . . . etcetera, etcetera.

CHAPTER 14

"THE State intends to show," says State's Attorney Bolivar Dodd, "that the late Mrs. Abby Bridewell met her death by willful murder while alone in her home at Quahog Point on the evening of April eleventh; that this murder was committed between the hours of nine and eleven. . . ." And so on. And so on. "And that her elder son, the defendant Earnest Bridewell, thus motivated, entered his mother's house unobserved, and, finding her solitary, availed himself of the opportunity. . . ." And so on. "And we will prove that the murder weapon belonged to the defendant and, *ispo facto*, was used by the defendant upon the helpless person of his aged mother."

So much for the prosecution. What sayeth the defense?

"The defense will prove," says Vernon Bibbs, Esq., "that the defendant, Earnest Bridewell, is innocent of the crime with which he has been summarily charged. We will show that this charge is the confection of malicious plotters—debtors, political rivals, vipers seeking to feed a taste for intrigue by stabbing in the back this innocent fellow townsman who. . . ." And so forth. And so forth. "Wherewith, if I may paraphrase Shakespeare, these bloody instructions, having been taught, will return to plague the inventors." And so forth. "Finally we shall prove beyond a shadow of a doubt that the defendant was nowhere near the scene of the alleged crime at the time of its alleged commission. Since it is physically impossible for a man to be in two different and distant places at once, it will be manifest that the defendant is not guilty of the atrocious crime in question."

Defense counsel retires.

There ensues the usual legalistic sparring that marks the opening of the average trial. Defense dominates the forenoon session with an effort to provide Earnest Bridewell with the character of a saint. Lunch is a welcome respite. Court resumes at one o'clock.

Judge Cottonwood folds meaty hands on the mahogany before him, and addresses the State's Attorney.

"You may call your first witness."

"I call Doctor Tompkins."

"Do you solemnly swear to tell the truth, the whole truth, and nothing but the truth so help you God?" asks the clerk.

"I do," sighs Tompkins. Seated he awaits Dodd's query.

"Now, Doctor Tompkins, you were the medical examiner who performed the official autopsy on the body of Mrs. Abby Bridewell?"

"I was."

"Please describe to the court your findings and professional deductions. . . ."

The medical examiner's findings were as follows:

The deceased lying on a bed. A cut under her right eye and the bone exposed. The whole right side of her face contused and scratched. A bruise and swelling on the left temple. Swelling on the top of the head, but no skull fracture. Two wounds on the top of the head.

While moving the body from bed to table for purpose of performing autopsy, discovered that deceased's neck was broken. Further examination disclosed body bruises. One on left knee (an old bruise). One on left breast (perhaps more recent). Bruise on arm (fairly recent). Right hand bruised, palm lacerated. Hand injury doubtless caused at time of death.

The medical examiner's deductions: Cause of death was fracture and dislocation of neck vertebrae. He had examined cellarway where body was found. Although steps made steep flight (almost like a ladder) he could not understand how Mrs. Bridewell "got two wounds on the top of the head of the same character by falling down the stairs." *

The State's Attorney: Doctor Tompkins, I show you this small bag partly filled with lead shot. It weighs a little over a pound. Would you say that the wounds on the head could have been caused by such a weapon?"

Tompkins: Yes, I would.

Lawyer Coulter: Objection! We have no evidence that this bag of shot or anything like a bag of shot caused the wounds in question. The implication that *this* was the murder weapon is based wholly on the imagination of the—

Attorney Dodd: Your Honor, the State will prove that this could indeed have been the murder weapon. If the learned counsel for the defense will permit—

Judge Cottonwood: Objection overruled.

Dodd: Thank you, Your Honor. Now, Doctor, do you see bloodstains on this bag?

Tompkins: I see dark stains resembling blood.

Dodd: And from the size, weight and shape of this shot-bag, you think the wounds on the top of Mrs. Bridewell's head could have been made by such a bludgeon?

Tompkins: I think that possible.

Erasmus Coulter (cross-examining): Doctor Tompkins, could the wounds on Mrs. Bridewell's scalp have been made by something *other* than that particular bag of shot?

Tompkins: I suppose they could.

Coulter: By a club, say? Or by an andiron?

Tompkins: Well, I wouldn't say by a firedog, unless maybe it

* Verbatim quote from the record.

was wrapped in something. A blunt instrument would be more like. Maybe a wooden club.

Coulter: Could they not have been made by the deceased striking her head against the sidewall of the cellarway when she fell?

Tompkins: As I said, I couldn't see how she'd get two wounds of the same character in falling down those steps.

Coulter: Yet she *might* have?

Tompkins: I would say the wounds were caused by something hitting her on the top of her head.

Coulter: It could just possibly have been done with a half-filled bag of shot. That is your opinion.

Tompkins: Well, I think I could make a wound on your head like that.*

Coulter: You do? With the hair I have there? *

Laughter.

Judge Cottonwood: Order in the court! . . . I believe these speculations may lead us far afield, and I would adjure those at the bar to eschew as far as possible a tendency to trespass over the borders of the incompetent, irrelevant and immaterial . . . Let the hearing proceed. . . ."

"I call Doctor Lemuel Hatfield."

"Do you solemnly swear to tell truth, whole truth, nothing butta truth, s'help . . . ?"

"I do."

"Doctor Hatfield, you were the Bridewell family physician?"

"Up to the death last year of old Captain Nathan Bridewell, paralytic. Attended his case for years. Rest of the Bridewells, too."

"So you knew the Bridewells intimately. Mrs. Abby Bridewell, the defendant Earnest Bridewell, his brother Lionel?"

"Brought the boys into this best of all possible worlds. Attended Mrs. Abby Bridewell. . . . But after her husband died last year,

* Verbatim quotes from the record.

I wasn't called to the house but once. Up until the morning of this past April twelfth."

Answering State's Attorney Dodd, Dr. Hatfield reviews his long acquaintance with the Bridewell family. He remarks internal dissension going back for several decades. The boys had long been at odds with their mother. Earnest especially. Money problems, of course. But (here was a new element) Earnest had latterly gone around saying that his mother had maltreated the old Captain when he was bedridden. Did not give him proper care. Wouldn't fetch the poor old paralytic so much as a pitcher of water. One time, about a year before the old Captain's death, Earnest had bawled out his mother in front of neighbors. Had accused her of neglecting the old man.

"Doctor Hatfield, were you attending Mrs. Bridewell's husband at that time?"

"I was."

"Did you notice such neglect on Mrs. Bridewell's part?"

"No."

"Was the invalid suffering from neglect?"

"I saw no signs of it. Of course, he was in this top floor bedroom. Kind of tucked away."

"But not maltreated?"

"He had plenty of drinking water. They had a servant to take care of him."

Nevertheless, Earnest continued talking against his mother. Everybody in the neighborhood knew there were stormy parlor scenes.

"Abby Bridewell spoke to me several times about it." *

"What did she tell you?"

"She told me Earnest said—"

"Objection" Coulter is bellowing on his feet. "Hearsay! The witness is reporting something allegedly said by the defendant. If it please the Court—"

"Objection sustained."

"Very well, Doctor Hatfield, will you tell us if you spoke to the defendant about his conduct toward his aged mother?"

* Verbatim quotes from the record.

"I did for a fact. When I learned from her there was such bad feeling. I met Earnest down near Town Hall. Last election day, it was. His mother had told me he said to her—"

"Objection!"

"Sustained."

"Go on, Doctor. What did you say to the defendant on that occasion?"

"I said, 'Whatever you do, keep your hands off your mother.' " *

"Order in the court! Any more of these disturbances, and this courtroom will be cleared!"

Dr. Lemuel Hatfield goes on. Guided by State's Attorney Dodd, he gives a blow by blow account of what he knows about the "ill-feeling" between Senator Earnest and Old Abby. Finally he comes step by step to the cellar stairs. He goes down the steps to the body. Dead, he would guess, about nine hours, maybe ten. Which meant the deceased met her death between nine and eleven the previous evening.

"Doctor Hatfield, did you recommend an autopsy?"

"I did."

"Did the defendant seem reluctant?"

"He seemed reluctant."

"Thank you, Doctor. No more questions."

Erasmus Coulter sidles forward with a narrow-eyed look at Dr. Hatfield. Then: "If it please the Court, I would like to cross-question this witness at a later time."

"If the State does not object."

Bolivar Dodd did not object.

"The State calls Mrs. Cornelia Ord."

"Here."

"Will you please take the stand, Mrs. Ord."

* Verbatim quote from the record.

"All right."

"You solemnly sweara tell truth, whole truth'n nothing but. . . ."

"Yes."

"Mrs. Ord, will you kindly tell us of your relationship with the late Mrs. Abby Bridewell?"

"Niece once removed."

"I mean your social relationship."

"Saw her occasionally."

"What does that mean?"

"It means I occasionally saw her."

Obviously Cornelia was answering in a manner which today would have won her the designation of "hostile witness." Bolivar Dodd was forced to work on her with forceps, so to speak. Her responses had to be drawn as though they were teeth. But defense counsel, cross-examining, had equal difficulty with these molar-like extractions. Cornelia did not like appearing in court. It had taken a subpoena-threat to get her there.

However, Dodd finally drew from her the story of her visit to her aunt's house on the evening of April 11 (as previously related in my simulated inquest testimony). He also drew from her the account of her experience in the early-morning gloaming of Wednesday, April 12.

"So you were there in your aunt's kitchen with Doctor Hatfield on emergency call?"

"Yes."

"You looked down and saw your aunt's body at the foot of the cellar steps?"

"Yes."

"What did you notice, Mrs. Ord, on the stone steps?"

"They were slick. Fruit sirup."

"Did you notice anything else on the steps?"

"Well, some broken glass."

"And?"

"Some blood."

"Anything else?"

"A rat."

"You mean a thing of false hair? The sort of bun you ladies wear?"

"*I* don't wear one."

"I can see that in your case such an item would be the height of superfluity. But was not the article you saw on the cellar steps—let me call it a female toupee—the sort of topknot a lady would fasten on her head if her hair was thin on top?"

"Yes."

Good point, and neatly extracted. One could only believe that a forceful blow on the skull had dislodged this hirsute adornment. Coulter, cross-examining, let it lie.

"Mrs. Ord, you said the steps looked slick?"

"Yes."

"Something sirupy was on them?"

"Yes."

"Would you say this sirup was pear juice?"

"How would I know? I didn't go down and taste of it."

The witness may step down.

Millicent Hatfield, Mercy Grimes, Hester Purdy. All swore, so help them God. The rumpuses they had heard from time to time when they passed the Bridewell homestead. The voices raised in angry recrimination. They had seen Earnest drinking.

Evangeline Goodbody, so help her, had heard a row the Sunday before Abby was murdered. "Their windows was open; you could hear plain as day. Earnest was hollering about money."

Robert Babcock (whole truth and nothing but, I do) remembered Earnest yelling at his mother in the store. "About money. Earnest was mad about the old man's will."

Jasper J. Jones, a "distant relative" of Mrs. Abby Bridewell, testified (whole truth, etcetera) that Earnest had forced the old father to transfer some property into his, Earnest's, name. Had flattered and cajoled the invalid Captain. But had wanted to put his father under a guardian. Abby Bridewell wouldn't hear of it. After the old man died, Jones had witnessed a furious family argument over probate proceedings.

Wilbur Hatfield (sworn) identified himself as a Notary Public. He testified that late in 1910 Abby Bridewell had called him to the house about some documents. While they were going over these papers—deeds and things—Earnest came into the parlor. Abby picked up one of the documents, saying she would keep charge of it. Earnest snatched the paper from her. Then, as Mr. Hatfield worded it: "A struggle followed, and Mrs. Bridewell fell to the floor. There seemed to be a good deal of feeling between her and her son on this occasion." *

So many neighbors and fellow townsmen heard disputatious shouts echoing from the Bridewell house that it convinced me a new twist should be applied to an old aphorism. Adults should be seen and not heard.

And there are occasions when it would be best for some adults if they were not even seen. At least four witnesses testified to seeing Earnest swig from a bottle late in the afternoon of Tuesday, April 11, so help them God.

Charlie Ravens, bartender, Center Saloon, stated: "The Senator come in about five P.M. Bought him a bottle of Weybosset Gin. Uncorked it and had him a drink before he left. He drove off in the direction of his mother's."

Nettie Gamber, nee Purdy, housewife, stated: "The Senator stopped his buggy under a tree before my house at about ten after five. I saw him take a drink from a bottle, then drive on."

Hornsby J. Styles, helper at Grimes' Smithy, stated: "Seen the Senator go by the blacksmith shop at a quarter after five. I was paring a hoof on Mrs. Babcock's mare. He pulled up down the road and took him a tilt from a bottle."

And, of course, Mrs. Smeizer of the telescopic eye noticed the gin-bibbing. "The Senator drove into his mother's yard about five-twenty. Before he went in the house he pulled a bottle from his coat and took a long one. Then he threw the bottle away into the bushes."

* Verbatim quote from the records.

Coulter rose to each statement to cross-question the witness. How big was the bottle? Witness Ravens could not exactly remember. Witnesses Gamber, Styles and Smeizer were not certain. But Bartender Ravens, his memory joggled, finally recalled it as a half-pint flask. Not a great deal of gin, surely. Yet more than enough to cast doubt on Senator Bridewell's sobriety when he called on his mother just before suppertime on the evening of April 11.

Of course Abby Bridewell had not met her death before suppertime on the evening of April 11. Earnest had called, spoken his highly audible piece, and left. Witnesses had seen him on the southbound road about six o'clock. His wife testified that he had reached her table in time for supper. Vacuous Alvin supported this domestic testimony. There could be little doubt that the Senator had been at his "south-side place" between six and eight on the evening of April 11. The State's attorney made no effort to contend otherwise. Evidently he was satisfied with the facts thus far developed.

Prosecution had established motive: Earnest Bridewell was in desperate need of funds.

Prosecution had established attitudes: Earnest Bridewell had for years been at loggerheads with his mother and had quarreled violently with her over the treatment of his late father and the disposition of his late father's estate.

Prosecution had established aptitude: Earnest Bridewell had displayed a pernicious temperament, a savage temper when "in liquor," and a recent habit of placing himself "under the influence."

There remained the business of establishing opportunity, developing the aptitude theme to the point of performance, and proving guilt by directly associating the accused with the murder weapon. State's Attorney Bolivar Dodd now produced his big guns.

Asa Goodbody (surprise witness).

Mrs. Smeizer (recalled).

Hobart Cudworth (body-finder).

Lionel Bridewell (accused's own brother).

When the barrage was over a betting observer would have wagered that State Senator Earnest Bridewell was a dead man.

"The State calls Asa Goodbody."

"Do you solemnly swear. . . ."

"Do."

"Mr. Goodbody, will you please tell what occurred, to your knowledge, about breakfast time, Wednesday morning, April twelfth?"

Goodbody relates the episode recounted in my reconstruction of the inquest records. Concluding with his statement that Earnest Bridewell had asked him to say, if questioned, that relations had always been above reproach between him and his mother.

"And was that all Mr. Bridewell asked of you?"

"No, t'warnt."

"What else did he want you to do or say?"

"Wanted I should make a statement in his behalf."

"To what effect?"

"Huh?"

"What did he want you to say?"

"If any question rose about it, he wanted me to say that I was with him at his south-side place 'long about nine to eleven, evening of April eleventh. I was seeing a man about a horse close to there. But anyhow I wasn't with Earnest Bridewell, since he wasn't there."

"Objection!"

"On what grounds, Mr. Coulter?"

"The State's Attorney is well aware of the grounds. This witness could not have known whether the defendant was at his south-side place or not."

"Objection sustained! And counsel will please address their remarks to this Bench rather than to each other. . . . The witness will please confine his answers to the questions asked."

"What was the question?"

"Just this, Mr. Goodbody. What did the defendant, Earnest Bridewell, ask you to say?"

"That I was with him between nine and eleven the evening his mother was killed."

"Did he offer you anything in return for such testimony?"

"He said he'd give me ten acres of land."

Defense passes on cross-examination. Through Goodbody, the State has scored a body blow that leaves Earnest Bridewell looking pale and winded.

"The State calls Mrs. Bertha Smeizer."

"Swearwholetruth, nothinbutthatruth. . . ?"

"I swear."

"Mrs. Smeizer, will you please tell what you heard and saw at the Bridewell house on the evening of April eleventh and at breakfast time, April twelfth?"

She said she would. She did. The gist I have already recounted. Considerably abridged in the interest of avoiding redundancy, and pruned of numerous interruptions by objecting defense counsel. Bolivar Dodd, however, employed tautology to emphasize theme. One point he particularly wanted to drive to the hilt.

"Please tell us now what you saw after dark on the evening of April eleventh."

"I've told you I saw the dressmaker leave the Bridewell house about eight, at which time Mrs. Ord went in. Some time later she came out and went away."

"What did you see after that?"

"Well, it was dark. I was looking out of the window. Just sitting and looking. . . ."

Did the front door of the Bridewell house open and shut? She was sure it did. Did the kitchen door slam a short time later? Well, some sound directed her attention to the porch at the side. She saw a figure there. A shadow.

"Do you think it could have been Earnest Bridewell?"

"Objection! Calls for a conclusion by the witness."

"Sustained."

"Mrs. Smeizer, did you see Earnest Bridewell at that late hour on the kitchen porch?"

"In the dark there. I think it was him."

"Objection!"

"All right. I'm sure. It was him."

"Now, Mrs. Smeizer. As a close neighbor, did you often hear quarreling at the Bridewell house?"

"Often. Whenever Earnest and Lionel was there, why—"

"Please, restrict your answer to the question, Mrs. Smeizer."

"Yes, I heard quarreling."

"Did you know of particularly bad feeling between the defendant Earnest Bridewell and his mother?"

"They were not so very friendly. One time Earnest threw his mother on the floor and she struck her head against the table.* Or so Abby Bridewell told me."

"Objection! Objection! Objection!"

"Sustained. The Bench must warn the witnesses in this case that hearsay allegations are not permissible."

"If Your Honor please—"

"Do not try the Court's patience."

"Your witness, Mr. Coulter."

"Mrs. Smeizer. For all your friendly and neighborly interest in the business of others, isn't it a fact that—no, let me rephrase the question. Isn't it true that several years ago you had a quarrel with Mr. Earnest Bridewell?"

"We had some words, but I hold no ill feeling. He—"

"One more question. Mrs. Smeizer, do you wear glasses?"

"Only for sewing. Otherwise I'm far-sighted."

"No more questions. But I should like permission to recall this witness."

The witness steps down. I could imagine her almost missing the step.

"The State calls Hobart Cudworth."

"Do you swear. . . ."

"Yessir."

* Verbatim quote from the records.

"Now, Mr. Cudworth, will you tell. . . ."

He told. About going to the Scenic Palace with Walter Jones on that fateful Tuesday evening. Coming home and going straight to bed. Up at six A.M. to build a fire. To the yard and back into the kitchen. Noticing the cellar door ajar. Looking down on death. Racing to Earnest Bridewell's place on the south side of the Point.

"Mr. Cudworth. While serving as Abby Bridewell's hired man, did you notice animosity between her and the defendant?"

"If that means was they at loggerheads, I would say plenty. Snapping turtles in a box."

"You witnessed quarrels between them?"

"Seemed like every time the Senator seen her they had a squabble. It was over money."

"What sums did you hear mentioned?"

"Something about a will. The old Captain's money, and where was it?"

"Was it a large amount you heard mentioned?"

"Three thousand dollars. The Senator kept nagging the old woman—lady, I mean—about three thousand dollars. Also money she'd took in from selling three horses."

"Did Mr. Bridewell abuse his mother?"

"Well, he swore at her a little. He called her a liar, and she called him a liar." *

"Did he physically abuse his mother?"

"Yes, one time. He knocked her down and bruised her up." *

"Did you see this?"

"Not exactly, but I heard—"

"Objection! Really, Your Honor—!"

"Your Honor! This witness is trying to say that he heard the fight—not about the fight. This is something quite different from hearsay. If the distinguished defense counsel would hold his fire until there is something to shoot at—"

"Objection overruled. The witness will continue."

"Well, this night I'm in the kitchen, and there's this set-to in the dining room."

"Between Earnest and his mother?"

* Verbatim quotes from record.

"That's right. He wants a paper some kind. She won't give it to him. I hear a whack. Then a sound of falling down. I look in. It's her."

"Mrs. Bridewell was down?"

"On the floor by the table. He—the Senator—is standing over her with his fist clenched."

"As though he had just knocked her down?"

"Objection! The State's Attorney is calling for a conclusion by the—!"

"I will rephrase the question. . . . When you saw the defendant standing with fist clenched over his aged mother who lay prostrate, did the defendant look angry?"

"His face was back to me."

"But his posture was combative, his fist was clenched, and you did not see him help his aged mother to her feet?"

"No."

"Your witness."

Coulter (cross-examining): "Now, Mr. Cudworth, how did you get along as hired man at the Bridewell homestead?"

"Well enough."

"But you did occasionally object to the food."

"Sometimes."

"Were you ever scolded by Mr. Earnest Bridewell for neglecting your duties and loafing on the job?"

"Objection!"

"Overruled."

"What was the question?"

"Did Mr. Earnest Bridewell ever ask you to pay attention to your job and quit loafing?"

"He was at me a couple of times."

"Did you ever with your own eyes see Mr. Earnest Bridewell strike his mother."

"No. Like I said, that time I heard the—"

"Please confine your answers to yes or no. Did you ever actually see the defendant strike his mother?"

"No."

"Or ever lay hands on her?"

"No."

"But you do say you heard him discussing household funds with her?"

"Objection! Defense counsel is putting words in the witness's mouth. Household funds, indeed!"

"Your Honor, my question refers to budgetary funds such as every mother and son might well discuss."

"In that case the objection is overruled."

"Mr. Cudworth, then?"

"I forgot the question."

"Did you ever overhear the defendant and his mother discussing household funds."

"I don't know what the funds were. Except the three thousand dollars they wrangled about—"

"Mr. Cudworth!"

"Well, you asked me, didn't you?"

"Very well. You say you heard words between them—something about three thousand dollars. Would you mind telling the Court how many times you heard that particular sum of money discussed?"

Doubtless after due head-scratching, Cudworth came up with an answer that might well serve as a standard substitute for the classic but overworked "I don't remember."

He said: "Gee, you've got me." *

"The State calls the defendant's brother, Lionel Bridewell."

Tension in the courtroom. A sudden cessation of scuffing and coughing. Stretching necks. Craning heads. "There he is," a woman voices an excited whisper as handsome Lionel rises from a seat on the aisle and strolls to the witness stand.

Did he wear padded shoulders, peg-top trousers and button shoes? Or were the newer styles on him—the longer coat; the three-

* Verbatim quote.

inch starched collar that choked the neck, flushed the complexion, and kept the chin angled like the bow of a dreadnaught? I am sure that whatever he wore, his habiliments met the fashion requirements of what in those days was called a "fusser." I imagine, too, that he exuded that faint but aromatic scent of cloves and spice that went with the orange pekoe man. Spice, anyway. A clove in the teeth was a good breath deodorant after a quick drink.

"You solemnly swear mmmmmmm . . . ?"

"I swear."

"Mr. Bridewell, the State is aware that this is a most painful duty for you—especially with the mourning band for your unfortunate mother still fresh upon your sleeve—and we will confine our questions to recent events only in an effort to abbreviate your ordeal. Will you tell the Court, please, when and how you first heard of your mother's lamented death?"

"I received a telegram about noon of April twelfth, from my brother Earnest, saying she was badly hurt. Would I come at once."

"You repaired immediately to Quahog Point?"

"On the afternoon boat. Soon as I got home they told me she was dead from an accident. I went over to Meck's right away."

"Who is Meck?"

"Horatio Meck, the undertaker. I wanted to see my mother, naturally."

"Naturally. And that same evening, then, you viewed the—the remains?"

"I viewed them. And I didn't like it a damn bit. . . . Excuse me, Your Honor. But, you see, it was mother."

The Judge nods. Lionel blows his nose. Bolivar Dodd, sympathetic, waits. Then—

"Will you state, Mr. Bridewell, what it was that you most particularly did not like? That is, aside from your natural distress at your mother's loss."

"Well, her face looked bruised. She had wounds on her head."

But his brother had already made funeral preparations. He did not quite know what to do about it. He went to see Dr. Hatfield, who wasn't in. Then he called on neighbor Goodbody. Of course he asked Goodbody about the accident. Wanted to know how the old lady had gotten beaten up like that.

"Did your neighbor voice an opinion?"

"Objection!"

Overruled. The witness is not asked to express an opinion; he is asked to report a conversation. He may reply to the question.

"Well, Goodbody did say that when he saw my mother down the cellar steps . . . his words were . . . 'It looked bad.' "

"Mr. Bridewell. Were you aware that your mother was planning to pack up and leave the old homestead?"

"Yes, I was. She intended to come and stay with me in Lookout Hill. She wrote me a letter to that effect."

"Mr. Bridewell, what were the relations between your mother and your brother?"

"They weren't pleasant. Earnest was frequently abusive to her. When my father died, he left three thousand dollars. Earnest would often ask mother what she had done with the money. On one occasion she replied, 'The money was given to me by your father to pay the necessary expenses and to provide you with a living.' " *

"What was your mother's attitude toward Earnest?"

"She was very much afraid of him. I have seen her pull down the curtains of the house and then get away from in front of the windows when the lamps were lighted." *

"I have here a bag of shot. I ask you if you recognize it?"

"Yes. It belongs to my brother Earnest."

"When and where was the last time you saw it?"

"In his bedroom at mother's house the weekend before she was killed. I saw it lying on the bed. Near the pillow." *

Coulter rises. "Objection! Reference to this bag of shot is irrelevant and immaterial."

Dodd flares, "If the Court please—"

Judge Cottonwood barks, "Sustained."

"But Your Honor, I intend to show that this shot-bag belonging to the defendant—"

* Verbatim quotes from the record.

"The objection is sustained!"

"I bow, of course, to the decision of the Bench. Defense counsel may cross-examine."

"Defense counsel thanks the State's Attorney for this rare opportunity to cross-examine an individual who would appear against his own brother. If the—"

"Your Honor! Defense counsel *knows* that such deleterious commentary—"

"The defense counsel will address his remarks to this Bench and hereafter the State's Attorney will refrain from advising the Bench in a tone of rebuke or any tone whatever. . . . Proceed with the cross-examination of this witness."

"Mr. Lionel Bridewell, what were *your* relations with your mother?"

"We got along well."

"And with your brother, the defendant?"

"I didn't like the way he treated our mother."

"Did *you* ever quarrel with your mother and brother over money?"

"Objection! The witness is not on trial!"

"Sustained."

"Your Honor, defense counsel wishes to show that this witness could have an ulterior motive in appearing against—"

"The objection is sustained!"

"Very well, then. I ask this witness, Mr. Bridewell, did you ever see your brother do physical violence to your mother?"

"No, but she was afraid—"

"I asked if you ever saw him do her violence?"

"No. But he threatened her."

"Threatened to place her in an institution? Isn't that what you mean?"

"No. One day last November. Earnest says to me, 'If I had you here in the house and you refused to answer my questions, you wouldn't get out alive.' And my mother said, 'There, you see, Lionel? He's threatening your life as well as mine!' " *

Erasmus T. G. Coulter gives the witness a frozen stare. The dam

* Verbatim quote from the records.

of silence breaks. Furor floods the scene. Exclamations. Onlookers surging to their feet. Someone calls out, "You tell 'em, Lionel!" Coulter's "No further questions" is drowned out by Judge Cottonwood's gavel. "Order!" the Judge pounds. "Order!"

No more questions, no more hearing for that day. With a last lusty wallop, Judge Cottonwood brings down the curtain. It falls at five minutes after six, with lengthy shadows of evening reaching into, and englooming, the courtroom.

Perhaps the longest shadow in the courtroom was the one suspended over the head and neck of State Senator Earnest Bridewell.

How did he feel about Brother Lionel's deadly asseverations? I found the answer scrawled in the margin of his scrapbook, opposite an encircled news report of Lionel's testimony.

"Liar!"

CHAPTER 15

"THE prisoner was brought into court this morning by Deputy Sheriff Cal Fiske and he presented a much more cheerful appearance than on his last appearance in the courtroom. He was asked how he was feeling, and he replied that he was feeling good."

So had stated the *Seaboard Herald* of May 3, 1911. That was the day it was first "rumored in court circles" that the case against Earnest Bridewell would collapse for want of a shred of evidence. It was that same week that Earnest Bridewell wrote to the Milk Street Orphans' Home requesting that Walter Jones be allowed to remain at Quahog Point as the key defense witness.

As of Saturday, May 27, it seemed the State had assembled all the shreds of evidence needed for the weaving of a ten-foot hangman's rope. And Earnest Bridewell stood in want of all the defense anyone could muster. The *Seaboard Herald* made no mention of his appearance as he entered court that morning. The previous day's climax must have convinced him a trip to the gallows was highly possible, and he doubtless spent that night packing the suitcases under his eyes.

Did young Walter Jones actually hold the key to Earnest's salvation? Privy to the scrapbook letter, I was eager to learn just how the orphan boy might accomplish the Senator's deliverance.

I could imagine Earnest sweating out the approach of that day's courthouse session. Bibbs and Coulter offering him those crisp, impersonal reassurances that surgeons give a patient facing a major operation. Now, now, Senator, don't be too alarmed. You have nothing worse than acromegaly of the corpus callosum of the brainpan with some complications causing tumefaction of the bump of cupidity. If neglected, your case could lead to a fatal separation of the medulla from the spinal column. However, if subornation fails, we shall try cunctation. As specialists, we have every confidence that we can pull you through. . . . No, don't worry about the bill. . . . Later perhaps. . . .

Clinical note: The patient did not eat a hearty breakfast. . . .

Vernon Bibbs, Esq., opens with classic formality.

"Your Honor, the defense moves that the case against the defendant, Mr. Earnest Bridewell, be discontinued on the grounds that the State's testimony has not borne out the charges in the warrant."

Judge Cottonwood replies with the classic retort. "Motion denied."

"The defense calls Norman Purdy."

"Do you solemnly . . . truth . . . whole . . . nothing but . . . ?"

"Yep."

"Did you say yes?"

"Yep."

"Will you please tell us your occupation?"

"Me? I drive a delivery wagon. Babcock's Store."

"You made grocery deliveries to the Bridewell home over a period of years?"

"Yep."

"Did you ever see the defendant strike his mother?"

"Nope."

"What *were* their domestic relations, to your knowledge?"

"He was her oldest son."

"But delivering charcoal one Saturday, you heard an argument between them? Mr. Earnest Bridewell protesting her treatment of his father?"

"Objection! Defense counsel leading the witness."

"Overruled. The witness may answer."

"Yep."

"What was the the argument about?"

"About the old man up in the attic. Why his room wasn't warmer. And such."

"You heard the defendant upbraid his mother? On that score?"

"Yep. The Senator said his father wasn't treated right."

"Your witness, Mr. State's Attorney."

"No questions."

"Will the Reverend Winfield Scott Palding please take the stand."

"Do you solemnly swear . . . ?"

"So help me God."

"Reverend, what is your faith?"

"Millerite by conviction. Used to be Jemimakin. Church at Quahog Point since closed. I also practiced a modicum of faith-healing. My grandfather knew Phineas Quimby."

"Will you state your connection with the Bridewell family?"

"Some years ago, after Captain Nathan was stricken by a stroke, I was called as male nurse for a time. My church had closed, you understand. The old Captain had occasionally attended. He believed in absent treatment. I went there to give it to him."

"Will you describe the defendant's attitude toward his father at that time?"

"The Senator felt his father much neglected. One reason he wanted me to look after him, personal. I did so for about three years. Up to a year before he died."

"Did you notice signs of neglect?"

"Deplorable. His bed was often unmade. He complained to me about the food—said his wife, Abby Bridewell, never gave him enough to eat. One time she wouldn't bring him a pitcher of water. He needed a lot of attention, and he didn't get it."

"Did the defendant protest this deplorable situation?"

"Frequently. I did my best to aid the poor old paralytic. But I was not hired to wait on him. There was a servant girl. I also felt that his wife, with all due respect, God rest her soul, was insufficiently attentive. Absent treatment demands a constant flow of what I call germicidal thoughts and prayers—"

"Yes, of course. And these—ah—emanations did not issue from the mind of Mrs. Abby Bridewell?"

"I did not feel them radiating in the atmosphere."

"But Mr. Earnest Bridewell was concerned about his father?"

"Most. In my presence he adjured his mother on numerous occasions. She did not take kindly. I believe she was influenced by Doctor Hatfield's insistence on materia medica. There were times, too, when she seemed mentally unbalanced. At least to me."

Bolivar Dodd cross-examines brusquely. Is the Reverend Palding a licensed practitioner? No. Is he a reader, Science and Health? No. Is he an ordained preacher? No, Millerite didn't have to be. Isn't it true that one time a Quahog Pointer suggested *his* incarceration in a mental institution? But that man was an infidel, an atheist, and—

"No further questions."

Defense called Tansy Thorn to the stand. Duly sworn, Miss Thorn testified that she had never, on any occasion whatever, heard a violent exchange between the defendant and his mother. If she heard anything, the name-calling was one sided—by Abby Bridewell. According to Tansy, Earnest was a good, kind, courteous and considerate gentleman. He always tipped his hat to her on Center Square. She had attended school with him as a child. One time at a taffy-pull, and another time on a hay-ride—Miss Tansy became confused. But anyway, Earnest in her opinion was a prince. No cross-examination.

Defense called Lizzie Robinson, dressmaker. I have reported the substance of Lizzie's testimony in simulation of inquest statement. The force of her courtroom story was, in effect, a negation of the implication that Earnest had "bruised up" his mother. Lizzie saw no bruises on Abby Bridewell as of eight P.M., Tuesday, April 11th. The Court recessed for lunch.

The afternoon session began at one o'clock. Now was the time for all good witnesses to come to the aid of the party in the dock. And for the quick brown fox to jump over the lazy dog.

"The defense calls Doctor Lemeul Hatfield to the stand."

"The doctor is already sworn."

"Now, Doctor Hatfield, yesterday you stated that when you first were summoned to the Bridewell house on the morning of Wednesday, April twelfth, you thought Mrs. Abby Bridewell had suffered an accident. If you thought her death accidental, what caused you to change your mind?"

"When I thought over the situation. Earnest Bridewell's attitude toward his mother. I went back to the house next day to examine the cellarway again and—"

"Doctor, not so fast, please. Were you not aware that the defendant's attitude toward his mother was incurred by her neglect of his invalid father, as described here this morning by the Reverend Palding?"

"Humph! Palding is a constipated old weasel and a fraud. He—"

"Doctor Hatfield, I must remind you that this is a courtroom hearing."

"I'm sorry, Your Honor. All right. I take it back. The Reverend Palding, as he calls himself, is not constipated. As a matter of fact, the last time he requested my professional services—"

"Doctor Hatfield! Will you please restrict your replies to the questions put by Counsel."

"Certainly. What was the question? Was I aware . . . ?"

"That the defendant's attitude toward his mother was incurred by her neglect of his invalid father."

"No, I wasn't aware of that, because I didn't think the old man was neglected. It was three flights up to his room, and he was ringing the bell all the time. You can't take care of—"

"Excuse me, Doctor, but you have answered. My next question is: If you did change your mind about Mrs. Abby Bridewell's death—that is, you rather belatedly came to the conclusion she did not die by accident—why didn't you promptly report it to the authorities?"

"I did."

"Before the funeral?"

"Yes."

"Then it was your report that caused the State's Attorney General to act?"

"I did file a report with the Attorney General's office."

"Order in the court! The Bench will not tolerate these outbursts of whispering."

"Now, Doctor, this question. Aren't you in debt to the defendant Earnest Bridewell?"

"If you call a mortgage being in debt."

"Isn't it a rather sizable mortgage?"

"The interest rates are sizable."

"Haven't you owed interest payments for some time?"

"Yes, but Mr. Bridewell agreed to—"

"As a matter of fact, aren't there two mortgages held by him on your Quahog Point property?"

"A first and second, yes."

"And you are in arrears on both?"

"With his consent at compound interest."

"Isn't the property of Wilbur Hatfield—the Notary Public—also mortgaged to Earnest Bridewell?"

"I don't mind my cousin's business."

"Didn't your brother, Rufus Hatfield, run against Earnest Bridewell for Senator last election?"

"Yes, but I don't see—"

"No further questions."

"Will Mrs. Smeizer please take the stand."

"You are already sworn, Mrs. Smeizer. You are still under oath."

"I'll tell the truth."

"Please do, Mrs. Smeizer, in answer to this question. . . . Isn't it a fact that you and your husband, Harold, have long been in debt to the Bridewells?"

"We owed the Trawler Company a few dollars for a boat, yes."

"And in talking with some neighbors at the Post Office one day this spring, didn't you call Mrs. Abby Bridewell a rich old pussycat and haven't you referred to her behind her back as Tabby Abby?"

"Well, I—I don't remember."

"Isn't it a fact that on another occasion you told the ladies of your sewing circle that Mr. Earnest Bridewell had been pressing your husband on a loan, and that Mr. Bridewell was a tight-fisted, dirty skinflint, and you didn't like him?"

"But I do like Earnest Bridewell! I do!"

"Order in the Court! I ask the door guard to remove that person who just 'meowed.' Any more catcalls from the back row and I will order the court cleared. . . . Proceed with this witness."

"No more questions."

"Defense calls Mrs. Floss Bridewell."

"Do you solemnly swear . . . ?"

"I do."

"You are the defendant's wife?"

"Yes."

Floss Bridewell gave a good account of herself on the stand. Through her prompt and forthright answers, she convinced me, at least, that she merited the appellation of "better half." Under lengthy questioning and sharp cross-questioning she told a straight story. One that must have sounded loyal and sincere. If she missed a large hole in the middle of her account, a novelist was to blame. I could only hope that a book of mine might be as fascinating. To wit:

Earnest's wife stated that on the evening of Tuesday, April 11, her husband came home around six o'clock. Was he sober? To her he seemed "perfectly sober." She gave him his supper. Then he repaired to the sitting room to listen to the reading of a novel. The title? *The Prisoner of Zenda.* Anthony Hope. *Antoinette de Mauban was in a loose white robe, her dark hair streamed over her shoulders, her face was ghastly pale, and her eyes gleamed wildly in the light of the torches. In her shaking hand she held a revolver, and as she tottered forward she fired it at Rupert Hentzau.*

Earnest liked to be read to. Floss's old father and mother, residing for the time with their daughter, listened in. (The prosecution might have given Earnest's wife a hard time about the couple, for the old lady was extremely near-sighted, and the old man was admittedly very deaf. Obvious question: How did he listen in?) That was the scene. Floss reading. Earnest and the old couple in their chairs.

About eight-thirty P.M. (Floss's testimony) Earnest left the room and went out to water the horse. According to his wife, he was gone about fifteen or twenty minutes. When he returned, he took his chair, and listened to the end of the book. About ten o'clock the family retired. Earnest did not leave the house during the night.

Under cross-questioning, Floss Bridewell stated that her husband had usually slept at Mrs. Abby Bridewell's house while old

Captain Nathan was alive. Had only stayed there a few times since his father's death.

Bolivar Dodd (cross-examining): "Mrs. Bridewell. Did you not call on a neighbor, Sally Ross, and ask her to say that she saw your husband come home sober at six o'clock the evening of his mother's murder?"

"I did, because Sally did see him. I thought it ought to be known. When I heard the things Mrs. Smeizer was saying, I thought my husband would need help."

"No further questions."

"The defense calls Walter Jones."

"Walter, I want you to tell us what you did on the evening before Mrs. Abby Bridewell was found dead, and on the morning that followed when her body was found."

I have already told that portion of Walter's courtroom story. But in reconstructing his inquest testimony, I went no further in my research than his bedtime retirement and subsequent appearance next morning on the kitchen porch. No, he had heard nothing during the night. Had been aroused by Earnest Bridewell shouting at Cudworth to fetch the doctor. Had peeked down at the body in the cellar when Doctor Hatfield arrived. Then had run to town to send the telegram to Senator Bridewell's brother.

"Now, Walter, after you sent that telegram what did you do?"

"I ran back to the house."

"What did you see?"

"Doc Hatfield was just leaving and Mr. Bridewell and Mrs. Ord was in the yard."

"Anyone else?"

"Mrs. Smeizer."

"What then occurred?"

"Mr. Bridewell and Mrs. Ord went back into the house. I didn't want to, on account of the body."

"You stayed out in the yard?"

"Yes."

"With Mrs. Smeizer?"

"That's right. She went this way with her finger, and I went up to her."

"She beckoned to you, wagging her finger.'

"Like I showed. So I went up to her."

"What did she want?"

"Me to walk home with her. She said she was nervous after what happened to old Mrs. Bridewell. So I walked with her. Across the road and up."

"What did she say to you, Walter?"

"She asked what did I know about Mrs. Bridewell being killed."

"And you said?"

"I didn't know nothin'."

"Then?"

"She asked me did I know about Mr. Earnest Bridewell having fights with his mother. I said I guessed they'd had some, like."

"What did Mrs. Smeizer tell you then?"

"She told me she was going to get even." *

"Will you speak up louder, please. I would like the Judge to hear you."

"Mrs. Smeizer said she was going to get even. She said her and her friends would fix him now. She said this was her chance to get square with Mr. Senator Earnest Bridewell."

"Order! Order! Order! Everybody sit down. This is the last demonstration the Bench will tolerate in this courtroom!"

"State's witness."

"No questions."

"That's all right, Walter, you can go now."

I could visualize State's Attorney Bolivar Dodd standing there like a frustrated exclamation point. How could a prosecution lawyer grill a kid on the stand? Especially a homeless orphan.

But, thirty years later, I had in mind a cross-question. And I'd have given a lot to know the answer.

When Walter Jones took the witness stand, was he wearing a new corduroy suit?

* Verbatim quote from the records.

Two final defense witnesses. Surprise! The bright pennies in the birthday cake. By way of anticlimax, their contribution was a two-cents' worth. But it added up to a nice finishing touch. Probably an astute one, too. Squires Bibbs and Coulter were doubtless unwilling to risk a decision on the testimony of a minor.

So the defense called to the witness stand a Mr. Victor McVest, and after him, a Mr. Marvey Garvy. I would have appreciated a mental picture of the two. But in reading their statements, I could only draw a blank. Two expressionless vacancies. Rather like a pair of weather-beaten ciphers. Down East version of Tweedledee and Tweedledum. They hailed from New Bedford.

McVest was a cattle dealer. Garvy was his assistant. On the evening of April 11, the pair had been combing the fields on the south side of Quahog Point "looking for southdown sheep." Following a path through the bayberry, the stock men skirted the south-side place occupied by Earnest Bridewell and his wife. About half past eight, McVest was approaching the gate. He saw a man (the defendant) come out of the house with a bucket in his hand. McVest called to the man. The man came up and they chatted for several minutes. (About what? The conversation was not specified.) McVest went on with the sheep-hunt. Joined Garvy in the lower field. About nine-thirty or ten o'clock, they came back to the road and walked past the same house. Both McVest and Gravy sighted the Senator standing at a front window "smoking a pipe."

Bolivar Dodd did his best. But his cross-examination failed to shake either witness. Both men were positive in their assertions. McVest had seen Earnest Bridewell manifestly about to water a horse at eight-thirty. And Garvy as well as McVest had seen the defendant at a lighted window on south-side locale "about nine-thirty or ten."

Reading the above testimony from the distance of today, it strikes one as far from decisive. It contains the same hole that appears in the testimony offered by the defendant's wife. Namely, the time element of Earnest's departure and return from "watering the horse." Floss Bridewell supposed "fifteen or twenty minutes." But people who have read *The Prisoner of Zenda* recall it as a book they could not put down. Could it have been possible that Floss lost herself somewhere between Ruritania and Lower Strelsau in the never-never country close to Graustark? And could it have been that her deaf old father went to the window between nine-thirty and ten, pipe in teeth? No one will ever know.

It is hard to doubt the word of two New Bedford men. Even though they be cattle dealers.

Vernon Bibbs, Esq., faced the courtroom and boomed, "Lionel Bridewell please take the stand."

No answer.

"I call Lionel Bridewell!"

State's Attorney Dodd, rising: "It was not understood by the witness that he would be recalled."

Bibbs sends a glare on a slow sweep across the courtroom, left to right. Then he stalks to the defense table for consulation with Erasmus T. G. Coulter. The two lawyers make a show of head-shakes and chin-wagging. Then Bibbs holds out his hands to the Bench as though about to launch an appeal. Instead, he drops his arms in a gesture of resignation.

"The defense rests."

Bolivar Dodd came down the home stretch limping. There was really not much left for him that day. But he had to follow the courtroom protocol with a final run of witnesses. These were minor and did nothing to reinforce his tottering case.

"The State rests."

An expected recess did not eventuate. After a pointed glance at the clock, Judge Mather P. Cottonwood ruled that thirty minute summations were now to begin.

As usual defense summarized first. Coulter took the floor. He began by speaking of the case's immense importance. The fantastic atrocity charged against the defendant. Matricide! The murder of one's mother. Heaven forbid that such a crime should stain the pages of this fair State's history. He was happy to feel that his client was innocent of so hideous a felony. Nay, he *knew* the defendant was innocent. The State had been unable to show the slightest connection between Mr. Earnest Bridewell and the death of his aged mother. Rumor—gossip—vengeful calumny—these were the witnesses who had spoken against the accused. It was sheer persecution. Malice. Slander without equal in local memory.

"Defense is sorry to learn that there are people in this fair State who are so revengeful that they color their testimony at whim and do not hesitate to commit rank perjury. Consider the statements made by a trusted neighbor. I refer to Mrs. Smeizer."

Coulter reviewed Mrs. Smeizer's testimony. He denounced it as a pack of falsehoods dealt by a harpy determined to "get even." It was obvious, said Coulter, that a camarilla had joined forces to undo Earnest Bridewell. Political chicanery motivated this group. Quahog Point had long suffered from a faction controlled by the Hatfields. Who could doubt that this faction drove the knife of Brutus into the back of honest Caesar. But these Catalines were spurred by a deeper motive. Almost all who spoke against the defendant were his debtors. And then there was his own brother—"a man of mystery"—most treacherous of all. Where was *he*—Lionel Bridewell—at the climax of his brother's ordeal? Gone! Fled! Doubtless with the mantle of shame drawn across his eyes. But this Judas brother who would sell out his own flesh and blood, betray his next of kin, would never reap the thirty pieces of silver—to wit, the estate he clearly hoped to gain through his brother's removal to the gallows. Ah, this was the unkindest cut of all. Worse than Brutus. Worse than Iscariot. This was the blow of Cain.

Defense prayed that His Honor would release the defendant from the thrall of this horrid plot and cleanse the blot from his escutcheon. "The case is in your able hands."

Summarizing for the State, Bolivar Dodd got *his* second wind.

He agreed the charge was vastly serious, the crime heathenishly atrocious—nobody should murder an old mother. He said the State had proved that murder was committed. A long chain of circumstantial evidence linked the crime to the accused. Admittedly there was much conflicting testimony. He agreed with learned counsel for the defense that perjury had reared its ugly head in this court proceeding. But the question was, which witnesses were the perjurers? The State wished to spare His Honor a blizzard of forensics. The State's Attorney was confident that the magistrate on the bench had been able to weigh the evidence presented. "Justice will therefore prevail."

Judge Cottonwood cleared his throat. Harrumph! "The State has spoken. The defense has spoken. This has been an extraordinary hearing. . . ."

Judge Cottonwood reviewed the case. It was, he said, one beyond his jurisdiction—the most important he had yet heard. The defendant had rights which the Bench was bound to consider. If the Bench erred, the decision could be reviewed by a higher court.

Judge Cottonwood conceded that evidence pointed to Earnest Bridewell as the possible murderer. Motive—attitude—these spoke against the defendant. But proof that he had done physical violence to his mother had not been established. There was evidence of murder, but no evidence directly connecting the accused with the crime. The accused had established an alibi. His wife's testimony might be open to question. The testimony of a minor might be open to question. But here were two disinterested parties—out-of-towners—gentlemen from New Bedford. They had volunteered their statements, and had no apparent interest other than seeing justice done. Add these factors, and it would seem that the defendant had not been on the scene of the crime when it was committed, and had indeed been victimized by local enemies.

In closing, the Judge had this to say: "Some of the witnesses in this case have deliberately lied. It has always been my experience while on this bench for the past seven years that in Quahog Point cases—and there have been many of them—the witnesses from that town have been disposed to perjure themselves. Invariably, in the matter of an alibi from that place, the defense has been disposed to perjure itself. It is too bad. But that is the fact observed after years of experience in this Court." *

The Judge added that the "people of Quahog Point were the biggest liars in the country." Therefore he attached considerable weight to the evidence offered by the good men of New Bedford.

"The State has not made out its case, and I will discharge the defendant upon the strength of the evidence introduced." *

Earnest Bridewell shot to his feet. Bibbs got him by one arm; Coulter by the other. The surgeons were beaming. The patient was saved.

A newspaper reporter rushed out to write: "There was no demonstration, but the defendant was immediately surrounded by his friends, who seemed quite numerous, and gave hearty handshakes and words of cheer. Many even went to the Judge to commend him on the fairness of his decision, as it seemed to them (*sic*)."

Earnest's private reaction to the Court decision was succinct. I found it in the margin of his scrapbook, entered as a footnote to the Judge's closing verdict. It was: "Ha! Ha!"

I quote the curtain-line of the story published in the *Seaboard Herald:* "The trial had taken two full days, held the witnesses away from their homes until Sunday afternoon, and caused all sorts of inconvenience for the lawyers who had made other plans for Saturday."

I was staring at that final paragraph. Wondering what other plans those lawyers could have made for Saturday. Wondering what Earnest had planned and what plans Lionel must have made. Certainly Brother Lionel must have had an important date. I could think of only one pastime that could have whisked him out of the courtroom on so dramatic an afternoon. No doubt she would have worn a picture hat tilted like the side of a roof, a princess-line coat, an ankle-length skirt, and the daintiest little

* Verbatim quote from the records.

cloth-topped shoes. I could see her waiting at a stage door, her gloved hands folded on the knob of a long-handled parasol. I could almost hear them.

"You may call me Lil."

"Call me Lion."

A voice behind me said, "Evening." Earnest Bridewell's scrapbook sprawled to the floor as I swerved around.

Fishbait Fred Fox leaned in the vestibule door. "Didn't mean to startle you," he said. "I was lookin' for Ed Brewster."

"He and his wife are out," I said.

Fishbait eyed me. He wore a wholly incongruous tuxedo jacket, a white vest, brown trousers and yellow oxfords. The straw hat on the back of his head was in character. He said, "I see you're still doing your homework."

"I've been reading about the Bridewells. Earnest Bridewell's trial."

"That was something, wasn't it? Get to where the Judge jumped on Quahog Point for telling fibs?"

"What do you think of it?"

"Think he hit the nail on the head. Except, maybe, Mrs. Smeizer."

I could not conceal my surprise. "Mrs. Smeizer?"

Fishbait eyed the ceiling. "My Aunt Nellie knew her quite well." He paused to insert thumb and finger into his mouth. Groping carefully, he took out a denture, frowned at it, then adjusted it back in place. "Mail-order teeth," he said bitterly.

"You were saying about Mrs. Smeizer?"

"Oh, yes. It was that night Abby Bridewell was done in. Bertha Smeizer told my Aunt Nellie that she saw the front door open and shut. It was night, you know, and she saw the yellow light. She was on her porch. And—this never got in the testimony—when the door opened she heard a man's voice. Sounded like it was here in the parlor."

"She heard a man?"

"Plain as day. He says something like, 'This is Neddy' or 'This is Ed.' "

"Neddy?" I exclaimed. "Or Ed!"

"That's all she heard. But she told my Aunt Nellie it was God's truth. Only she didn't get a chance to say so at the trial."

"Who could it have been, Fishbait?"

"Damfino." He rounded from the door and sauntered out into the kitchen. I heard the kitchen door slam. A moment later a car pulled into the drive.

Luke Martin burst in from the night. "Get your bag, we're going."

"How did you do, Luke?"

He stormed, "It got away! The biggest one I ever saw. It got away!"

But as we drove out of town that night, I was convinced that Luke's fish was not the only big one that ever got away at Quahog Point.

With the charges against Earnest Bridewell dismissed, the case ends as abruptly as one of those amputated news items in previous reference. And as unsatisfactorily, needless to add.

For if the evidence pointed to murder, as Judge Cottonwood conceded, why was the criminal investigation dropped? Why did the State's Attorney General shelve it as though it were a worthless old hat which some bumpkin had inadvertently left in his office?

Certainly a great many obvious questions were left hangfire. To enumerate a few:

Convinced as the Judge was that the Quahog Pointers were errant perjurers, why did not the State bring formal charges against them?

Why did Senator Bridewell's lawyers fail to bring similar charges against the witnesses who had presumably maligned him?

Why did the Court tolerate the testimony of a thirteen-year-old orphan who was "bound out" to Senator Bridewell and who could easily have been bribed or pressured?

Why did the officers who visited the scene of the crime fail to look for fingerprints on the cellar wall or on the door at the stair-top? Since 1900 or thereabouts the Bertillon System had been employed in America. And New England police were considered innovators, among the constabulary avant-garde.

What became of Exhibit A—the bag of shot? Harvard, Brown and other nearby universities contained scientific equipment which might have been put to better use than the examination of jumping cigar-store Indians. Indeed, the medical savants had for some years been assisting in police work. At hand, then, were facilities for a microscopic study of the alleged murder weapon, which might conceivably have uncovered a wisp of hair, a smear of face powder, or some other revelatory clue. Why was no scientific examination made in this case?

Defense averred that Dr. Hatfield, with the Hatfield axe to grind, offered adverse testimony and urged other Quahog Pointers to testify against Earnest Bridewell. A political vendetta was alleged. Why was this allegation never investigated?

In court Lionel Bridewell was denounced as a scoundrel who would frame his own brother. Why was there no police reaction to this allegation which added a fratricidal plot to matricide?

Finally (and it would seem rather importantly) if Earnest Bridewell did not slay his mother, who did?

"The State's evidence was that murder had been committed." And possessed of such evidence the State drops the affair. A pack of witnesses who are manifest perjurers. A village where liars are reputedly thicker than fiddlers in hell. Manifestations of an ugly family feud. Obvious political skullduggery. Clues as numerous as fleas on a dog. Motives in homicidal abundance. But? Case closed.

Surely this was a unique attitude on the part of law enforcement officials.

When the State's Attorney General shelved it, the Bridewell affair was an anthology of mysteries.

Certainly the trail was zero cold when, thirty-five years later, I spread the notes across my desk in New York.

CHAPTER 16

No COLLECTOR of true crimes and criminological curiosa is surprised to come across an unsolved murder mystery. Only the most naive layman believes the myth that "murder will out."

But a murder mystery in a microcosm, in a flyspeck community of 700 people, an anthill packed together in "togetherness." Here are no jungly terminals where smog provides cover for a human carnivore, no asphalt canyons teeming with strangers in hurrying anonymity. In this one-street town you know your neighbor like a book, and he is equally informed on you. Murder in concealment? As well try to hide a blacksnake in a goldfish bowl. It was this goldfish bowl aspect of the Bridewell case that made it, to me, most intriguing.

Physical geography, if nothing else, virtually precluded a chance slaying by a vagabond intruder. By the same token it ruled out a revenge killing by rum-runners or some professional hireling. At remote Quahog Point, vagrant strangers would have been spotted by eyes behind every window curtain.

No, it almost had to be a local job. Sea pirates and alien smugglers could be scratched from any list of possible suspects.

Going over my notes, I composed such a list. I summarized: "Someone well acquainted with the Bridewells. Conversant with the habits of the family. Familiar with layout of house and grounds. Had access, and could make or seize opportunity."

Almost any neighbor or fellow townsman could qualify. Yet the suspect list could again be whittled down by evidence which strongly indicated an inside job.

I wrote: "An intimate of the household. Probably in the bosom of the family. Must reckon with ambush potential of parlor, dining room, pantry, kitchen, the many doors."

Rationale: the death-blow had been lightning swift. Delivered with the hair-trigger timing and deadly precision of a mousetrap. But this was a better mousetrap. And it had been set at the best possible vantage point. Had the victim been struck down in the kitchen, parlor or anywhere else in the house, there would have been blood-stains on carpets to reckon with, or linoleum to wash, or other traces to hide. Only those brutal cellar steps would do to lend the appearance of accident.

And would a neighbor have been likely to discern the cellarway's strategic potential? To know the pitch of those stone steps, the insecurity of the handrail, the ugly outcroppings of the sidewall? And the tricky detail involving Earnest Bridewell's bag of shot. How would a neighbor have come into possession of that fantastic item?

Would a neighbor have been liable (a) to filch the bag, and then (b) risk the planting of the bag in an upstairs bedroom? In addition to the murder risk downstairs, such an awkward maneuver upstairs would have been extremely hazardous. What excuse can a neighbor offer if surprised upstairs with a hand under the mattress of your bed?

"Mrs. Bertha Smeizer," I wrote. "Possible, but unlikely for reason of ambush strategy and business of shot-bag. Modicum motive, but negative opportunity."

The same applied to other neighbors and townsmen. Many may have harbored private reasons to do away with Old Abby. Quahog Point seems to have been Grudge Harbor. However, all the visible signs indicated a house intimate, someone who knew his, or her—and the victim's—way around.

So I ruled out a Madame Sophie on the score that a town Venus would have had even less opportunity than a backfence busybody. For maternal, if not financial, reasons a state of cold war doubtless existed between Abby Bridewell and Lionel's lady friends. Which seemed to militate against the possibility of some trull intimately acquainting herself with the Bridewell homestead. Certainly Abby would never have invited one of the Cyprian sisterhood to tea, nor would a doxie have been there at garden parties with the King's Daughters. Sophie was too shady a lady to begin with.

Sybil Bridewell—I crossed her off, too. She *was* a ghost. Another character as unsubstantial as an old wives' tale. Not an iota of historicity supported the stories told about her. One could as reasonably list Ghostly Mary as a suspect.

Joao Gero? One could think about it. A man who presumably knew his way around the Bridewell house and grounds. Who knew the byroads and backroads of Quahog Point.

And conceivably the type to stage a vendetta. If there was any truth in the story about him and his daughter. If the girl had actually been seduced by Lionel Bridewell. If Abby had hustled the Geros away. If Magdalena had died in childbirth. If—if—if. All supposition. All conjecture. I had to cross Gero off. Hearsay cannot stand as valid testimony, and assumption spun from hearsay is a rope of sand.

"Cornelia Ord," I wrote. And let the name stand for contemplation.

One could build a case against Cornelia. Motive and opportunity. Well acquainted with the house. A family intimate. And she could have been there.

And yet? For a Cornelia Ord the cellarway ambush seemed out of character. A formidable woman. A stubborn soul. Probably would have held a grudge for two hundred years—as a matter of principle. But contrive a cunning mousetrap? Strike from concealment? Furtiveness is not consistent with the type of stubborn formidability that saves a man's biscuits for 17 years.

Nor did Cornelia seem the type to plant decoy evidence in an effort to incriminate an innocent man. That is the device of a scorpion mind, of a poisoner and back-stabber. Cornelia may have been determined and unforgiving. Mulishness is not a synonym of craft. Bent on execution, Cornelia would have probably told you off, and clouted you in the face with a flatiron.

The fact remained: she could have gone back to the house; she *could* have been on the crime scene that evening. Reluctantly I left her on the list of possible suspects.

"Walter Jones."

I had been able to learn little about the orphan boy. Ed had mentioned him only in passing.

Walter was thirteen years old. Was he a young thirteen or an old thirteen? The age differential in boys of thirteen could be important. A boy of thirteen could be mostly child. A boy of thirteen could be part man. And in a place like Quahog Point of the Gaslight Era, a boy of thirteen could be worked like a man. And kicked around like a man.

Earnest Bridewell may or may not have brutalized his mother. But a country squire who bickers over buying his ward a suit sounds like a nasty scrooge, and the evidence to this was in his own scrapbook. Then he headed his household in a day when spare the rod and spoil was a shibboleth which gave many a martinent a chance to exercise a temper. All of which suggests rough treatment for Walter Jones.

An oppressed boy can become as dangerous as an oppressed Choctaw. Goaded by miseries fancied or real—perhaps if only deprived of a coveted corduroy suit—the boy may rebel like an adult, or a whole Colony of adults.

But whereas a Colony of adults may raise an ideological flag (Taxation Without Representation is Tyranny!) the barefoot boy, incoherent, may seek redress in primitive terms of "getting even." Boy-like, he might dream up a savage ambush, complete with a scalping. It would not be beyond his man-child cunning to invent a decoy contrivance with a bag of shot. Destroy the old lady and place the blame on Earnest. A dandy way to kill two birds with one stone.

The record is unclear. But apparently Walter was on the scene of the crime soon after Abby Bridewell's body came to light. Where was he while it lay in the dark? He stated that he'd gone straight to bed the previous evening after attending a movie. His statement went unquestioned. Seemingly it occurred to no one that the boy could have climbed out of bed five minutes after he climbed in.

But Walter Jones had piped up as a friendly witness for the defense. On the stand he could have ruined Earnest Bridewell. Instead, he ruined Bertha Smeizer's adverse testimony. This performance scarcely accorded with any boyish desire to "get even," much less cover a murder.

Of course, the youngster's testimony could have been bought. On the face of it, bribery seemed likely. Yet the fact that he was probably a suborned witness did not rule him out as a savage who could have scalped Old Abby. So I did not cross off Walter Jones.

"Hobart Cudworth," I wrote, relieved to be done for the moment with Walter.

Here was a party to conjure with. I had pictured him as a straw-chewing clodhopper. It now occurred to me that the portrait had been evoked by the term "hired man" and by his name. Cudworth.

But the point is that names are not character indicators. Cudworth could have been a handsome stripling, as tall, lean and athletic as a pole-vaulter named Arrowsmith. Or he could have been as rolypoly as Santa Claus and as sloppy as a shirttail.

Fat or lean, handsome or homely, Abby Bridewell's hired man had to be analyzed by the record alone. What were the recorded facts concerning Cudworth?

He was born a "Pointer." (That came out at the trial.)

He had not been very long in the Bridewell employ.

Had apparently done his work efficiently enough to satisfy an exacting taskmistress and her splenetic elder son.

On the evening of April 11 had accompanied young Walter Jones to the picture show.

Had returned with the said boy and, like him, had gone straight to bed.

We next hear from Cudworth at six-thirty the following morning. He states that at that hour he was in the kitchen, performing a routine chore. While engaged in this task he noticed the cellar door standing ajar. He went to the cellar door. And at that juncture (to my way of thinking) Cudworth's story invited suspicion.

He looked down the cellarway. Why? Your normal reaction on seeing a door casually ajar is to walk over casually and close it. If, as he implied, he had no reason to expect someone down there, what caused the hired man to peer down into the darkness?

Looking down, he spied the body. To do so, he must have held a lamp, for at that hour of the morning the kitchen windows would have been gray and the cellar-hole black as pitch. So a casual glance would not have sufficed. Lamp in hand, he must have deliberately peered.

Spying Mrs. Bridewell's body at the foot of the steps, he called down to her. What did he call? "Mrs. Bridewell, are you all right?" Or: "Mrs. Bridewell, what's the matter?" No, he testified that he merely called her name. But it seems inane to call down anything at all to an old lady sprawled prostrate at the foot of steep, stone steps.

When she failed to answer, Cudworth did not go down the steps. Instead, he bolted from the house and "went for help." Surely this was an odd reaction. One might think the man, seeing the old lady lying there, would have gone down to her aid. Well, the yokel may have panicked. But then—

Going for help, he went all the way to the other side of town. Bypassing nextdoor neighbors. Ignoring Dr. Hatfield's down the road (extraordinary on the face of it). Footracing more than a mile to the home of the one "Pointer" least likely to give a damn about Old Abby's welfare. In the hour of dire emergency Cudworth goes for Earnest Bridewell instead of the family doctor.

Of course, Cudworth may have been a handsome rattlebrain. Or he may have been a loutish dolt. He could have been something else, however. As no one else immediately involved in the case, Cudworth enjoyed a clear field of opportunity.

He lived in the house. He knew its appointments. He was there on the night of the killing—in domicile with the old lady and a thirteen-year-old boy.

Like Walter Jones, Hobart Cudworth could have climbed from his bed five minutes after he climbed into it. Had he so desired, he could have prowled the downstairs rooms from eleven P.M. to six A.M. In this respect, he had a considerable advantage over Walter. As hired man, Cudworth could have fabricated some reasonable excuse for being up and about after bedtime. On some pretext or other, he could have summoned Abby Bridewell to a midnight ambush.

Or suppose he arises at five A.M. with murder in mind. He is there in the kitchen when Abby comes down for an early breakfast. With an appetite for pickled pears, she goes down to the cellar. Now is Cudworth's chance. A weapon? As handy as a chunk of kindling wood. And what bludgeon could have been more easily disposed of?

After the deed is done and the stove properly stoked, Cudworth makes a quick search for a decoy weapon. Ah, the shot-bag stained with pheasant blood! Now to pin the job on nasty Earnest. He catfoots upstairs to tuck the bag under Earnest's mattress.

That Cudworth had little use for Earnest Bridewell was apparent in the hired man's courtroom testimony. He did not overdo it. He said that the Senator swore at poor Abby "a little." And: "He throwed her down and bruised her up." Violence, yes. But perhaps no more than one might expect of a squire exasperated by his mother. Delivered in this tone of restraint, Cudworth's testimony doubly damned the accused. A witness who knows how to insinuate nuances is nobody's simpleton.

However, a simple question weakened the case against Hobart Cudworth. Mainly, *why*? To what end would he have slain Abby Bridewell?

Surface facts left the hired man without a patent murder incentive. Robbery? Nothing was stolen. Vengeance? But Cudworth was not "bound out." A tyrannized hired man usually quits before the yoke drives him to homicide.

Cudworth stood to gain nothing tangible by Abby's demise. In fact, it cost him his job.

However, he could have been ordered to carry the pitcher to the well once too often. He could have revolted against a single reprimand or against lumpy oatmeal. He could have nursed a spite acquired when he wore kneepants. Because of such imponderables and the uncertainties of human thermodynamics, I left the hired man on my suspect-list. I rated him "maximum opportunity, minimum motive."

"*Lionel Bridewell,*" I wrote finally. Underlining the name.

I liked Lionel as a suspect. I liked him a lot. It seemed to me that much of Lionel could go on the discredit side of the ledger. No need to review in detail the obvious motive and character factors. Incentive: total inheritance. Reputation: unsavory. Attitude: reptilian. Deportment: bad. The man was a natural.

One should think that the minions of the State's Attorney General, and surely the County Sheriff, would have grilled the eye teeth out of Brother Lionel. If not for an accomplished matricide, certainly for an attempted fratricide with that shot-bag device. With the case against Earnest evaporating, suspicion positively coagulated around Lionel.

In court he was described as "a man of mystery." He was branded a scoundrel who would try to hang "his own flesh and blood." Before his brother's fate was decided, he slipped away from the courtroom. He looks virtually as guilty as Cain.

With the reputation of a wastrel and a rake, Lionel Bridewell is his own worst character witness. Of course, sexual rakery is not homicide—if it were the dockets would be jammed with some surprising mass murderers. But confirmed rakes are mistrusted by the average layman who, with some logic (and perhaps from experience) may reason that it is but a short step from knavery to foul play.

Expensive indulgences: wine, women and song. According to town talk, Lionel had indulged them all. And, according to bill collectors, such indulgence costs money.

Two barriers stood between Lionel and money—Mother Abby and Brother Earnest. Reduced to fundamentals, the Bridewell case seemed to boil down to a dual-purpose effort to dispose of both. No individual involved in the case had a motive factor as large and as dually inclusive as Lionel Bridewell's.

But on the debit side—a frustrating negative—was apparent lack of opportunity. Lionel had removed himself from the old homestead. His Lookout Hill address was a long way from Quahog Point. He claimed he was in Newport on business, Tuesday, April 11. Claimed he returned to Lookout Hill late that evening. At any rate, he was in his office at Lookout Hill on the morning of the 12th. To have included Quahog Point in this itinerary would have taken some doing.

Well, it just could have been done. Peddling orange pekoe, he could have been in Newport on midday of April 11. Caught the afternoon boat for Quahog Point. Sneaked to the old homestead during the evening. Walked the peninsular road during the night. Caught an "inland" bus to Lookout Hill and made it by breakfast time. But!

At best he would have needed extraordinary luck to clear the time and space hurdle. The steamer to Quahog Point from Newport was often late. So was the average get-out-and-get-under motorbus. I could not believe that a native so familiar with the regional transportation problem as Lionel would have burdened a murder scheme with this hazardous obstacle race. For any hitch that delayed him on the final lap from Quahog Point to Lookout Hill, anything that prevented his return to base by breakfast time, and his geographic alibi was "jiggered."

In addition, there would have been the problem of traveling incognito. A nondescript Joao Gero might have attracted little attention on the road. Lionel was known to the seaboard area, and the nearer he drew to Quahog Point the greater the risk of recognition.

What were the known facts? Lionel was seen in Newport at midday on the 11th. He was seen in Lookout Hill on the morning of the 12th. By a long, long stretch of highspeed travel he could have reached Quahog Point during the night of April 11–12. If he *did* reach Quahog Point, he *could* have slain his mother. But I had to rate him almost zero opportunity.

Still, I left Lionel Bridewell on my suspect-list. In italics.

Mrs. Burton Smeizer.
Cornelia Ord.
Walter Jones.
Hobart Cudworth.
Lionel Bridewell.

I stared at the abbreviated list. Who else was there?

There *was* another—?

To mind came a prickly thought. A name that sent a little breath of frost down the back of my neck. Why hadn't it occurred to me before? Occuring to me now, it was scary.

I formed a resolve to return to Quahog Point and continue my research on locale. Current events intervened, and I did not see the Point again until after V-J Day.

CHAPTER 17

ED SAID, "It's been a long time."

I said something fatuous about Hitler, and asked Ed if Luke Martin and his wife, Bengta, had been at the Point recently. He said not for a couple of seasons.

I noticed Gillion's Wharf had been smartened up with some new timbering and paint. Fishbait Fred Fox's hotel had a new roof and a brand new wing. The distant Seagull boasted a small Neon sign.

Ed explained, "Government's put some money in here. The State is going to build a bunch of highways."

Farewell to Quahog Point as a Currier and Ives antique. But its primitive face had not yet been lifted. It still retained its Grandma Moses background, Winslow Homer waterfront and Howard Chandler Christie hotels.

Except for some enlargement of the girth, my host had not changed much, either.

"Come to fish?" Ed asked as we tooled along a familiar shoreside road. "The mackerel's been running."

Uncomfortable, I said, "I came to do some writing. I have to go back Sunday."

We passed the Anchor Saloon. Ed took a back road which skirted the Center, and presently we arrived at the house.

He had made some alterations. The hedges were trimmed, the gnarled trees had been cut down, a new driveway went around to the side. Arched over the drive was a rose arbor.

I was sorry to see the old barn no longer there.

"Hurricane last September," Ed said.

But the front vestibule was familiar. The Victorian parlor was little altered, although the Eye had gone.

"Yes," Ed nodded with a rueful smile, "and the rest of it may go. We had a paying guest last season who was a decorator. Sold Annette on the idea of remodeling the whole place."

"Change and decay," I thought, "change and decay." Another few years, and the last Victorian nicknack might be gone. Another few years after that, and the house itself might disappear. Nothing on earth is possessed with permanence. The Gaslight Era was a matchflare between the Oil Lamp Period and the day of the Mazda Bulb. Our own Atomic Civilization might be no more durable.

"There's Massasoit," I noted. "If you ever do sell that statue, I'd like a chance to buy it. That picture, too—*Morning, Noon and Night.*" Offhandedly I led around to the gramophone. "But I don't suppose you'll ever part with the phonograph."

"That stays," Ed said firmly. Then he shook his head. "Unless Annette makes me sell it to get a television."

I saw I was just in time. One more season, and vestigial Bridewellia might vanish entirely. Into the limbo of the forgotten past might go the last bit of concrete evidence, the last reliable clue to the killing of Abby Bridewell. Another unsolved murder case wiped off the books by history's inexorable statute of limitations.

To mind came some remembered copybook lines from Christina Gabrielle Rossetti.

> Come, gone—gone for ever—
> Gone as an unreturning river. . . .
> Gone as the year at the dying fall—
> Tomorrow, today, yesterday, never—
> Gone once for all.

I felt a disturbing sense of urgency. As though the Bridewell house were dissolving around me in the twilight, and tomorrow would be too late. Did I still have time?

That was hard to say when I was not quite sure what I was looking for.

For supper we had grilled mackerel, a platter of chicken lobster and a goose the size of a wild swan. On the steamer passage to the Point I had read a newspaper item on the unusual number of swans in the region that spring. Its concluding paragraph advised that poachers would be fined five hundred dollars for shooting the protected birds. Recalling Ed's rack of shotguns, I wondered. But that was not the reason my appetite began to hurt my conscience.

Annette said, "You were here before in April. I remember how it rained."

I said, "Yes, I was."

Ed beamed. "We had a good time spinning yarns. Remember?"

I nodded, ill at ease. My discomfort was heightened when Ed reminded, "We went over all those old papers on the Bridewell case. Earnest's scrapbook and all. You thought you might write an article about the mystery."

"Yes."

"Did you ever write it?" Annette inquired.

Glad to shift my eyes from Ed, I told her, "I never finished it."

I was relieved when the topic took another turn. And relieved when Ed said that he and Annette had made a date to go with friends to the Scenic Palace; would I excuse them that evening.

"Do you mind," I asked, "if I look over some of those old books and things in the attic? Don't bring them down."

"The Bridewell stuff? Sure, go ahead." Ed grinned. He said that he himself hadn't yet found time to go through all of it. "There's reams in that old Saratoga trunk. I clear it out a little now and then."

Annette protested, "The whole place needs clearing. Ed goes up to do it, then sits down and reads the old magazines."

He winked at me. "*Police Gazettes.* That's why I installed electric lights up there last year. Go on up, help yourself."

When you aren't sure what it is you are looking for, you may find everything or nothing, or everything *and* nothing. I found both that evening. And something quite unexpected.

I intended a final look at the Bridewell cellar. But on the off chance of discovering a skeleton in some closet, I looked first up under the eaves of the Bridewell attic. If I could not find a closeted skeleton, at least I might discover some clue—a hint—a key.

The only skeletal item in visible evidence was the black, high-bosomed dress form. When I snapped on the overhead light, the form, standing in center floor, cast a disturbing shadow on the rough brickwork of the chimney—the silhouette of a headless and truncated female torso.

I shoved the form into a dark corner. There were enough shadows in the Bridewell attic without that one.

Old books.

The household's intellectual boneyard. Therein I might find *something*. In uncut pages, the culture rejected. In worn-out bindings the family's education—the sources of its information or misinformation, its basic thinking, its opinions, inhibitions, prejudices—its ideology. I was curious about the Bridewell mentality, but my research was primarily aimed at a lower level. People sometimes leave scraps of paper, mementoes or revelatory marginal notes in old books.

The Bridewells had rejected Ruskin.

They had not read *The House of Seven Gables.*

The Lay of the Last Minstrel—"With Happy Memories to Lionel from Opal"—had apparently been read by Lionel. (He was deceived by the title? And who was Opal?)

Lalla Rookh, Don Quixote and the *Personal Memoirs of U. S.*

Grant had been left to the consumption of bookworms unrelated to the genus Bridewell.

Well, the first-generation household had read the brass-bound family Bible. Until the hasp had broken off and the vellum had worn shabby. Then it had been consigned to the attic. Even the Good Book must be dressed up if it is to sit in the parlor.

I suspected the Alger books had been next in favor for assiduous reading. Here was pabulum for the juvenile minds of youthful Earnest and Little Lionel. *Phil the Fiddler; Brave and Bold; Sink or Swim; Bound to Rise.* In spite of immense vicissitudes which were usually based on poverty, the commercially-minded Alger hero always rose. The formula keynote was struck on the flyleaf of *Wait and Hope, or a Plucky Boy's Luck.* Illustrated was a youthful necktie salesman displaying his wares. The caption read: *"There's lots of ways of making money. Do as I do—'Wait and Hope.'"*

The boys had bypassed gift copies of *Ben Hur, Silas Marner* and *Vanity Fair.* They had evidently plodded through *The Last of the Mohicans*—required reading of the gaslight school, until Mark Twain scalped Fenimore Cooper with a tomahawk criticism that exposed the latter's brain as a fountainhead of literary nonsense.

Ten Nights in a Bar Room—that, too, was probably required reading in this Sabbatarian household. So was a copy of *Pilgrim's Progress.*

In his formative years, Earnest Bridewell had been subjected to John D. Quackenbos. *Quackenbos's Practical Arithmetic. Quackenbos's Mental Arithmetic. Quackenbos's History of the World.*

Standard texts in the American school system of the Gaslight Era, Quackenbos's arithmetics were similar to those in use today. Two times two seems to equal four in any age.

It was evident, however, that the same scientific consistency did not apply to the study of history.

Opening the Quackenbos text at random, I found the following passage concerning Charlotte Corday, heroine of the French Revolution.

> "Death by the guillotine she had expected, and she met it with the utmost composure. *When the brutal executioner*

buffeted her severed head, her cheek flushed at the indignity." *

At that point the Professor's cheek should have flushed. Thousands of little Americans would believe this and similar hogwash, word for word; in fact, they stood to be birched if they refused to believe it. Aesop had nothing on Quackenbos.

In addition to quack history and geography, Earnest and Lionel Bridewell had been dosed with *Barnes's New National Reader*. From it they were compelled to absorb massive quantities of verse. And because elocution was then in educational vogue, they were called upon to disgorge the stanzas with gestures. Professor Charles J. Barnes tells them how. His text opens with a treatise on the subject of "Expression." To quote:

> "EXPRESSION includes in its treatment the consideration of Tone of Voice, Rate or Movement, Force, Pitch, Emphasis, Pauses, Inflection and Modulation."

The Professor does not stop there. He dissects these various categorical elements into sub-elements. For example: "*Tone* is regulated by sentiment . . . The *Conversational Tone* is that used in expressing quiet or unemotional thoughts . . . A *Full Tone* is used to express such sentiments as great joy, sublimity, lofty courage, reverential fear, exultation and others of similar nature . . . The *Calling Tone* is used in loud exclamations, in addressing persons at a distance, and in unbridled passion."

Ah, yes, those yesteryears of the little red schoolhouse—take us back to those good old days when training was "old school." Teachers tolerated no nonsense back then. Courses were stiff, and there was plenty of homework. Education *was* education.

All right, class, this semester you will memorize the following from Barnes—

Sample:

CURFEW MUST NOT RING TONIGHT

. . . *Wild her eyes and pale her features,*
Stern and white her thoughtful brow,

* Emphasis supplied.

And within her secret bosom Bessie made a solemn vow.
She had listened while the judges read without a tear or sigh,
"At the ringing of the curfew, Basil Underwood must die . . ."

And:

THE BURIAL OF SIR JOHN MOORE

. . . Slowly and sadly we laid him down,
From the field of his fame fresh and gory!
We carved not a line, we raised not a stone,
But we left him alone in his glory. . . .

And:

VIRGINIUS

"Then clasp me round the neck once more, and give me one more kiss;
And now, mine own dear little girl, there is no way but this."
With that he lifted high the steel, and smote her in the side,
And in her blood she sunk to earth, and with one sob she died.

And with gestures, mind! Waving your little arms. Posturing. Striking your forehead with anguish. Holding up your hands in appeal. . . . There in the Bridewell attic I could almost hear and see it. Earnest with arm upraised, preparing to smite with steel the "dear little girl." Lionel practicing the Calling Tone as used in "unbridled passion."

Five books remained to the attic stack. By the copyright dates and state of repair, I gathered that this residue marked the high tide of the household culture.

Two of the volumes dealt with humor—a copy of Bill Nye, and *Aunt Samantha Goes to the Centenniel.* Here was a side of Abby Bridewell I had previously missed. I wondered if she read these adult comics to her invalid husband.

I wondered, too, if Old Abby was the reader who had dog-eared a trashy romance entitled *Captain Rudolph's Secret.*

The next book at hand did belong to Abby, for the flyleaf bore a signatory demand that the potential borrower return it. A book of poems containing *Songs of Many Seasons* by Oliver Wendell Holmes. I was surprised at Abby's concern for this volume, until I sighted a marginal mark which called attention to a poem entitled *Our Banker*. Of course. And it seemed in keeping that the following stanza was underlined:

Old Time, in whose bank we deposit our notes,
Is a miser who always wants guineas for groats,
He keeps all his customers still in arrears
By lending them minutes and charging them years.

I picked up the last of the books. This was the strange little paperback with the intriguing title: *From the Ball Room to Hell; Facts About Dancing*. Between the covers of this 1894 booklet, the Glad Tidings Publishing Company issued a warning "to parents who are blind to the awful dangers there are for young girls in the dancing academy." I wondered at this opuscule turning up in a household unblessed with daughters. A glance at the contents informed me that the "facts" as presented might have been interesting to certain sons.

Once started, one cannot put the booklet down. But at last, and all too soon, it comes to a final summary.

> "Two-thirds of the girls who go to dancing school are ruined . . . Did you ever know a lady, who danced to excess, to live to be over twenty-five years of age? If she does, she is in most instances broken in health physically and morally. Beside the harmful exercise there is great danger from the exposure a girl is so often subjected to in a ballroom. She gets in a perspiration during the dance and as soon as it is over rushes to an open door or window with arms and chest exposed. Is there any wonder that so many women of today are unhealthy? The average age of the excessive male dancer is thirty-one."

Today it seems unbelievable that American moralists ever poured out such slop. This outpouring did not occur in the year of Puritan judges and Salem witch trials. The date was 1894—on history's calendar the day before yesterday. The waltz, indeed! Why, by 1911—less than eighteen years later—the nation was two-stepping, syncopating and bunny-hugging from Maine to California. Everybody's doing it! Doing what? Turkey-trot! Give us Alexander's Ragtime Band! Give us the Vernon Castles!

So all the girls expired at the age of twenty-five. All the young men, aged thirty-one, dropped dead. America became a bleak and silent cemetery. Only the pious censors and the sinless moralists lived on to roam among the tombstones of fallen dancers.

How had either of the Bridewell boys managed to retain a semblance of sanity? On the one hand, the Bible: *It is harder for a rich man to get into heaven. . . .* On the other hand, Alger: *There's lots of ways of making money. . . .* The moralist: *Dancing is death!* Professor Barnes: *To die is glorious!* The sixth Commandment: *Thou Shalt Not Kill!* Newspaper headlines of 1898: *Remember the Maine!*

Well, it seemed to me you couldn't have it both ways, unless you were a schizoid—one of the world's more dangerous characters. The schizoid's, of course, is the maddening dilemma of the person who tries to carry water on both shoulders. Sooner or later he loses his balance, drops one bucket or the other, or both, in an emotional smash that sends him amuck.

Staring at the dusty books, I shook my head. They offered a psychological clue, perhaps. But where did that lead? As well identify the killer as a member of the human race.

Yet such blanket identification, too, contained a fallacy. The obvious fallacy of generalization. For there were many men and women who led worthy lives of good will in the Gaslight Era. Led them in spite of wretched schooling, homicidal nationalism and moralistic hysteria.

Perhaps Quackenbos and Barnes were no more harmful than chickenpox, and as soon forgotten. Perhaps Earnest and Lionel Bridewell learned something of value from the "old school" curriculum. Arithmetic, anyway. And possibly a mastery of elocutionary gestures took Earnest to the State Senate. Possibly Lionel's "Calling Tones" won him an entree to the better guest rooms of the Surf and Sand.

I was back where I had started. The books clued nothing, solved nothing.

I turned to the Saratoga trunk.

A surprise lay in store.

CHAPTER 18

OLD trunks.

This one had leather strappings. On the side was a dim label: *Wescott Express.*

The dry hinges creaked.

Peering inside, I felt a little like the opener of an Egyptian mummy-case.

What had the household buried in this coffer? What do most people bury in attic trunks? Unwanted wedding gifts. Junk. Outgrown garments. *Memento mori.* Articles of no earthly use, but too valuable to be thrown away. Articles of no value whatever, but preserved because of magpie instinct.

Such as:

Twelve large, domed butter dishes, German silver, the metal tarnished an ugly black. Type of dish once used in center table for homemade butter. (Value? A couple of dollars. And why in the world would anyone have acquired *twelve?*)

One patchwork quilt, some of the patches missing.

One souvenir spoon, "Niagara Falls."

One china teapot, the spout broken off.

One high-button lady's shoe, right foot.

One lady's bonnet, deaconess type.

Some sheet music including *Oh, Promise Me* by Reginald de Koven, and Eben E. Rexford's *'Tis Only a Pansy Blossom.*

And, at figurative barrel bottom, a small packet of letters and old bills.

Since Ed Brewster had previously been through most of this Bridewell residue, I had a feeling I was again in barren territory. Still, his eye could have missed something. I skimmed through the sheaf of bills.

So I was the one who almost missed it, there, in the dunnings for hay and grain, chickenfeed, carpet-sweepers, taxes, charcoal, wallpaper, horseshoes and kerosene. Plain as the bills themselves —indeed, their content—was the fact that the Bridewells were being dunned.

Wealthy tycoons? In 1908 several firms were threatening to turn Bridewell accounts over to collection agencies. In 1909 the village blacksmith was hammering at Old Abby. So was the local coal dealer. Earnest's Kelp Company was mortgaged. The Trawler Company was mortgaged. *Please Remit. We cannot renew. You have just thirty days. Principal and interest expected by next ins't.* In 1910 the Tax Office warned Old Abby that severe penalties impended. Surprised, I stared at the tax notice.

Perception came slowly, but it came. The realization that the Bridewells could not have been the rich overlords pictured in local legend. That, far from being a plutocrat, Abby was not what even the localites would have deemed "comfortably off."

But the truth was there in the Bridewell attic. Abby Bridewell was no opulent chatelaine, no bucolic Hetty Green. The family had never been rich. They had lost the Surf and Sand. I found a frayed letter which indicated that the hotel was sold to remote relatives on the Sybil Bridewell side of the clan. Apparently Captain Nathan had retained a small interest in the enterprise. But long before Lionel's incumbency as manager the ownership had passed into the hands of a Chicago concern. Evidently Abby had procured the management job for Lionel, and it was equally evident that Lionel had posed as proprietor. What easier way to impress (or enchant) a guest?

And the New Years' banquets given by Abby? The bills told that story, too. It seemed that village memory could inflate a chowder supper into a cotillion at the Waldorf-Astoria. But the audits suggested what vernacular called "sociables"—the kind undoubtedly expected of a State Senator's mother. Reading between expenditures, I could see Ed Brewster's big-eyed lobster thermidor reduced to a tuna fish salad, and the palatial crystal chandelier shrinking to a small cluster of glass bangles.

As for the Bridewell holdings in the P. and Q. Rapid Transit

Company, they had amounted, it appeared, to a total of some forty shares. Par value, four thousand dollars. Ultimate value, nothing. A gaudy brochure listed the company's original assets which, so far as I could see, consisted largely of Alger-type hope. I could not find Earnest Bridewell's name on the Board of Directors. In a sea-bound community which had little or no comprehension of capital investment, I suppose a few shares of stock had grown in imagination to half of Wall Street. And because Abby may have advised a townsman or two that she thought the trolley line a good venture, she was Jim Fisk in skirts when the venture came to the end of the line.

Apparently the three-thousand-dollar legacy aired at the murder trial constituted the sum and substance of the Bridewell "fortune." The rest of the family's reputed wealth was so much helium. The income, if any, from Earnest's meager enterprises was hypothecated. Lionel had saved little but debts. The Bridewell house and grounds were burdened with back taxes. Perhaps with taxes paid, the estate could have cleared two thousand dollars.

So Abby Bridewell had pinched pennies. She may not have been as gracious about it as Whistler's Mother. Whistler's Mother was never compelled to hold out against two nagging, badgering, foxy, unscrupulous and avaricious adult-delinquent sons. Earnest bullying, Lionel scheming. And the widow's savings, such as they were, dwindling away.

No wonder Old Abby had tried to collect monies owed her. No wonder she had pressed Cornelia Ord on a mortgage loan—if that story, too, was not so much local helium.

I did find an invoice which seemed to credit a down payment on a grand piano. It came to me—the idea could never be proved —that Old Abby could have bought Cornelia's Steinway to keep it in the family. Intending, perhaps, to return it to Cornelia if and when the Ord fortunes improved. Why not?

Evidently Abby had liked Cornelia, or she would not have invited her to the house. Regretting the forced sale of the piano, the old lady could have retrieved the heirloom from the dealer. Could have arranged its installation in the Surf and Sand because of insufficient room in the Bridewell parlor. Could have planned to bestow it on Cornelia after the final payments were made. Wouldn't a generous construction of Abby's motives be as valid as village gossip construing the contrary? Why else, when her purse was threadbare, would the harassed old lady have purchased a Steinway?

Among her papers I found evidence suggesting charity on Abby's part. Many of the receipts were unidentifiable. Over a period of years she had paid out regular monthly sums—ten dollars—fifteen dollars—for something unspecified.

The receipts were initialled, but I could make nothing of the initials. (Not blackmail. Blackmailers do not offer receipts.) The sums had gone to charity? To some missionary fund? To some needy person—Sybil Bridewell, say?

Sybil. Of course. Someone must have supported her—a recluse with no income. Someone must have paid for those baskets of groceries left week in, week out, at Sybil Bridewell's door. The baskets must have been sent from Babcock's, the only grocery in Quahog Point. For several decades Abby Bridewell had been part owner of Babcock's store. Who else would have provided for Sybil Bridewell? Old Abby was her sole remaining relative, unless Earnest and Lionel were counted. As I saw it, when it came to charitable contributions the Bridewell boys were of no account.

But I was seeing a new picture of Abby Bridewell. Not the Victorian matriarch in black bombazine and choker collar portrayed in the family album. Not the dowager Captain Bligh of local legend. Those were public images.

The album portrait of Abby Bridewell did not show her sending a check to an orphan asylum in New London. The public image did not display her as making a similar donation to a Providence orphans' home. I found the cashed checks and letters of thanks. Also a card acknowledging a donation to a foundling home in Newport. Another thanking Abby for contributing to a fund for homeless children in Gloucester.

To Old Abby, herself hard-pressed, such offerings must have been by way of widow's mites. And I found something else which controverted the public image. Evidently abetted by her Senatorial son, rumor had painted Abby as a virago who would deny an invalid husband a glass of water. Even Doc Hatfield, no friendly witness, had spoken up to refute this calumny. But what Hatfield apparently did not know—what her own sons apparently did not know—was that Abby herself bore the mark of a fatal pathological impairment.

In the attic residue I found the evidence. Apparently mistrusting Doc Hatfield, she had, in the summer of 1910, visited a celebrated surgeon then vacationing for a few days at the Surf and Sand. He must have given her discouraging word. A cryptic note advised "immediate treatment." Early in 1911 she had written to a sanitarium in Hartford, describing recurrent symptoms. The answering letter had doomed her with a diagnosis as coldly positive as a death sentence. We regret to inform you that our specialists here, etcetera, etcetera. The progress of your complaint as you describe it, etcetera. In a few more months, at best a year, and so on. While we must decline to operate on a patient of your years, we can hope to make you comfortable until such time as the Lord in His mercy, and so forth.

She was, as they called it in those days, "host to the worm." Evidence of malignant cancer. She had refused to confide in Doctor Hatfield. Had never told her sons. Too long she had held her knowledge within her. By January 1911 it was killing her.

I doubted if she were actually in her eighties. Victorian women seldom confided their age, although they were supposed to dress and act like grandmothers at forty. But she must have been at least seventy, suffering the nerves and anxieties which modern geriatricians tell us are buzzards that haunt the old. Too, Abby had other buzzards to cope with. Earnest and Lionel. And the realization that her days were numbered.

But she was not a usurious old Tartar.

Not a mercenary and skinflint grimalkin.

Not a domineering duchess ruling the lives of her sons.

She was a lonely old woman with shadows closing in around her. An aged widow struggling to maintain a competence for a pair of sleazy incompetents. She must have been weary, forlorn, frightened. She was selling her horses to pay her debts, leaving her home, preparing to live in an alien town with a son who did not want her. Her minutes were being charged against her at the hourly rate, as in the mournful verses she had underlined.

Above her hovered the mental buzzards. Fear. Anxiety.

And over her chair hovered Earnest and Lionel. Waiting. Hoping.

But it seemed that someone—perhaps one of the boys—couldn't wait. I could taste the irony in my mouth.

Abby Bridewell, poor old soul, was already dying when a bludgeon struck her down.

The attic trunk contained two more surprises. These I came upon, dramatically enough, in the last of the correspondence—a packet tied with black ribbon—mostly letters of condolence penned on paper decorated with black fringe.

> *Dear Earnest: Heard the sad news, and know that to you and Lionel the loss must have come as a blow. . . .*

It had come as a blow all right, I thought caustically, but not to Earnest and Lionel. The only blow in evidence was the one that smote their mother on the forehead. And glancing through the condolence mail, I could not help wondering what the condolers thought when they subsequently heard of Earnest's arrest for murder and of Lionel's shady involvement.

Could Lionel have actually believed his brother the murderer? It was a possibility I had not considered. On the stand Lionel had virtually accused Earnest. He had identified the bag of shot as belonging to Earnest, and had said he had seen it upstairs on Earnest's bed. Everyone, myself included, had supposed Lionel was lying.

But could he have told the truth? Unregenerate he may have been. Shifty. Slick as pomade. Yet what if he *did* see the shot-bag in Earnest's bedroom? What if he had, indeed, been convinced that Earnest was his mother's killer?

"Dear Earnest: We know your mother's passing was a shock to you. . . ."

Could Earnest have killed her? Certainly the testimony against him sounded like it, and his frantic efforts to establish an alibi looked black. His acquittal, however, rested on an alibi that seemed unshakable—the word of strangers, disinterested witnesses. The cattle dealers, McVest and Garvy.

"Wait a minute!" I thought aloud.

If McVest and Garvy were strangers, how was it they were able to recognize Earnest Bridewell with such absolute certainty? And if they were disinterested, why had they volunteered such vital information to Earnest's lawyers? The two Bedford men had left Quahog Point three days before the murder charge was leveled. They could not have heard of the case until they read about it in their home-town papers three days later. A man in Quahog Point is up for murder. *They* were in Quahog Point, yes, three days ago, when the murder presumably occurred. Well, it says here an old lady was killed in a house on the north side of the Point. *They* were on the south side. But now they were prepared to vow that a man they had seen on the south side—total stranger to them—was the accused. Did they recognize this man from a picture in the paper? (I saw no photographs of Earnest in the newspapers.) Even if they saw a newspaper photograph, what made them certain of their man? A figure seen at night in a dooryard and momentarily glimpsed later in the evening at a lamp-lit window?

I told myself I should have smelled that rat from the first. But when a case is alive with rats, you can miss a fast one. At any rate, Dear Earnest was back on my suspect-list.

However, "Hold your horses," I advised myself. "Once bitten, twice shy. What do you know about the real Earnest?"

Then I came to the surprising letters. There were two of them. As though by contrived suspense, the last of the packet. At the tag end of the condolence missives. Held together by a rotted rubber band.

The rotted band fell away, and I examined the time-browned envelopes. One ordinary envelope, one legal-sized envelope. Both letters were addressed to Earnest.

The first was postmarked May 1910, the year before Abby's death. Content as follows:

Provincetown, Mass.
May 7, 1910

Mr. Earnest Bridewell
Quahog Point
Dear Sir:

This is to certify that I have this day examined the infant born March 13, 1910, at the house of L. N. Gotch in Provincetown.

Height 19 inches. Good growth of hair. Bones of head ossified, in contact at sutures. Fingers and toenails fully developed. Baby sound. Cried loudly. In my opinion this is a full term baby.

The infant has been placed in a home.

Respectfully,
H. Ž. Rauschbush, M.D.

So there *was* a baby! And it must have been Earnest who—!

"Good God!" I said aloud.

The rape had been blamed on Lionel. Earnest had held silent, had let Lionel bear the obloquy. How wrong could a public image get?

And no wonder Lionel had taken the stand against his brother. He must have known Earnest had ravaged the girl, since he himself had not done it (who else was there?). Yet he, Lionel had been forced into semi-exile. What a chance to repay the injury when Earnest faced a charge of matricide!

Tense, I examined the second letter. The legal envelope was postmarked August 1915. The letter read:

HASKINS, HASKINS & ARKWRIGHT
ATTORNEYS AND COUNSELLORS AT LAW
404 WATER STREET
NEWPORT

August 2, 1915

Earnest Bridewell, Esq.
Quahog Point
Dear Mr. Bridewell:

In reply to your query of recent date in behalf of you and your brother, I beg to state that, inas-

much as you and your brother are the inheritors of the estate formerly belonging to your mother, this property became yours at the time of your mother's death, and you have an absolute right to take possession as legal heirs and joint owners.

You are right in assuming that tax liens must be satisfied by the inheritors. Our assessor concurs with your estimate that the estate's value, after taxes, is approximately $500.

Yours very truly,
H. H. Haskins, Att'y.

Scuttled! I was back to Nowhere! The Bridewell brothers now applying for joint ownership! Earnest and Lionel, arm in arm, hand in glove, in mutual and fraternal effort to acquire the Bridewell inheritance.

It was all wrong. It did not add up. I could not believe that a five-hundred-dollar estate could be salve enough to compensate Lionel for the odium sloughed on him by Earnest; quittance enough to requite Earnest for the perfidy attributed to him by Lionel. To forgive is surely divine, but I could not imagine five hundred dollars endowing Earnest and Lionel with that much divinity.

Five hundred dollars!

It came to me that this meager inheritance was hardly enough to incite a man to his mother's murder. The sons must have known that house and grounds were virtually at pawn. That the estate, after taxes, would look like a turkey after Thanksgiving. Kill Mother Hubbard when you knew what was in the cupboard? Risk the gallows for five hundred dollars?

There went the murder-for-profit motive. At least, so far as Earnest and Lionel were concerned.

But someone else, someone who did not know. . . .

"An outsider," I said aloud, staring at the letter. "Someone deceived by the public image. . . ."

A voice behind me said, "So you found the letters."

Startled, I wheeled about-face.

Ed Brewster was standing at the top of the attic stair. He

regarded me with a sleepy smile. From his big right fist dangled a small, brown, pear-shaped bag.

CHAPTER 19

"HAVE some more saltwater taffy," Ed said.

We sat in the dining room with coffee cups before us. He extended the brown paper bag.

"No thanks," I said.

He peeled the colored tissue from three or four taffys and tucked them into an amiable smile.

With his cheek pouched, he said, "Sorry we was so late at the movie. Double feature. Film broke just when Ava Gardener was kissing this hunter—he wasn't her husband—there in the jungle. Took them twenty minutes to fix it. The film, I mean. . . . No more taffy?"

"No, really."

Ed bellowed toward the kitchen, "How the fritters doing, Nan?"

Annette called, "Coming."

Ed said, "I always like a midnight snack if we're up." He licked a thumb, wiped his hand on his woollen shirt, and squinted. "You look kind of peaked. Find anything *in*-tresting in the attic?"

"I always like old papers and things."

He chuckled, and said he did too.

Annette brought in the fritters, coffee, butter and sirup. "Men!" she said accusingly. "Food!" She took the complaint back with a cheerful smile, and bid us goodnight. At the stair door she paused to ask if I wanted an early breakfast; was I going fishing?

"I'm afraid I can't, Mrs. Brewster. I have to go back tomorrow. I thought I'd take the early boat."

When she had gone, Ed said regretfully, "I thought you were staying over to Sunday."

"I can't. I remembered some things I have to do."

We ate in silence for several minutes. Wonderful flapjacks. Pure maple sirup. And I seemed to be swallowing mouthfuls of flannel.

Then Ed said, "You could take the steamer goes at four P.M. and make almost as good time as the two o'clock. The early one stops Stonington, *and* Groton, and New London."

"I know. I thought I'd like to see Groton."

"You city guys," Ed said. "Come here Friday and go back Saturday. All alike. Luke Martin can't wait to leave the minute he gets here. Ants in his pants! Business! . . . I'd really like to take you out in my fishing boat. Just the two of us."

I said, coughing, "I'd like to sometime."

He stood up.

"Well," he sighed, "see you in the morning. I got to go turn up the water heater. A new one I just put in . . . Want to see it? It's in the cellar."

"I'm rather fagged, Ed. If you'll excuse me, I'll go on up to bed."

Four rye on aspirins finally solved the sleep problem. And when I woke up with the morning sun streaming through starched curtains, and saw the chair I had wedged under the doorknob, I felt a considerable fool.

Against whom or what had I reared the barricade? Ghosts? Earnest Bridewell? Lionel? Cornelia Ord? Cudworth? An evil house spirit—some poltergeist? But underneath my skin I knew.

There was no lock on the door (country people seem to think a lock inhospitable) and I had been too uneasy to sleep. It was nonsensical of me. Ridiculous. Uneasy was not the word for it, either. The person underneath my skin had been scared. Not physically frightened, exactly. Mentally scared. What was the line from *Macbeth* about fear? . . . *A dagger of the mind; a false creation proceeding from the heat-oppressed brain.*

Then I saw the chair had been forced a little askew. Someone had tried to open the door. . . .

Down in the dining room Annette was clearing breakfast dishes. She greeted me with hospitality and domesticity.

"Ed's eaten and gone into town to get the car fixed. Do you want your eggs scrambled or sunnyside?"

"Thank you, Mrs. Brewster. Just toast and coffee."

"French toast, then," she insisted. She started out, then paused. "I hope Ed didn't wake you. He thought you might like to drive into the Center with him. He went up to call you a while ago and found your door fastened."

A dagger of the mind.

I had to get out of the house. Out into the sun-bathed morning, the sea-washed wind. Away from the Bridewell parlor, the Bridewell attic, the lurking poltergeists of murder, hatred, trickery, mendacity, secrecy, suspicion.

After breakfast, I walked.

Under shade trees that were bowers of springtime leafage, between banks of elderberry, chinaberry and beach plum, the road wandered pleasantly villageward.

But I could not get away from the Bridewell case.

Smeizer said the first mailbox down the road.

Grimes said a box farther on.

Before I realized it I was in the Center striding past *Babcock's Grocery and General Store* (still in business!), *Ord's Seafood House* (something new), *Horatio Meck, Jr., Fine Liquors* (a variant of embalming fluid), and *Hatfield's Beach Shop.*

The Seagull Hotel sprawled half the length of Main Street. I passed the dry fountain. I passed the shabby façade of the Scenic Palace. It was not shabby, nor did it wear a plaintive sign insisting "Movies Are Better Than Ever" when Hobart Cudworth and Walter Jones went there on the long-ago evening that was Abby Bridewell's last.

Lodge Hall—abandoned, boarded up. Center Church—carpenters repairing the steeple. The Bayberry House—a teetering relic with the roofline sagging. On a slope beyond, the Surf and Sand with its long, and now rickety, verandah.

I took a side road to avoid the Surf and Sand. I wanted to get away from the good old days—Victorianism—the remnants of the Gaslight Era that clung to this remote landfall like driftwood half buried on a beach. So I hurried on up a hill, strode over a crest that gave view to open sea, and walked into a cemetery.

Headland Cemetery.

At Quahog Point, it seemed, there was no getting away from yesterday and its people. Here they were, all of them, in family groups and uneven hedgerows.

And since I was there, I might as well go ahead and meet them—the entire lot of them facing me with their final public images. . . .

A pause, there, Stranger as You Pass By,
As You are Now, So Once was I.
As I am Now, So You will Be.
Prepare for Death, and Follow Me.

That was Isaiah Robinson, "b. 1794, d. 1869." A cheerful prognosticator, to say the least. "Prepare for Death." Most of the older headstones, the slabs of flaky, reddish sandstone, offered that somber advice.

Our very hopes belied our fears,
Our fears our hopes belied,
We thought him dying when he slept,
And sleeping when he died.

That was one Uriah Purdy who "passed away of a flux" in 1875 "while in the very flower of his youth."

Dust, to its narrow house beneath,
Soul, to its place on high,
Toll the Knell for Lily Belle.
She too was born to die.

Yes, she too. Probably they had reminded Lily Belle Ross of that fact from the day she was a little girl in the 1840's to the day she died in 1900. Death is coming. Dissolution is nigh. Life was a prolonged preparation for the grave in the Victorian period. The only compensation lay in the assurance that when you died you made an exit from this vale of mortal misery and woe wherein you were constantly reminded that Death had your number. The tomb was an escape hatch.

Two hands upon the breast,
And labour's done;
Two pale feet crossed in rest,
The race is won.

So Abigail Goodbody was compensated for a long sprint that had kept her ahead of the Grim Reaper for a lifetime. How inconsistent all this was. You won when he caught you, yet you did your mortal best to outrun him.

At least, Prudence Jones had made a brisk and almost cheerful "departure from this life."

In Eighteen Hundred and Ninety-two
The heavens opened, and Prue went through.

That was all right. I could see where Cornelia's practicality had come from. She was there beside her mother in an assortment of Joneses. *Cornelia Jones Ord,* "b. 1851, d. 1917." No epitaph. Enough said.

Eustace Meck had more to say, borrowing some lines from *Hamlet.*

Who builds stronger than a mason, a shipwright or a carpenter? When you are asked this question next, say 'a grave-maker.' The houses that he makes last till doomsday.

Posthumous advertisement. The realtor in the midst of his suburban development. But some of Meck's "houses" were already tumbling down, going to seed. I found Grampa Bryce's monument standing a-tilt in a patch of brambles. Naturally, local legend had exaggerated this small granite trylon into a marble cenotaph. The legend on the pedestal was equally exaggerative, referring as it did to the departed's naval service in 1847.

Nor shall your glory be forgot
While Fame her record keeps,

Or Honor points the hallowed spot
Where Valor proudly sleeps.

And who today, I wondered, ever thinks of Churubusco, Chapultepec, Molina del Rey? Our modern histories tend to skip the Mexican War.

I came across the Ords behind a castiron picket fence, their name lettered on the base of a stone angel which had a bird's nest for a halo. I noticed an undated "Lost at Sea" for Wallace Ord. Had Cornelia preferred to rest in the Jones lot, fearing another Enoch Arden return?

Poe was engraved on a neighboring stone to "Little Gloria Hatfield."

Come, let the burial rite be read,
The funeral song be sung—
A dirge for her that doubly died
In that she died so young.

By all means, read the rite and sing the dirge. Life is fleeting. The graveyard waits. And if you've come this far up the cemetery path and don't believe it, keep walking.

Here is the word from Junius Grimes, "gored by a bull."

Life is not as idle ore,
But iron dug from central gloom
And heated hot with burning fears
And dipt in baths of hissing tears,
And batter'd with the shocks of doom.

And from Letitia Grimes, widow of Junius Grimes.

So vanishes our state, so pass our days,
So life but opens now, and now decays.
The cradle and the tomb, alas! so nigh,
To live is scarce distinguished from to die.

Truly the Gaslight Era was incredible. What had come over these people? And not just these hardshell "Pointers." This acute morbidity had been epidemic in America throughout most of the Nineteenth Century. It had been cultivated as a part of the way of life. If it was not sheer hypocrisy, then it was certainly a manifestation of schizophrenia. A national personality split in two. On the one hand bustling, building, expanding, shooting it up, living it up—going like a steam calliope. On the other hand glooming, sighing, sermonizing, brooding over dirges and death-knells—mourning like the Miserere.

But enough of this graveyard with its lugubrious public imagery, its solemn warnings. Lifting my heels, I headed crosslots for the road. Then I saw the small brownstone mausoleum.

BRIDEWELL

A gateway led to the doorstep, but I did not go in. From the gate I could see who was in residence.

Captain Nathan Bridewell
R.I.P., 1910
Abby Bridewell, his Widow
R.I.P., 1911

In the corner of the lot there were numerous other Bridewells. I made out Sybil Bridewell's headstone. But neither Earnest nor Lionel seemed to be on locale.

More than willing to be elsewhere, myself, I proceeded across the grass. My retreat brought me up against a granite angel labeled "Smeizer." The epitaph read:

I hear a voice you cannot hear,
Which says I must not stay,
I see a hand you cannot see,
Which beckons me away.

By one of those odd coincidences, I heard a far-off voice hail my name at that moment. Turning to glance down the slope, I saw a black sedan at roadside. The driver had an arm out of the window with a finger upraised in that gesture which says taxi.

It was Ed Brewster.

But I was somehow reminded of an old Irish legend. The ghostly hearse that draws up before the house of the unsuspecting. The driver who leans out and calls to the victim, "There's room for just one more."

Ed said, "We'll take a shortcut back to the house. We won't have much time if you're going to get that two o'clock boat."

I said, "Thanks for picking me up."

"Nan said you'd went for a walk. She's fixed you a lunch."

The car swerved in ruts, and trailed a plume of dust. We passed an abandoned farm and a yawning gravel pit. Then another abandoned farm.

"That's the place Earnest Bridewell lived for a time. After he married Floss Grimes."

"Ed," I inquired, "what became of Earnest and Lionel Bridewell? I didn't see them back there in the cemetery."

"They're there." He could not tell me exactly where. "Maybe in the new part. You were in the old part."

"Oh."

"Well, Lionel died some time around World War One. After, maybe. He'd left Quahog Point. You heard a lot of stories. There was one he tagged after a burlesque queen. Just a yarn, I suppose."

"I can imagine."

Ed frowned. "You know how it is. Some sailor says he seen Lionel at a burley house in Bridgeport or somewhere. Maybe it was Lionel, maybe it wasn't. Next thing you know, it's around that Lionel is married to one of those big pink Mae Wests. Or maybe that he's selling candy up the aisle between the acts."

This last was an evocative suggestion. The finale of the rake's progress. The curtain descends on a brassy rendition of "Sugar Blues." The house lights go up. And then, in the smoky lull of intermission, the candy hawker starts up the aisle. It is Lionel (or what is left of him) in straw hat and shirtsleeves, his eyes glazed, his false teeth shining, addressing the audience in cracked Calling Tones. "Prize in every package! Getcha chocolate-covered cherries!"

"I don't really know what did happen to Lionel," Ed mused. "Nothing out the ordinary, I expect. . . . Here! Here's somebody, though, can tell you about Earnest."

He slowed the car, then brought up at roadside where an elderly man in overalls was standing with a fishpole. We picked up Roy Goodbody.

After introductions, Ed said, "Roy, we was talkin' about the Bridewells up at the cemetery. You knew the State Senator."

"Sure. We all knew him."

"What was that about his trouble after the trial? I was telling my friend here."

"Why, he died."

"I mean before that. Didn't they make him Road Commissioner?"

"Oh, that. Sure." Our passenger rubbed his chin thoughtfully. "A couple of years before the World War. The first one."

"What happened?"

"To Earnest?" Roy Goodbody shrugged. "I don't know what you mean, unless it was about him going back to jail."

I asked Roy Goodbody why Earnest Bridewell had gone back to jail.

"Well, he'd had this other trouble," Roy said. "About his mother. After that blew over, the County kind of relented. So they fixed him up with this Road Commissioner appointment. It was too bad, eh, Ed?"

Ed Brewster shook his head. "I never heard all the details."

"Why, Earnest kind of played it sharp. He got to padding the payroll with names off tombstones. Mecks, Purdys, Robinsons, Thorns. Even old Grampa Bryce. On the County payroll after they'd been dead for years. He might've got away with it if he hadn't started taking some of the slabs, well as the names."

I echoed, "Some of the slabs?"

"Well," Roy Goodbody told me, "taking names from a cemetery was one thing. Kind of usual in politics around election time and all that. You sort of expected it, back then, in ballot boxes and county payrolls . . . Earnest went too far. You don't like to walk into someone's barn and find a stable paved with flagstones that say 'Pythias Ross, Rest in Peace,' or 'Bertha Smeizer, Gone but not Forgotten.' "

"That was in Earnest's place back up the road near the cemetery?" Ed asked.

"Convenient," Roy nodded. "I don't calculate it's true, but I heard the hearth inside the fireplace had Doc Hatfield's name on it."

We had come to a road-fork near the Bridewell (which was to say Ed Brewster's) house. Roy Goodbody climbed out.

As we drove on, Ed said, "Don't believe everything you hear. But they did send Earnest up for a couple of years. He died a short time after he got out of prison. His wife Floss was a good woman. Went away. Stepson Alvin, or whatever he was, died of paresis a few years back. That orphan, Walter Jones, died in an insane asylum."

"How soon after that did you acquire the house, Ed?"

"This place?" as we turned into the drive. "Some years after. Like I told you, it was vacant for a long time."

We pulled up at the side porch. Ed looked at his watch and then at me. "You've got about half an hour. . . . Let's see what's cooking."

I followed him to the kitchen door. As Ed stepped into the kitchen, he called, "Nan!" When she did not answer he grumbled something that sounded like "down the road for eggs," and stood aside to let me go ahead of him.

The kitchen was shadowy and quiet. Coffee simmered, aromatic, on the stove. I was conscious of the wall clock ticking. Then I was conscious of something else.

Ed said, "Use a beer? I got a keg down cellar. We can bring up a couple of pitchers if you'll come down and hold—" Then he paused to see what I was staring at.

My attention had gone to the cellar door ahead of him. "Isn't that a new door?" I asked.

Ed eyed it admiringly. "Yes, it is. Hung it myself some time ago. Ever try to put up one? It's a job."

"But the old one! The antique!"

"Chopped it up," Ed said. "It wasn't really any good. Warped cockeyed, and too thick for the frame. The old hasp was worn out and wouldn't latch. It kept swinging open, and give Annette the creeps. Every time she'd look up, the door would be moving ajar like someone was coming up out of the cellar."

"I suppose it would make one a little nervous."

"More than a little after what happened on those cellar steps."

"You mean Abby Bridewell."

"Not just her," Ed said. "Me, too. The damndest thing. It scared me out of a year's growth."

I looked at him. "What happened?"

"Huh!" he exclaimed. "It was the autumn after you first came here. I was fixing a water pipe down cellar. We'd had a storm warning that morning, and I wanted to get the job secured before a gale set in. I come in through the kitchen door with a three-foot pipe on my shoulder. Nan was in here fiddling around. I recall she asked me to fetch the laundry basket from the washroom so she could go bring in the laundry off the line before it blew away. I asked her couldn't she see I was busy. So she said she'd go fetch it herself. Anyway, she was out of the kitchen when I started down cellar."

Demonstrating, Ed went to the cellarway. He pulled open the cellar door. He said across his shoulder, "There wasn't *nobody* behind me, I'd swear to that. There wasn't nobody in the house, I'd swear, except Annette. And *she* says she didn't come near this end of the kitchen. . . . Look. . . . Here she comes now. She can tell you."

Breezy, Annette Brewster came in through the kitchen door. She was carrying a loaded laundry basket and pouting a mouthful of clothes pins. Before one of us could help her she dumped the basket on the table and palmed the pins.

"Speak of the devil," Ed said. "I was just telling about the time you went out for the laundry and I got clobbered going down cellar."

I exclaimed, "Clobbered?"

Ed rubbed the back of his head. "Damn near brained! It was dark down the cellarway, so I was extra careful on the steps. But I got it just the same. I'm about five steps down, and wham! Like across the back of the neck with a baseball bat."

Ed pointed down the dark cellarway. I moved to his side to peer down.

"See that lumpy sidewall?" He aimed a thick finger. "I must've bounced off that with a beautiful header. Whatever I got slugged with, it caught that iron pipe on my shoulder and like to broke my neck. I came to at the bottom—it seemed a long time afterward—with Annette sponging my face."

I turned to look at Annette. Her expression was woeful.

She said unhappily, "I couldn't imagine what had happened. I saw him start for the cellar and I went into the washroom there, and got the laundry basket and went out to the porch. Just as I stepped out on the porch and closed the door, I heard this muffled bang or something—almost like a gunshot—and then a falling, clanging sound."

"The iron pipe," Ed explained. "Bouncing with me down the steps."

"You were on the porch," I prompted Annette fatuously.

"Well!" she exhaled. "I came right back in. I just knew it was Ed. I ran to the cellar door and looked down. There he was."

"You saw nobody in the kitchen?"

"Of course not."

"The cellar door?"

"Partly open, just as Ed left it. Those steep steps! You should have seen him. He might have killed himself!"

Ed said darkly, "Or been killed."

But on the way to Gillion's Wharf, Ed confided that he supposed he had actually slipped.

"After all," he said ponderously, "I'm no rich old widow sitting on top of a fortune. I'm no Hetty Green."

Thus legends, once launched, are seldom dispelled. Fable would give Abby Bridewell a Dun and Bradstreet rating no matter the contrary evidence exhumed by basic research.

Ed parked the car at the pierhead. Then he escorted me to the gangway of the S.S. *Cremolian*—an old walking-beam steamer of the Bay & Ocean Line. Most of the passengers had already boarded. The captain peered down from the bridge, and deck hands stood ready to cast off.

In parting, Ed said, "Going to write up that mystery?"

"I might," I said.

Rubbing his neck, he said, "It would be interesting if someone would ever solve it."

The steamer blew the whistle on us, giving me no time to tell Ed Brewster that he had that day supplied me with a solution. Actually I was most relieved about this outcome, and at the same time embarrassed by the sense of relief. But, however erroneous the suspicion, in a murder mystery all principals are suspect until cleared by the solution, whether the case be factual or fictional. Given possible motive and opportunity, a twelve-year-old newsboy could be as deadly as the next man. After all, Ed did acquire the gramophone, and—

Daggers of the mind! And fool's logic. Begin with a false premise, build assumption on supposition, and, as Lincoln or some other wise man once observed, you could prove a horse chestnut was a chestnut horse.

The steamer shuddered and backed away from the pier. Ed waved. Feeling happier than I had for some time, I waved back.

Later, I stood topside at the taffrail watching the headland and the lighthouse diminish astern. A whippy saltwater breeze helped to clear my head of attic cobwebs, Victorian epitaphs and other mental blocks. By the time the long peninsula was a chalkline far astern, I had all of the key jigsaws in place.

And so (to borrow the period rhetoric of a once nationally famous travelogue) I said goodbye to Quahog Point—last outpost of the Gaslight Era, and favorite resort of Ananias, Baron Munchausen and Professor Quackenbos—and sailed off in the tinted light of a golden afternoon, confident that I had found the answer to at least one mystery.

At any rate, I was almost certain that Earnest Bridewell had caused the death of his mother. And I was equally certain that I knew how he had done it.

CHAPTER 20

Earnest Bridewell must have killed his mother. Easy enough to see the *modus operandi.* Not to be mistaken for the *deus ex machina.*

Consider his supposedly ironclad alibi: He was at his farmhouse on the south side of Quahog Point throughout the entire evening of April 11. True, he left the house for a while. But according to his wife, he, Earnest, supposedly remained on the premises from suppertime until bedtime—a statement presumably substantiated by the testimony of the Bedford cattle dealers, McVest and Garvy.

Dissolve that crucial alibi, and Earnest could have been anywhere on Quahog Point. The solvent of what used to be called "horse sense" readily dissolves it. Not only do twilight and evening star shadow the alibi. The intention of the witnesses is open to doubt.

However, let us take them at their word and believe the cattle men testified in good faith. "We were out looking for southdown sheep, and I twice saw this man that evening," McVest could aver with hand on Bible, and perhaps swear to it honestly. Yet the inherent fallacy is obvious. When you're looking for ewes and rams, you are hardly paying attention to someone glimpsed in a dooryard or seen at a window.

The cattle dealers were in a hurry. They wanted to get their business over with. Their search for strays led them over rough terrain, through thickets of sapling and head-high bayberry. Probably they cast frequent and anxious glances at the evening clouds. A weather change was setting in. The wind off the sea was chill. Preoccupied with sheep and mare's tails, the two Bedford men could have remained entirely unaware that Earnest Bridewell had quit the farmhouse and taken the northbound path through the orchard.

Around nine o'clock, then, Earnest arrives at the old homestead unobserved. Perhaps he sees Cornelia Ord emerge from the house. With no particular affection for this "vaguely related" cousin, he waits for her to go. Or, possibly, he arrives at the Bridewell homestead just after Cornelia's departure. At any rate, his mother is in there alone.

Earnest walks up the hedge-screened path to the front door (unnoticed by Mrs. Smeizer, for all her infra-red night vision) and enters the vestibule. The downstairs seems deserted. His mother is not in the lighted parlor. She must have just quit the room because the gramophone is playing *"This is an Eddy-son reckord"* over and over, the needle stuck in the groove (the voice Mrs. Smeizer heard!). Abby cannot have been gone long, or the machine would have run down. Earnest shuts it off.

Scowling, he looks for his mother in the dining room. Nobody. The sewing room is dark. A lamp is burning in the kitchen, so she must be somewhere in back. Earnest walks into the kitchen. He notices the cellar door standing open. Ah, his mother is down there.

So Earnest goes about his business. What business? A man could visit his mother's house on any one of a thousand conceivable errands. But Earnest will never tell. Could he say he visited the house to retrieve a hat from a closet? To get his pipe? To look for a wallet he'd left upstairs in his old bedroom? To borrow or return a book? No story he could tell in court would be believed. The more inconsequential such an errand, the more unbelievable it would become. Least of all could he aver that he just dropped in for a minute to see his mother.

After what happens, he must swear that he was nowhere near his mother. After what happens, he must go on oath that he was nowhere near the old homestead when it happened.

What happened?

Since no one witnessed it at the time, no one could say with absolute certainty thirty-five years later. But laws of probability are not invalid in logic, nor in scientific analysis.

During that same month of 1911 when Abby Bridewell was killed, the Philadelphia publisher, Craige Lippincott, was found dead one morning in the drawing room of his mansion on Rittenhouse Square. He was in evening clothes. Near his hand lay a Colt revolver. He and his wife had been the previous evening to a Metropolitan Opera performance of *Quo Vadis*. Upon returning home, Mrs. Lippincott had retired. She said she had heard no shot. The police at first suspected a burglar, but the house was locked and nothing had been stolen. Then, no doubt, they wondered about Mrs. Lippincott. But her reputation was unimpeachable. When the medical examiner found powder burns, suicide seemed apparent. The question was settled when investigation disclosed that Lippincott had been temperamental, nervous, depressed, and had wept bitterly over the hari-kiri of Petronius in the opera. Of course, it may not have been a *felo-de se* in the publisher's case. But the chances are a millon to one that he committed suicide.

Abby Bridewell did not commit suicide. By all the laws of probability, death caught the old lady exactly as it almost caught Ed Brewster. In Ed's case, it knocked him down the cellar steps, face forward, a stunning blow. In Abby's case, the blow smote her in the face—or, more exactly, on the forehead—as she was coming up through the cellar doorway, stooping a little on the climb.

Slam! Just that. Even as Earnest Bridewell opened the back kitchen door, as did Annette years later, and stepped out on the porch, caught the door against an outside gust, and then pulled it shut with a whack.

Annette heard Ed go plunging with the iron pipe. But Earnest, doubtless in a hurry and probably a little drunk, heard only a door slam, and thought nothing of it. And the wind galing through the kitchen on that system of inner doors and drafts had caught the cellar door as a squall catches a sail, and had slammed it crashing into the face of Abby Bridewell.

A man slams a kitchen door as he leaves a house, and he kills his mother on a cellar stairway without knowing it. In the dark he walks off in all innocence. He returns to his own domicile where he is glimpsed puffing a briar in a lighted window. Next morning he shocks awake to the fact that he is bound in a deadly web of circumstantial evidence. Motive, opportunity, appearances, almost everything adds up to a murder charge and possible conviction. He is a man who has made enemies, quarreled with relatives, alienated his own brother. Now the chickens are home to roost. Choking in fear and despair, he has a foretaste of the hangman's noose.

One can forgive the man for trying to lie his way out of a potentially fatal trap. If the guilty flee when no man pursueth, at least they take advantage of a chance for flight. The innocent, under suspicion, dare not flee, for they know that flight implies guilt. At the outset Earnest Bridewell must have been desperate. He had no way of knowing that some moron would later try to frame him with that bag of shot, and thus inadvertently provide ammunition for his defense. Frantic, he made a clumsy effort to purchase an alibi. Probably he bribed young Walter Jones. But Earnest Bridewell was not guilty of matricide.

CHAPTER 21

Yes, it goes without saying that no murder was committed if Abby Bridewell was killed by a cellar door which was slammed in her face by a galing draft. Since big winds are a matter of weather, such disasters are usually defined by insurance men as Acts of God.

Yet it would seem that a murderer did enter the case. Whoever planted the shot-bag evidence against Earnest Bridewell certainly had murder in mind, and as a man thinketh so is he. Or she, if the thinker were a woman.

I am still holding that blood stained shot-bag as a jigsaw piece which fits no visible slot in the puzzle. Somebody tucked it under Earnest's mattress. If Brother Lionel did not do it, who did?

Who rigged that not so artful dodge? I would stake my claim on her forthright and unassuming tombstone that Cornelia was not guilty of the deceit. A vengeful Cudworth? An unhappy Walter Jones? A malicious neighbor? Some party rival with a political axe he wanted to bury in Earnest's head? Reviewing the basic factors of motive and opportunity, and recalling his courtroom performance, one invariably comes back to Lionel.

Lionel, however, remains "a man of mystery." Somehow he apparently healed the breach with Earnest—at least, when it came to a settlement of the estate. And evidence suggests that he went into business among the "inlanders" and lived happily ever after, as the storybooks coin the term.

All of which would indicate that Lionel Bridewell ended his days at some worthwhile pursuit as a solid citizen. Indeed, he may always have been one, local gossip to the contrary.

Deservedly or undeservedly, public images were just clay pigeons at Quahog Point.

Yes, when it came to character assassination, Quahog Point seems to have been a shooting gallery. Evidently few in the village had even tried to pay lip service to the Ninth Commandment. Bearing false witness against a neighbor was a game two, and everybody else, could play.

As for truth, it would seem Diogenes with a searchlight could have found no grain of it in that beach resort. Probably the history of jurisprudence lacks the equal of the obiter dictum handed the community by the irate judge who sat on the Bridewell case.

"It has been my experience while on the bench for the past

seven years, in Quahog Point cases—and there have been many of them—that witnesses from there were disposed to perjure themselves. Invariably in the matter of an alibi from that place the defense is disposed to perjure itself. It is too bad . . ."

Yet here is another Scriptural admonition. Judge not, that ye be not judged. Victorian Quahog Point was not Sodom. Neither was it Gomorrah. It seems only fair to see the place as a product of its time—a ten-cent mirror which reflected the larger scene, the American scene, or the world scene, if you will.

If the "Pointers" traduced their neighbors, so did every major nation on the contemporary globe—in the presumed self-interest of national propaganda. And it would hardly behoove a modern to deplore this beam in the eye of the Victorian Period when one can scarcely see daylight for the mote in the eye of Today. Why, character assassination of nations, races and peoples has become a nonstop roundelay, with world capitals now trading traducements in the most impassioned Calling Tones. How would Diogenes fare in our modern world community?

So Quahog Point, like its day and time, had a tacky side. But perhaps that clamshell microcosm on the gas-lit beach was not so bad, comparatively speaking. For all its hypocrisy, back-biting and esurient libido, Victorian Quahog Point produced only one murder. Or were there two?

I visited the Point this year for a final look. And I found myself thinking the foregoing thoughts, and wondering.

Well, a new highway system roars out to the peninsula with cloverleaf underpasses and four-lane speedways. However, a billboard announces that the road will be closed in event of atomic attack. As a sign of the times it struck me as no improvement on the Past.

Nor could I see much cultural advance in the Neon glare which now replaces the Center's gaslight. Nor in the garish façades of the modernized beach hotels. Certainly none in the gaudy jukebox blaring a blather of rock-and-roll from the remodeled parlor of the New Surf and Sand.

So the Victorian "Pointers" were prudes? All right, old-fashioned prudery was no longer in evidence on the local beach. But it showed up new-fashioned in an item I chanced upon in the modern *Clarion-Journal.** Censors in the U.S. Post Office had currently barred from the mails an advertisement which displayed a reproduction of Goya's famous painting "The Naked Maja." Since the same nude appeared on a stamp issued in Spain, the U.S. Post Office was in hot water. I could imagine Madame Sophie (gay old lady) laughing at that one. Yesterday's prudes had tried to cancel *her*. Today's were trying to cancel an inch-size postage stamp!

Moral betterment? I drove out to the old Bridewell homestead. Ed and Annette had sold the place. Modern decorators had been there. A mobile dangles in the vestibule. Exotic furniture, all metal tubes and pastel plastic, replaces the plush of Abby Bridewell's time. The parlor's new picture window looks out on the wall of a garage. A twenty-inch TV stands where the gramophone talked. As I glanced in, a silly adult Western banged to its hackneyed finish, and an unctuous newscaster took the screen. The news? Wretched. Embracing the report of a highway graft that made Ernest Bridewell's zombie peculations so much petty larceny in comparison.

Once again I quit the Point with a conviction that Abby Bridewell deserved far better than she got from neighbors, family and Fate. She was one of those unsung women—and there were many of her time—who held a household of problem sons together with the might of maternal instinct and the main of feminine resolution.

However, errant Earnest may not have been as brutal as some of the localites averred. A little graft, perhaps; a little perjury; a little delinquency on the back stairs—after all, he *was* a political dignitary. At any rate, his villainies seem to have stopped short of matricide.

And I (who mistakenly prejudged him) confess to a real liking for Brother Lionel. I almost hope the rumor which gave him a mundane suburbanite status was as groundless as the gossip which painted him a rapist.

I would like to think of Lionel Bridewell ending his days as

* Press releases, March 1959.

a suave old roué—the type who dyes his hair jet black and whose white-browed eyes light up like matchflares every time they behold a young lady. (He restricts his hunting to rich widows, but he can dream, can't he?) I picture him wearing a burgundy velvet lounge jacket with padded lapels. And a cummerbund to hide his electric belt. He strolls into the parlor of some resort hotel. Sits down at the piano and regales the twittering feminine complement with such nostalgic old-timers as *Pony Boy, Tis Only a Pansy Blossom, The Last Rose of Summer* and *Ta-Ra-Ra-Bum-de-Yay.* Including, of course, that ghastly classic of yesteryear, *Just a Handful of Earth from Mother's Grave.*

Anyway, that's my verdict.

What's yours?